# First World War
## and Army of Occupation
# War Diary
## France, Belgium and Germany

18 DIVISION
54 Infantry Brigade
Duke of Cambridge's Own (Middlesex Regiment)
12th Battalion
27 April 1915 - 30 April 1919

WO95/2044/1

The Naval & Military Press Ltd
www.nmarchive.com
Published in association with The National Archives

Published by

## The Naval & Military Press Ltd

Unit 10 Ridgewood Industrial Park,

Uckfield, East Sussex,

TN22 5QE England

Tel: +44 (0) 1825 749494

www.naval-military-press.com

www.nmarchive.com

*This diary has been reprinted in facsimile from the original. Any imperfections are inevitably reproduced and the quality may fall short of modern type and cartographic standards.*

© **Crown Copyright**
**Images reproduced by permission of The National Archives, London, England, 2015.**

# Contents

| Document type | Place/Title | Date From | Date To |
|---|---|---|---|
| Heading | WO95/2044, 18 Division, 6 Btn Northants Regt July 1915-Aug 1919 | | |
| Heading | 18th Division 54th Infy Bde, 6th Bn Northamptons Jly 1915-Apl 1919. | | |
| Heading | 18th Division 6th Northamptons. Vol I. From 25-31 Jly 15 | | |
| War Diary | Codford. Wilts. | 25/07/1915 | 25/07/1915 |
| War Diary | Southampton | 25/07/1915 | 25/07/1915 |
| War Diary | Havre | 26/07/1915 | 26/07/1915 |
| War Diary | Longueau | 26/07/1915 | 27/07/1915 |
| War Diary | Talmas | 27/07/1915 | 31/07/1915 |
| Heading | 18th Division 6th Northamptons Vol. II From 1-28.8.15 | | |
| War Diary | Talmas | 01/08/1915 | 08/08/1915 |
| War Diary | Bonnay | 09/08/1915 | 13/08/1915 |
| War Diary | Suzanne | 14/08/1915 | 23/08/1915 |
| War Diary | Mericourt | 24/08/1915 | 28/08/1915 |
| Map | Morland | | |
| Map | Tank Routes | | |
| Heading | 18th Divn. 6th Northamptons Vol. 3. Sep 1.15 | | |
| War Diary | Mericourt L'Abbe. | 01/09/1915 | 03/09/1915 |
| War Diary | Meaulte | 04/09/1915 | 16/09/1915 |
| War Diary | Morlancourt | 16/09/1915 | 30/09/1915 |
| Heading | 18th Division 6th Northamptons Vol 4 Oct 15 | | |
| War Diary | Sector D.1 | 01/10/1915 | 01/10/1915 |
| War Diary | Of Trenches | 03/10/1915 | 03/10/1915 |
| War Diary | Morlancourt | 04/10/1915 | 11/10/1915 |
| War Diary | Sector D.I Of Trenches. | 11/10/1915 | 19/10/1915 |
| War Diary | Morlancourt | 19/10/1915 | 27/10/1915 |
| War Diary | Sector D.I of Trenches. | 27/10/1915 | 31/10/1915 |
| Heading | 18th Division 6th Northamptons Vol. 5 | | |
| War Diary | Sector D.I of Trenches. | 01/11/1915 | 02/11/1915 |
| War Diary | Morlancourt | 02/11/1915 | 10/11/1915 |
| War Diary | Sector D.I of Trenches. | 10/11/1915 | 18/11/1915 |
| War Diary | Morlancourt | 18/11/1915 | 26/11/1915 |
| War Diary | Sector D.I of Trenches. | 26/11/1915 | 30/11/1915 |
| War Diary | Morlancourt | 30/11/1915 | 30/11/1915 |
| Heading | 18th Div. 6th Northamptons Vol. 6 121/7931 | | |
| War Diary | Morlancourt | 01/12/1915 | 04/12/1915 |
| War Diary | Sector D.2 of Trenches. | 04/12/1915 | 11/12/1915 |
| War Diary | Buire | 11/12/1915 | 24/12/1915 |
| War Diary | Sector D.2 of Trenches. | 24/12/1915 | 31/12/1915 |
| Heading | 10th Div 6th Northants Vol. 7 | | |
| War Diary | Sector D.2 of Trenches. | 01/01/1916 | 02/01/1916 |
| War Diary | Morlancourt | 02/01/1916 | 02/01/1916 |
| War Diary | Sector D.2 of Trenches. | 10/01/1916 | 18/01/1916 |
| War Diary | Morlancourt | 18/01/1916 | 26/01/1916 |
| War Diary | Sector D.2 of Trenches. | 26/01/1916 | 31/01/1916 |
| Heading | 6 Northants. Vol 8 | | |
| War Diary | Sector D.2 of Trenches. | 01/02/1916 | 04/02/1916 |
| War Diary | Meaulte | 04/02/1916 | 04/02/1916 |

| Type | Location/Description | From | To |
|---|---|---|---|
| War Diary | La Houssoye | 05/02/1916 | 16/02/1916 |
| War Diary | Pont Noyelles | 16/02/1916 | 29/02/1916 |
| Heading | 6th Northants Vol 9 18 A | | |
| War Diary | Pont Noyelles | 01/03/1916 | 01/03/1916 |
| War Diary | Corbie | 02/03/1916 | 07/03/1916 |
| War Diary | Bray | 07/03/1916 | 07/03/1916 |
| War Diary | Bronfay | 08/03/1916 | 08/03/1916 |
| War Diary | Sector A.2 of Trenches. | 11/03/1916 | 15/03/1916 |
| War Diary | Bray | 15/03/1916 | 15/03/1916 |
| War Diary | Sector A.2 of Trenches | 19/03/1916 | 23/03/1916 |
| War Diary | Bronfay | 23/03/1916 | 27/03/1916 |
| War Diary | Sector A.2 of Trenches. | 27/03/1916 | 31/03/1916 |
| War Diary | Sector A.2 of Trenches. | 01/04/1916 | 02/04/1916 |
| War Diary | Bray | 02/04/1916 | 08/04/1916 |
| War Diary | Sector A.2 of Trenches. | 08/04/1916 | 14/04/1916 |
| War Diary | Bronfay Farm | 14/04/1916 | 20/04/1916 |
| War Diary | Sector A.2 of Trenches. | 20/04/1916 | 26/04/1916 |
| War Diary | Bray | 26/04/1916 | 01/05/1916 |
| War Diary | La Houssoye | 01/05/1916 | 01/05/1916 |
| War Diary | Frechencourt | 02/05/1916 | 10/05/1916 |
| War Diary | Saisseval | 15/05/1916 | 15/05/1916 |
| War Diary | Bray | 15/05/1916 | 24/05/1916 |
| War Diary | La Houssoye | 15/05/1916 | 24/05/1916 |
| War Diary | Saisseval | 25/05/1916 | 07/06/1916 |
| War Diary | Picquigny | 11/06/1916 | 23/06/1916 |
| War Diary | Bronfay Farm | 23/06/1916 | 30/06/1916 |
| Miscellaneous | Special Order Of The Day by Brigadier General T.H. Shoubridge, C.M.G, D.S.O., Commanding 54th. Infantry Brigade. Appendix I | 02/06/1916 | 02/06/1916 |
| Heading | 54th Inf. Bde. 18th. Div. War Diary 6th Battn. The Northamptonshire Regiment. July 1916. | | |
| War Diary | | 01/07/1916 | 05/07/1916 |
| War Diary | The Loop | 06/07/1916 | 07/07/1916 |
| War Diary | Bois De Tailles | 09/07/1916 | 12/07/1916 |
| War Diary | Maicourt | 13/07/1916 | 14/07/1916 |
| War Diary | Since Reported Killed | | |
| War Diary | Maltz Horn Trench | 15/07/1916 | 17/07/1916 |
| War Diary | Copse D S. of Maricourt | 17/07/1916 | 17/07/1916 |
| War Diary | Bois De Tailles | 18/07/1916 | 20/07/1916 |
| War Diary | Citernes | 22/07/1916 | 22/07/1916 |
| War Diary | Wallon Cappel | 23/07/1916 | 27/07/1916 |
| War Diary | Bailleul | 28/07/1916 | 31/07/1916 |
| Miscellaneous | Appendices 2, 3, 4 & 5 | | |
| Operation(al) Order(s) | Operation Order No. 10. by Colonel G.E. Ripley, Commanding 6th (S) Bn. Northamptonshire Regiment. Appendix 2 | | |
| Miscellaneous | Plan of Attack. | 22/06/1916 | 22/06/1916 |
| Miscellaneous | The Attack. | 22/06/1916 | 22/06/1916 |
| Miscellaneous | Position of Units 54th Inf. Bde. Immediately before Zero hour. Appendix "A" | | |
| Miscellaneous | Acquittance Roll (All Arms). | | |
| Miscellaneous | Grenades. Appendix "B" | | |
| Miscellaneous | Acquittance Roll (All Arms). | | |
| Miscellaneous | Dumps. Appendix "C" | | |
| Miscellaneous | Acquittance Roll (All Arms). | | |

| Type | Description | Date From | Date To |
|---|---|---|---|
| Diagram etc | N.B. All Trenches Not Marked With An Arrow May Be Used In Either Direction. | | |
| Map | Appendix D | | |
| Miscellaneous | Extract From O.O. 18 | 27/06/1916 | 27/06/1916 |
| Miscellaneous | The Following Messages Are To All Concerned. Appendix 3 | 01/07/1916 | 01/07/1916 |
| Miscellaneous | Operations In Trones Wood Appendix IV | 14/07/1916 | 14/07/1916 |
| Map | Montauban. | | |
| Miscellaneous | 6 Nov. R July 1916 Appendix 5 | | |
| Heading | 6th (S) Bn The Northamptonshire Regt. | | |
| War Diary | N.W. of Bailleul. | 01/08/1916 | 04/08/1916 |
| War Diary | Rue Marle Armentieres | 05/08/1916 | 11/08/1916 |
| War Diary | Camp near La Motte | 11/08/1916 | 14/08/1916 |
| War Diary | Rue Marle | 15/08/1916 | 15/08/1916 |
| War Diary | B.2 Sector II Army | 16/08/1916 | 23/08/1916 |
| War Diary | Erquingham | 24/08/1916 | 25/08/1916 |
| War Diary | Bailleul Aux Cornailles | 26/08/1916 | 31/08/1916 |
| Operation(al) Order(s) | Operation Orders No.1 by Colonel G.E. Ripley, Commdg. 6th (S) Bn. Northamptonshire Regiment. Appendix 6. | 15/08/1916 | 15/08/1916 |
| Miscellaneous | Operation Orders by Colonel G.E.Ripley, Commanding 6th (S) Bn. Northamptonshire Regiment. Appendix 6.A | 22/08/1916 | 22/08/1916 |
| Miscellaneous | Officer Commanding, 6th. (S) Bn. Northamptonshire Regiment. | 05/10/1916 | 05/10/1916 |
| War Diary | Bailleul Aux Cornailles | 01/09/1916 | 08/09/1916 |
| War Diary | Buneville | 09/09/1916 | 09/09/1916 |
| War Diary | Sus St Leger | 10/09/1916 | 10/09/1916 |
| War Diary | Arqueves | 11/09/1916 | 22/09/1916 |
| War Diary | Hedauville | 23/09/1916 | 23/09/1916 |
| War Diary | S. Bluff Authville | 25/09/1916 | 25/09/1916 |
| War Diary | Thiepval | 26/09/1916 | 26/09/1916 |
| War Diary | S. Bluff | 27/09/1916 | 28/09/1916 |
| War Diary | Mailly Maillet Wood | 29/09/1916 | 30/09/1916 |
| Miscellaneous | 6th (S) Bn Northamptonshire Regiment. Summary Of Casualties. | 02/10/1916 | 02/10/1916 |
| Miscellaneous | Distribution of 54 Bde Immediately before Zero Hour Appendix A | | |
| Map | K 36.-M 33. | | |
| Map | Plan Showing approximate position of 54th Inf Bde. on night. | | |
| Map | | | |
| Miscellaneous | | | |
| Miscellaneous | Preliminary Instructions For Attack. | 23/09/1916 | 23/09/1916 |
| Operation(al) Order(s) | Operation Orders No. 33. by Colonel G.E. Ripley, Commanding 6th (S) Bn. Northamptonshire Regiment. | 26/02/1916 | 26/02/1916 |
| Operation(al) Order(s) | Operation Orders No. 40. by Colonel G.E. Ripley, Commanding 6th (S) Bn. Northamptonshire Regiment. | 26/09/1916 | 26/09/1916 |
| Miscellaneous | Narrative of the part Played by the 6th S. Bn. Northamptonshire Regiment in the capture of Thiepval on the 26th September 1916. | 26/09/1916 | 26/09/1916 |
| Miscellaneous | 6th (S) Bn. Northamptonshire Regiment. Programme Of Work. Appendix 4. | 27/08/1916 | 27/08/1916 |
| Diagram etc | | | |
| Miscellaneous | 6th (S) Bn. Northamptonshire Regiment. Appendix 13. | 10/09/1916 | 10/09/1916 |

| | | | |
|---|---|---|---|
| Operation(al) Order(s) | Operation Orders No. 38. By Colonel G.E. Ripley, Commanding 6th (S) Bn. Northamptonshire Regiment. Appendix 14 | 24/09/1916 | 24/09/1916 |
| Miscellaneous | Appendix 15. | | |
| Miscellaneous | 18th. Division. Appendix 16. | 29/09/1916 | 29/09/1916 |
| War Diary | Mailly-Maillet | 01/10/1916 | 03/10/1916 |
| War Diary | Berneuil | 04/10/1916 | 14/10/1916 |
| War Diary | Beauval | 15/10/1916 | 15/10/1916 |
| War Diary | Warloy | 16/10/1916 | 16/10/1916 |
| War Diary | Bouzincourt | 17/10/1916 | 21/10/1916 |
| War Diary | Albert | 22/10/1916 | 25/10/1916 |
| War Diary | Trenches | 25/10/1916 | 28/10/1916 |
| War Diary | Albert | 29/10/1916 | 30/10/1916 |
| War Diary | Warloy | 31/10/1916 | 31/10/1916 |
| Miscellaneous | Subject. Operations. From. | 02/10/1916 | 02/10/1916 |
| Miscellaneous | 6th. (S) Bn. Northamptonshire Regiment. App 16. | 09/10/1916 | 09/10/1916 |
| War Diary | Warloy | 01/11/1916 | 03/11/1916 |
| War Diary | Albert | 04/10/1916 | 05/10/1916 |
| War Diary | Trenches | 06/10/1916 | 10/10/1916 |
| War Diary | Ovillers Huts. | 10/11/1916 | 11/11/1916 |
| War Diary | Warloy | 11/11/1916 | 12/11/1916 |
| War Diary | Albert | 13/11/1916 | 14/11/1916 |
| War Diary | Ovillers Huts. | 14/11/1916 | 18/11/1916 |
| War Diary | Trenches | 18/11/1916 | 19/11/1916 |
| War Diary | Ovillers Huts | 19/11/1916 | 21/11/1916 |
| War Diary | Warloy | 21/11/1916 | 21/11/1916 |
| War Diary | Herissart | 22/11/1916 | 22/11/1916 |
| War Diary | Boullens | 23/11/1916 | 23/11/1916 |
| War Diary | Berneuil | 24/11/1916 | 24/11/1916 |
| War Diary | Domqueur Le Plouy | 25/11/1916 | 25/11/1916 |
| War Diary | Oneux | 26/11/1916 | 26/11/1916 |
| War Diary | Neuf Moulin | 27/11/1916 | 13/12/1916 |
| War Diary | Canchy | 14/12/1916 | 31/12/1916 |
| Heading | 6th Northants Jan-Dec 1917 | | |
| Miscellaneous | British Salonika Force War Diary 12th Corps. | | |
| War Diary | Canchy | 01/01/1918 | 11/01/1918 |
| War Diary | Domqueur | 12/01/1918 | 12/01/1918 |
| War Diary | Fienvillers | 13/01/1918 | 14/01/1918 |
| War Diary | In The Line | 15/01/1918 | 31/01/1918 |
| Heading | 6/Northamptonshire Feb 1917 | | |
| War Diary | Mckenzie Huts | 01/02/1917 | 08/02/1917 |
| War Diary | Warwick Huts | 09/02/1917 | 12/02/1917 |
| War Diary | Gloster Huts | 13/02/1917 | 14/02/1917 |
| War Diary | Trenches | 15/02/1917 | 17/02/1917 |
| War Diary | Marlboro Huts. | 18/02/1917 | 18/02/1917 |
| War Diary | Bouzincourt | 19/02/1917 | 28/02/1917 |
| Miscellaneous | Narrative Of The Part Played 3 & 6th Northamptonshire Regiment On The Operations Adjutant S. Miraumont Trench Feb. 17.1917 | 17/02/1917 | 17/02/1917 |
| War Diary | Bouzincourt | 01/03/1917 | 01/03/1917 |
| War Diary | Thiepval Wood | 02/03/1917 | 14/03/1917 |
| War Diary | Pys | 14/03/1917 | 17/03/1917 |
| War Diary | Bihucourt | 17/03/1917 | 18/03/1917 |
| War Diary | Ervillers | 18/03/1917 | 19/03/1917 |
| War Diary | St Leger | 19/03/1917 | 21/03/1917 |
| War Diary | Warloy | 22/03/1917 | 22/03/1917 |

| Type | Location | From | To |
|---|---|---|---|
| War Diary | Villers | 23/03/1917 | 23/03/1917 |
| War Diary | Bocage | 24/03/1917 | 24/03/1917 |
| War Diary | Dury | 25/03/1917 | 28/03/1917 |
| War Diary | Thiennes | 28/03/1917 | 21/04/1917 |
| War Diary | Manguenville | 22/04/1917 | 26/04/1917 |
| War Diary | Bours | 27/04/1917 | 27/04/1917 |
| War Diary | NE Ville Vitasse | 28/04/1917 | 28/04/1917 |
| War Diary | In The Trenches | 29/04/1917 | 30/04/1917 |
| War Diary | In The Trenches W of Cherisy. | 01/05/1917 | 01/05/1917 |
| War Diary | Neuville Vitasse. | 02/05/1917 | 12/05/1917 |
| War Diary | Bivouacs N of Henin | 13/05/1917 | 31/05/1917 |
| Miscellaneous | Report on attack By 6th (S) Bn. Northamptonshire Reg. On Fontaine Trench By Lieut Colonel R. Turner D.S.O. | | |
| War Diary | Bivouacs N of Henin | 01/06/1917 | 03/06/1917 |
| War Diary | In The Trenches W. of Cherisy. B.H.Qrs. N.30.d. | 03/06/1917 | 06/06/1917 |
| War Diary | In The Trenches W. of Cherisy | 06/06/1917 | 09/06/1917 |
| War Diary | Support Trenches S of Heninel | 09/06/1917 | 11/06/1917 |
| War Diary | B.H.Q | 11/06/1917 | 13/06/1917 |
| War Diary | Bn.H.Qn In Shaft Tr. N. 35. C. | 14/06/1917 | 15/06/1917 |
| War Diary | Bn.Hd.Qrs In Concrete Tr. | 16/06/1917 | 16/06/1917 |
| War Diary | Camp S. 17 | 17/06/1917 | 18/06/1917 |
| War Diary | Andinfer-Wood. | 18/06/1917 | 18/06/1917 |
| War Diary | Warlincourt. | 19/06/1917 | 30/06/1917 |
| Miscellaneous | Proposed Scheme For Recapturing The Horse Shoe Trench about M.31.b.80.25. | 03/06/1917 | 03/06/1917 |
| War Diary | Warlincourt | 01/07/1917 | 04/07/1917 |
| War Diary | Billets & Bivouacs NW of Abeele | 04/07/1917 | 06/07/1917 |
| War Diary | Camp N.W. Dickebusch (Canal Reserve Camp) | 07/07/1917 | 22/07/1917 |
| War Diary | Dallington Camp Whippenhoek E. | 23/07/1917 | 24/07/1917 |
| War Diary | Bivouacs N.W. of Steenvoorde | 25/07/1917 | 29/07/1917 |
| War Diary | Micmac Camp West F Dickebusch | 26/07/1917 | 31/07/1917 |
| War Diary | Canal Reserve Camp. N.W. of Dickebusch. | 31/07/1917 | 02/08/1917 |
| War Diary | In The Line Bn Hd. Qrs S.E of Ignorance Crescent. | 03/08/1917 | 10/08/1917 |
| War Diary | In The Line | 09/08/1917 | 10/08/1917 |
| War Diary | Chateau Wood | 10/08/1917 | 10/08/1917 |
| War Diary | Chateau-Segard. H.30.a | 11/08/1917 | 11/08/1917 |
| War Diary | New Dicke-Busche Camp H.33.a. | 12/08/1917 | 12/08/1917 |
| War Diary | N.E. Of Steenvoorde K22.b.2.8 | 13/08/1917 | 15/08/1917 |
| War Diary | Billets at W Hoog Huys | 15/08/1917 | 31/08/1917 |
| Miscellaneous | Operation Orders By Lieut-Colonel R. Turner D.S.O., Commanding 6th. (S) Bn. Northamptonshire Regiment. | 07/08/1917 | 07/08/1917 |
| War Diary | Billets at Hoog Huys Hd.Qrs G.30.b.30.45. | 01/09/1917 | 03/09/1917 |
| War Diary | Billets N.E. of Arneke. | 04/09/1917 | 22/09/1917 |
| War Diary | Tunnelling Camp. F 27.a & C Sheet 27 | 23/09/1917 | 30/09/1917 |
| War Diary | Tunnelling Camp | 01/10/1917 | 16/10/1917 |
| War Diary | Canal Bank | 16/10/1917 | 17/10/1917 |
| War Diary | Poelcapelle | 18/10/1917 | 20/10/1917 |
| War Diary | Tunnelling Camp | 21/10/1917 | 23/10/1917 |
| War Diary | Birty Bucket Camp | 24/10/1917 | 28/10/1917 |
| War Diary | Billets N.E of Proven | 29/10/1917 | 31/10/1917 |
| War Diary | Padding-Ton Camp N.E of Proven F.3.6. | 01/11/1917 | 05/11/1917 |
| War Diary | Dykes Camp A 4.6 | 05/11/1917 | 10/11/1917 |
| War Diary | In The Line Eqypt House U.6.d.4.0. | 10/11/1917 | 13/11/1917 |
| War Diary | Canal Camp B.5.d | 13/11/1917 | 15/11/1917 |
| War Diary | Dykes Camp A.4.b. | 16/11/1917 | 22/11/1917 |
| War Diary | In The Line Egypt House U.6.d.4.0. | 22/11/1917 | 23/11/1917 |

| War Diary | In The Line Egypt House | 23/11/1917 | 25/11/1917 |
| War Diary | Baboon Camp B.6.c. | 26/11/1917 | 27/11/1917 |
| War Diary | Dykes Camp | 28/11/1917 | 04/12/1917 |
| War Diary | Egypt House | 04/12/1917 | 04/12/1917 |
| War Diary | In The Line Egypt House. | 04/12/1917 | 08/12/1917 |
| War Diary | Dykes Camp | 08/12/1917 | 16/12/1917 |
| War Diary | Bapaume Camp | 16/12/1917 | 31/12/1917 |
| War Diary | Baupaume Camp Haringhe H.1.5.0. | 01/01/1918 | 03/01/1918 |
| War Diary | Dykes Camp A 4.d. | 04/01/1918 | 10/01/1918 |
| War Diary | In The Line. Pascal Farm U.12.e.5.2. | 10/01/1918 | 10/01/1918 |
| War Diary | In The Line. Pascal Farm | 10/01/1918 | 11/01/1918 |
| War Diary | Abri Wood U 25d. | 15/01/1918 | 18/01/1918 |
| War Diary | Dykes Camp A4d. | 18/01/1918 | 21/01/1918 |
| War Diary | Dykes Camp | 22/01/1918 | 24/01/1918 |
| War Diary | In The Line Pascal Farm U.12.e.5.2. | 24/01/1918 | 25/01/1918 |
| War Diary | In The Line Pascal Farm. | 25/01/1918 | 26/01/1918 |
| War Diary | K.B.R.I Camp | 26/01/1918 | 30/01/1918 |
| War Diary | Camp E of Crombeke. | 30/01/1918 | 31/01/1918 |
| War Diary | Camp. W. of Crombeke X. 13.d.3.8. | 01/02/1918 | 08/02/1918 |
| War Diary | Morlincourt | 09/02/1918 | 10/02/1918 |
| War Diary | J.28. C & D (Sheet 70e.) | 11/02/1918 | 12/02/1918 |
| War Diary | Camp 700 & N. N.W. of Jussy. Map. Ref. St. Quenton | 12/02/1918 | 24/02/1918 |
| War Diary | Camp N.W. Jussy | 25/02/1918 | 25/02/1918 |
| War Diary | Billets At Caillouel | 26/02/1918 | 26/02/1918 |
| War Diary | Caillouel | 26/02/1918 | 28/02/1918 |
| Heading | 54th Inf. Bde. 18th Div. War Diary 6th Battn. The Northamptonshire Regiment. March 1918 | | |
| War Diary | Billets Caillouel E.24 | 01/03/1918 | 09/03/1918 |
| War Diary | Billets Jussy M.15.c | 10/03/1918 | 13/03/1918 |
| War Diary | Camp Jussy | 14/03/1918 | 21/03/1918 |
| War Diary | In Line Ly-Fontaine | 21/03/1918 | 21/03/1918 |
| War Diary | In The Line SE Jussy | 22/03/1918 | 23/03/1918 |
| War Diary | Caillouel | 24/03/1918 | 24/03/1918 |
| War Diary | Crepigny Grand Rue | 25/03/1918 | 25/03/1918 |
| War Diary | Babouef | 25/03/1918 | 26/03/1918 |
| War Diary | Andignicourt St Aubin | 27/04/1915 | 27/04/1915 |
| War Diary | St Aubin | 28/03/1918 | 30/03/1918 |
| War Diary | Gentelles | 31/03/1918 | 31/03/1918 |
| War Diary | In The Line N Of Hangard | 31/03/1918 | 31/03/1918 |
| Heading | 54th Inf. Bde. 18th Div. War Diary 6th Battn. The Northamptonshire Regiment. April 1918 | | |
| War Diary | In The Line N Of Hangard | 01/04/1918 | 05/04/1918 |
| War Diary | In The Line N of Hangard | 05/04/1918 | 08/04/1918 |
| War Diary | Boutillerie | 09/04/1918 | 18/04/1918 |
| War Diary | Cagny | 19/04/1918 | 20/04/1918 |
| War Diary | In The Line S.E. Of Cachy | 20/04/1918 | 25/04/1918 |
| War Diary | Gentelles | 26/04/1918 | 27/04/1918 |
| War Diary | Heucourt | 27/04/1918 | 30/04/1918 |
| War Diary | Heucourt | 01/05/1918 | 04/05/1918 |
| War Diary | G. La Mous | 05/05/1918 | 05/05/1918 |
| War Diary | Warloy | 06/05/1918 | 06/05/1918 |
| War Diary | In The Line E of Lavieville. | 07/05/1918 | 10/05/1918 |
| War Diary | In The Line S.E of Lavieville. | 18/05/1918 | 23/05/1918 |
| War Diary | In The Line E of Lavieville. | 11/05/1918 | 24/05/1918 |
| War Diary | In Camp On Terraces In C. 14 C. | 25/05/1918 | 31/05/1918 |
| War Diary | Warloy | 01/06/1918 | 04/06/1918 |

| | | | |
|---|---|---|---|
| War Diary | In The Line West of Albert. | 04/06/1918 | 13/06/1918 |
| War Diary | Bivouacs W of Henencourt Wood | 14/06/1918 | 20/06/1918 |
| War Diary | N.W. of Albert | 20/06/1918 | 04/07/1918 |
| War Diary | Henencourt-Bouzincourt Rd. | 05/07/1918 | 12/07/1918 |
| War Diary | Saisseval | 13/07/1918 | 29/07/1918 |
| War Diary | S.W. Frankvillers | 30/07/1918 | 30/07/1918 |
| War Diary | In The Line | 31/07/1918 | 31/07/1918 |
| Heading | 54th Inf. Bde. 18th Division 6th Battalion Northamptonshire Regiment. August 1918. | | |
| War Diary | Line W. of Albert | 17/08/1918 | 20/08/1918 |
| War Diary | Line S.W. of Albert. | 21/08/1918 | 25/08/1918 |
| War Diary | Fricourt | 26/08/1918 | 30/08/1918 |
| War Diary | In Line N. of Sailly Laurette. | 01/08/1918 | 02/08/1918 |
| War Diary | In Import N.of Sailly-Le-Sec | 03/08/1918 | 10/08/1918 |
| War Diary | Line W of Albert. | 11/08/1918 | 15/08/1918 |
| War Diary | Henencourt Wood | 16/08/1918 | 16/08/1918 |
| War Diary | Combles. | 01/08/1918 | 04/08/1918 |
| War Diary | E. of Guillemont | 05/08/1918 | 30/08/1918 |
| Operation(al) Order(s) | Operation Orders No.30 by Lieut, Colonel R. Turner, D.S.O., Commanding 6th. Bn. Northamptonshire Regiment. | 17/09/1918 | 17/09/1918 |
| Miscellaneous | The Attack of The 6th Northamptonshire Regt In That Past Of The 54 Infantry Brigade Attack South. | | |
| War Diary | SW. of Vendhuile | 01/10/1918 | 01/10/1918 |
| War Diary | Ronnsoy | 02/10/1918 | 02/10/1918 |
| War Diary | Molliens-Au-Bois. | 02/10/1918 | 16/10/1918 |
| War Diary | Nurlu | 17/10/1918 | 18/10/1918 |
| War Diary | Serain | 19/10/1918 | 20/10/1918 |
| War Diary | Reumont | 21/10/1918 | 24/10/1918 |
| War Diary | Bousies | 25/10/1918 | 31/10/1918 |
| Miscellaneous | Addenda to Diary for 24th | | |
| War Diary | Epinette Farm | 01/08/1918 | 10/08/1918 |
| War Diary | Le Cateau. | 11/08/1918 | 13/08/1918 |
| War Diary | Serain | 14/11/1918 | 07/12/1918 |
| War Diary | Elincourt | 08/11/1918 | 08/11/1918 |
| War Diary | Serain | 09/11/1918 | 11/11/1918 |
| War Diary | Walincourt | 12/11/1918 | 14/11/1918 |
| War Diary | Selvigny | 15/11/1918 | 15/11/1918 |
| War Diary | Walincourt | 16/11/1918 | 21/11/1918 |
| War Diary | Selvigny | 22/11/1918 | 22/11/1918 |
| War Diary | Walincourt | 23/11/1918 | 31/11/1918 |
| Miscellaneous | Photograph Of "B" Company At Divisional Review Held On 2nd December 1918. | | |
| War Diary | Walincourt | 01/01/1919 | 30/04/1919 |
| Miscellaneous | Copies Of App For Original War Diary | | |

WO95/2044
18 DIVISION
6 BTN NORTHANTS REGT
July 1915 - April 1919

18TH DIVISION
54TH INFY BDE

7TH BN NORTHAMPTONS

JLY 1915 - APL 1919

121/6607

18th Division

6th Northamptons
Vol: I
From 25- 31 July 15

Army Form C. 2118

# WAR DIARY
## or
## INTELLIGENCE SUMMARY
*(Erase heading not required.)*

Instructions regarding War Diaries and Intelligence Summaries are contained in F.S. Regs., Part II. and the Staff Manual respectively. Title Pages will be prepared in manuscript.

| Place | Date 1915 | Hour | Summary of Events and Information | Remarks and references to Appendices |
|---|---|---|---|---|
| BEDFORD, WILTS | 25.7 | 9.a.m | Advance Party, 106 all ranks and all transport entrained | |
| SOUTHAMPTON | 25.7 | 11.30 | Detrained and shifted all animals and wagons on board S.S. Time taken, 55 minutes. | |
| HAVRE | 26.7 | 8 a.m | Disembarked. | |
| " | 26.7 | 6 p.m | Entrained | |
| LONGUEAU | 27.7 | 11.50 a.m | Detrained and marched to Amiens, then turned N. to TALMAS. | Distance marched 13 miles |
| TALMAS | 27.7 | 4 p.m | Arrived without casualty. Went into billets. | |
| " | 28.7 | 9 a.m | The Battalion marched in having left to return on 26th July about 31 m. and crossed via Folkestone and Boulogne, thence by train to Talmas | |
| " | 29.7 | | Battalion in both Reserve | |
| " | 30.7 | | " " | |
| " | 31.7 | | " " | |

G Ripley Col.
6th Bn Northamptonshire Regt

18th Division

6th Northamptons
Vol: II
from 1 - 25.8.15

# WAR DIARY
## or
## INTELLIGENCE SUMMARY

*(Erase heading not required.)*

Army Form C. 2118

| Place | Date 1915 | Hour | Summary of Events and Information | Remarks and references to Appendices |
|---|---|---|---|---|
| TILQUES | 1.9 | | Battalion in both areas | |
| | 2.9 | 2.30pm | Inspection by General Monro, Commdg. 10th Army Corps | |
| | 3.9 | | Battalion in both areas | |
| | 4.9 | " | " | |
| | 5.9 | " | " | |
| | 6.9 | " | " | |
| | 7.9 | " | " | |
| | 8.9 | 4 am | Marched to fresh billets at BONNAY (12 miles) | |
| BONNAY | 9.9 | | Battalion in both areas | |
| | 10.9 | | " | |
| | 11.9 | | " | |
| | 12.9 | | " | |
| | 13.9 | 2.30 am | Marched to SUZANNE (12 miles) and attached to 1st E. Surrey Regt for instruction in trench warfare | |
| SUZANNE | 14.9 | 2 am | Machine Gun attachment, half Headquarters, C and D Coys entered trenches | |
| | 15.9 | | " | |
| | 16.9 | 10 pm | Half Headquarters, A and B Coys relieve half Headquarters and C and D Coys in the trenches. Draft of 39 men joined battalion. | |
| | 17.9 | | | |

G Whitby Colonel
1st Northumberland Fus.

Army Form C. 2118

# WAR DIARY
or
## INTELLIGENCE SUMMARY
(Erase heading not required.)

Instructions regarding War Diaries and Intelligence Summaries are contained in F.S. Regs., Part II. and the Staff Manual respectively. Title Pages will be prepared in manuscript.

| Place | Date 1915 | Hour | Summary of Events and Information | Remarks and references to Appendices |
|---|---|---|---|---|
| SUZANNE | 19.8 | 9 h.m | Half Headquarters, C and D Coys relieve half Headquarters, A and B Coys, in the trenches. 1 killed. | |
| " | 19.8 | | | |
| " | 20.8 | 4.30 a.m | Half Headquarters, A and B Coys relieve half Headquarters, C and D Coys in the trenches. 1 wounded. | |
| " | 21.8 | | 2 wounded. | |
| " | 22.8 | 6 h.m | Half Headquarters, C and D Coys marched to fresh billets at MERICOURT. | |
| " | 23.8 | 6 h.m | Remainder of Headquarters, A and B Coys march to MERICOURT. (11 miles). | |
| MERICOURT | 24.8 to 27.8 | | The Battalion whilst resting here were employed making 2nd line trenches, the two Coys. not so engaged working on alternate days. The senior officer of the Coys. not on the trenches was to be responsible for the station in Depot 132. | |
| " | 28.8 | | 1 draft of 10 men joined Battalion | |

J Hurley Lt Colonel
6th Bn Northamptonshire Regt

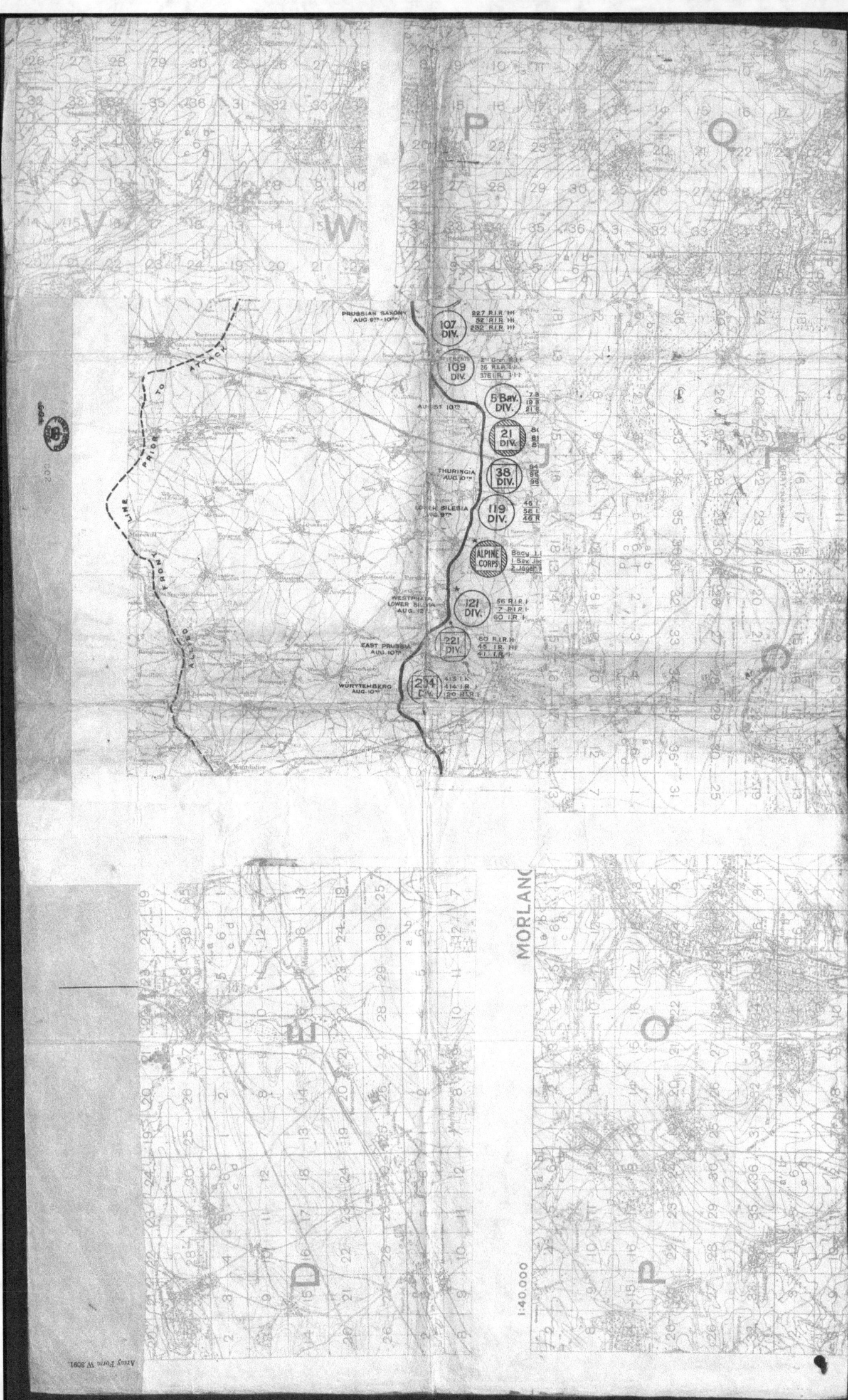

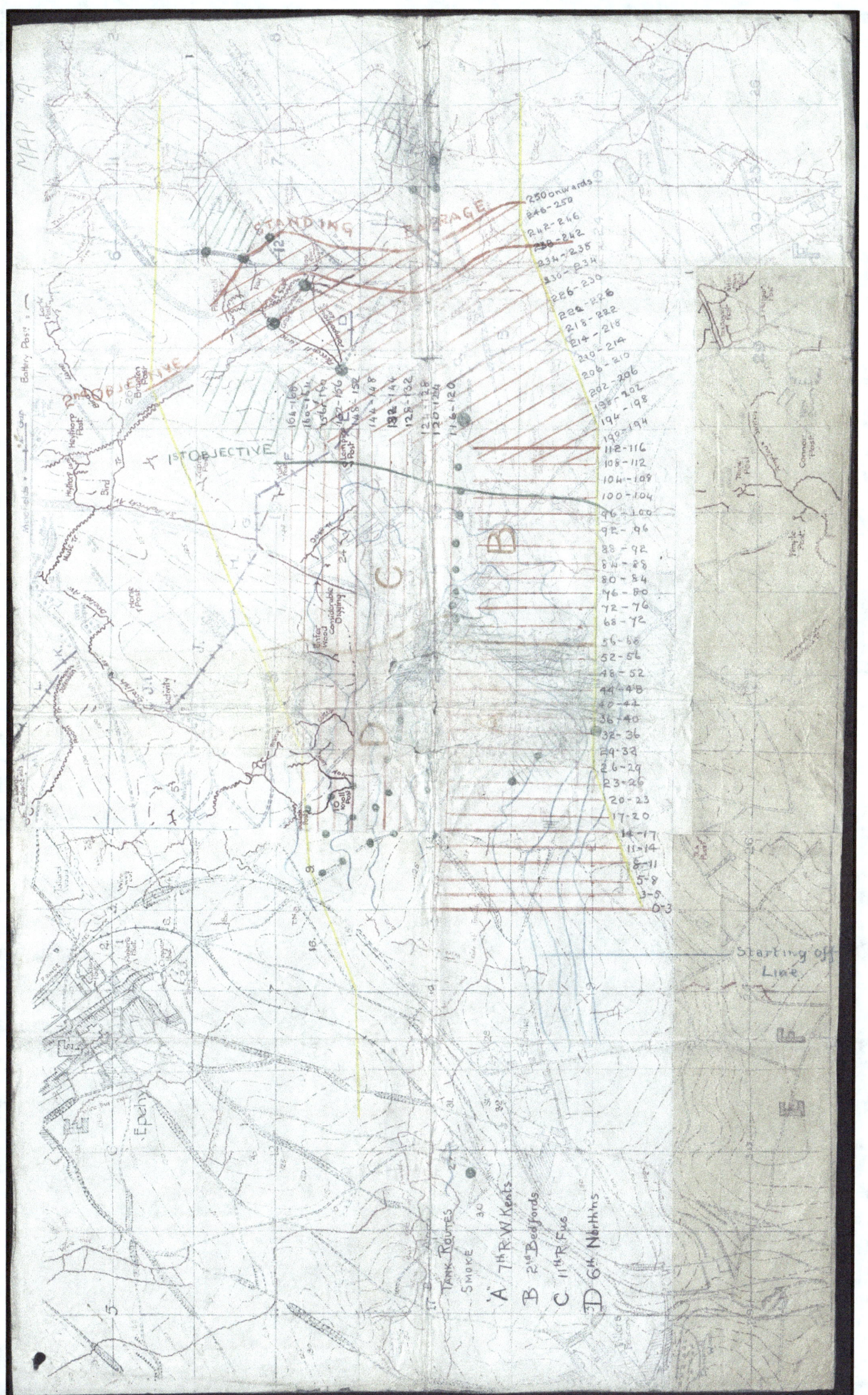

121/7198

18th Aug'n

6th Northamptons
vol: 3
Sep 1. 15.

1st Army
Gustin

Army Form C. 2118.

# WAR DIARY
## INTELLIGENCE SUMMARY.
*(Erase heading not required.)*

Instructions regarding War Diaries and Intelligence Summaries are contained in F.S. Regs., Part II. and the Staff Manual respectively. Title pages will be prepared in manuscript.

| Place | Date | Hour | Summary of Events and Information | Remarks and references to Appendices |
|---|---|---|---|---|
| MERICOURT L'ABBE. | 1915 1-9 | | Battalion in Bois Faucus. Employed in making 2nd line trenches. | |
| | 2-9 | | Half Battalion working at trench dugout. | |
| | 3-9 | 6 A.m. | Battalion marched to MÉAULTE (7 miles) leaving one of Bois Faucus and Dugouts Reserve. | |
| | 4-9 to 8-9 | | Remained in Brigade Reserve. | |
| MÉAULTE | 9-9 to 15-9 | 4.30 p.m | Relieved 11th R. Fusiliers in Sector D1. of trenches. 2 days in front line & 4 days in support. During this period there were considerable activity on both sides. The enemy exploded two mines on our front and we retaliated with one. We were the inflictors on the scheme of trenches etc. was severe. Total casualties, 4 killed, 14 wounded. The weather except on one day was fine and warm. | |
| | 16-9 | 7 p.m. | The battalion was relieved by the 11th R. Fusiliers and marched to billets at MORLANCOURT. | |
| MORLANCOURT | 16-9 to Sep 9 | | This time was spent in rest, one company being employed daily on 2nd line trenches. On the 19th a draft of 50 men joined. | |

Army Form C. 2118.

# WAR DIARY
## or
## INTELLIGENCE SUMMARY.
*(Erase heading not required.)*

Instructions regarding War Diaries and Intelligence Summaries are contained in F. S. Regs., Part II. and the Staff Manual respectively. Title pages will be prepared in manuscript.

| Place | Date | Hour | Summary of Events and Information | Remarks and references to Appendices |
|---|---|---|---|---|
| | 10/15 | | | |
| MORLANCOURT | 25.9 | 6 p.m. | The Battalion relieved the 11th R. Fusiliers in reserve D.I. of the trenches | |
| | 26.9 to 30.9 | | During this tour of duty there was little activity on the enemy's part. One mine was exploded by them on the 28th. Our casualties, 1 killed, + wounded Capt. + Adjt. E.W. Beacham was injured the Military Cross and Pte. Plowman the D.S.M. for good work on the occasion. Two companies Oxford + Bucks L.I. were attached for instruction. Weather fine and dry | WSH |

J Kirby Colonel
Commanding 6(S) Bn Northamptonshire Regt

121/7593

18th Kurourn

6th Southampton
Vol 4

Oct 15

# WAR DIARY / INTELLIGENCE SUMMARY

Army Form C. 2118.

6(S) Bn. Northamptonshire Regt.

| Place | Date | Hour | Summary of Events and Information | Remarks and references to Appendices |
|---|---|---|---|---|
| SECTOR D.1 OF TRENCHES | 1915 1st to 3rd Oct | | Battalion completed its tour of duty in the trenches. On the 2nd three men were wounded and on the 3rd 1 killed and 4 wounded. Weather fine. | |
| MORLANCOURT | 4th to 11th | | A draft of 11 men arrived on the 3rd. On the 5th the Battalion was inspected by the Brigadier and on the 6th by General Sir C. Munro, commanding 3rd Army, who expressed his opinion in the following words "An admirable Battalion, I am proud to have you under my command." On the 7th Capt. Dunham was presented with the Military Cross by Genl. Sir C. Munro in the presence of the Battalion. | |
| SECTOR D.1. TRENCHES | 11th Oct to 19th | | The battalion relieved 11th Royal Fusiliers. The enemy were very quiet during this period. Total casualties 2 killed, 6 wounded. Weather fine & warm. On the 15th a platoon were to assist the 12th Suffolks on our right, and one of their bombers had been blown up by a mine. | |
| MORLANCOURT | 19th to 24th | | The battalion returned to Morlancourt on the 19th being relieved in the trenches by the 11th R. Fusiliers. A wire was received from the Brigadier congratulating the battalion on their work in the trenches during 11th to 19th Oct. | |

# WAR DIARY 1/(5) Bn Northamptonshire Regt

## INTELLIGENCE SUMMARY

| Place | Date | Hour | Summary of Events and Information | Remarks and references to Appendices |
|---|---|---|---|---|
| SECTOR D1 OF TRENCHES | 1915 Oct. 24th to 31st | | The Battalion relieved the 11th R Fusiliers in the trenches on 24th Oct. Casualties:- 1 killed and 3 wounded on 29th and 2 wounded on 30th. | |

6th Northampton
Vol: 5

121/7788

18th Russian

Nov 15

Army Form C. 2118.

# WAR DIARY

## INTELLIGENCE SUMMARY.
(Erase heading not required.)

8th (S) Bn Northamptonshire Regt.

| Place | Date 1915. | Hour | Summary of Events and Information | Remarks and references to Appendices |
|---|---|---|---|---|
| Sector D.1. of Serre | 1-11 to 2-11 | | Three mines were fired by us simultaneously on the evening of Nov 1st. Some casualties to Lambries and 3 men killed, 5 men wounded. Weather wet. | A.W. |
| Morlancourt | 2-11 to 10-11 | 6 p.m. | 4 tents were received from the Engineers on their work. The Bn was relieved by 11th Royal Fusiliers on the afternoon of the 10th. | A.W. |
| Sector D.1. of Vaulx | 10-11 to 16-11 | | During this period the enemy exploded a camouflet on the 12th, we replied with a mine on the 13th. The enemy fired two mines, one on the 15th and another on the 14th. Total casualties 4 killed and 7 wounded. | A.W. A.W. |
| | | | Weather warm wet the first three days, after that, fine with slight frost at night. | |
| Morlancourt | 18-11 to 25-11 | 6 p.m. | The Bn was relieved by the 11th Royal Fusiliers & returned to rest billets. | A.W. |
| Sector D.1. of Vaulx | 26-11 to 30-11 | 6 p.m. | The Bn relieved the 11th R. Fusiliers. During this tenure of four days the enemy were fairly quiet. No mines were fired by either side. Trench casualties 3 killed & 2 wounded. Weather was cold, hard frosts at night. On the 29th the front trenches and the communication trenches were very much damaged owing to the trenches being heavy rain which caused much damage to the trenches. | A.W. |
| Morlancourt | 30-11 | | On the afternoon of the 30th the Batn was relieved by the 7th Bn. Bedfordshire Regt. and returned to rest billets. | A.W. |

A Hopley Col
Commdg 8th Northants Regt.

6th Northamptons
Vol: 6

121/7931

18th 1/21

Su5

incident of 20 men
being taken prisoners
by the enemy
on the 24/12/15

# WAR DIARY or INTELLIGENCE SUMMARY

Army Form C. 2118.

(Erase heading not required.)

| Place | Date | Hour | Summary of Events and Information | Remarks and references to Appendices |
|---|---|---|---|---|
| | 1915 | | 6th (S) Bn. Northamptonshire Regiment | |
| MORLANCOURT | 1-12 to 10 | | Battalion in Rest Billets. | |
| SECTOR D.2 | 11-12 to 11-12 | | The Battalion occupies D.2 sector for the first time relieving the 11th Royal Fusiliers. Weather was throughout. The trenches were in a very muddy state. Casualties:- 2nd Lieut. Wilkinson and 2 men wounded. | |
| BUIRE | 11-12 to 24-12 | | The battalion were relieved by the 11th Royal Fusiliers, and marched to new rest billets at BUIRE. | |
| SECTOR D.2 | 24-12 to 31-12 | | The Battalion relieved the 11th Royal Fusiliers. On the 24th our artillery fired about 800 shells into the trenches in and close to FRICOURT. On the 29th the enemy retaliated with about 2000 shells from guns and trench mortars on D.2 sector from 3.30 p.m. to 5.30 p.m. Among them were a number of gas shells. Towards the end of the bombardment a party of the enemy entered our trenches West of the Cemetery and surprised 20 of our men who had taken cover in a dug-out. These men were made prisoners and taken away to the German lines before the posts on their right and left became aware of the occurrence. | |

G Hicks Col

Army Form C. 2118.

# WAR DIARY
or
# INTELLIGENCE SUMMARY.

(Erase heading not required.)

| Place | Date | Hour | Summary of Events and Information | Remarks and references to Appendices |
|---|---|---|---|---|
| SECTOR D.2. J Trenches | 1915 24.12 to 31.12. | | 6th (S) Bn. Northamptonshire Regiment.<br><br>The point selected for the attack was ranged off by the enemy's fire during the operation and the barrage party blown in. A German soldier who had strayed from the party was shot by our men. Total casualties during this tour of duty in the trenches were 4 killed, 17 wounded, 20 missing.<br><br>The weather was continuously wet but mild and the trenches were in a very bad state. | Note Jan 1st |

Crisp Ly Colonel
Comdg. 6th (S) Bn. Northamptonshire Regt.

6th Merchants
Vol: 7

1st Div

Army Form C. 2118.

WAR DIARY 6th (S) Bn. Northamptonshire Regt.

INTELLIGENCE SUMMARY.

(Erase heading not required.)

Instructions regarding War Diaries and Intelligence Summaries are contained in F.S. Regs., Part II. and the Staff Manual respectively. Title pages will be prepared in manuscript.

| Place | Date | Hour | Summary of Events and Information | Remarks and references to Appendices |
|---|---|---|---|---|
| | 1916 | | | |
| Sector D.2 of Fricourt | 2nd Jan | | On 2nd Jan. the battalion was relieved by the 11th Royal Fusiliers in Sector D.2, facing FRICOURT and marched to Port killed as MORLANCOURT. Casualties during 1st and 2nd Jan, nil. Post killed. | |
| MORLANCOURT | 2nd to 10th | | | |
| Sector D.2 of Fricourt | 10th to 18th | | The Bn relieved the 11th Royal Fusiliers in Sector D.2, on the 10th. This period of eight days was a quiet one. On the 14th our artillery fired about 800 shells into and around FRICOURT. Weather fine and mild. Casualties, 1 killed, 5 wounded. | |
| MORLANCOURT | 18th to 26th | | The Bn was relieved by 11th R. Fusiliers on the 18th and returned to rest billets. | |
| Sector D.2 of Fricourt | 26th to 31st | | On the 26th Bn. returned to D.2, relieving the 11th R. Fusiliers. Weather fine. Casualties, 3 killed, 14 wounded. There was little activity on the part of the enemy during this period except in the matter of machine guns which were very busy. The majority of the casualties were caused by two shells which burst inside the men's billets at BÉCORDEL. | |

Chathams Vol 8

Army Form C. 2118.

# WAR DIARY
## INTELLIGENCE SUMMARY.
(Erase heading not required.)

February 1916.   6th (S) Bn. Northamptonshire Regiment.

Instructions regarding War Diaries and Intelligence Summaries are contained in F. S. Regs., Part II. and the Staff Manual respectively. Title pages will be prepared in manuscript.

| Place | Date 1916 | Hour | Summary of Events and Information | Remarks and references to Appendices |
|---|---|---|---|---|
| Sector D.2 S. of Meaulte | Feb 1st to 8th | | The Bn. completed its tour in the trenches on 8th Feb. when it was relieved by the 8th (S) Bn. Devonshire Regiment, and marched to MÉAULTE. The weather was fine except the last day when it rained heavily. 10 casualties 2 N.C.O's & 6 Wilrs and 1 man wounded. | |
| MÉAULTE | 4th | | | |
| LA HOUSSOYE | 5th to 16th | | The Bn. marched 8 miles to billets at LA HOUSSOYE, the 54th Bde. being now in Divisional Reserve. | |
| PONT NOYELLES | 16th to 29th | | On the 16th the Bn. marched two miles to PONT NOYELLES exchanging billets with the 7th (S) Bn. Royal West Kent Regt. The weather was wet with light winds and during the last week, snow. On the 28th 2nd Lt. B. Thankers was accidentally wounded. | |

J. B. Weston Major
Commdg. 6th (S) Bn. Northamptonshire Regt.

6th Northants
vol 9

18ª

Army Form C. 2118.

# WAR DIARY / INTELLIGENCE SUMMARY

(Erase heading not required.)

6th (S) Bn Northamptonshire Regt.

MARCH 1916

| Place | Date 1916 | Hour | Summary of Events and Information | Remarks and references to Appendices |
|---|---|---|---|---|
| PONT NOYELLES | MARCH 1. | | Battalion in Corps Reserve with remainder of 54th Infantry Brigade. | |
| CORBIE | 2. | 9 a.m. | The Battalion marched to CORBIE, 3 miles, and went into billets in the town. Weather wet, some snow. | |
| BRAY | 7. | | The Battalion marched to BRAY, 11 miles, remained there one night and the following afternoon marched to BRONFAY FARM and BILLONWOOD, 2 miles. One Coy | |
| BRONFAY | 8. | | + Hd Qrs being at the former and 3 Coys at the latter place. Col. G.E. Ripley + Capt + Lieut R.M.A. unclear unclear. | |
| SECTOR A.2. OF TRENCHES | 11. F 15. | 6.10 | The Battn. went into a new sector of front line trenches, A.2. just north of CARNOY village, replacing the 1st Bedfordshire Regt. The trenches, which had been occupied by the 30th Division, were in a very bad state of repair. The 21st Manchester Regt, 7th Division, were on our left and the 12th Middlesex on our right. The enemy fired a mine on the 13th. Weather fine. Casualties: Captain A.H. Burrows killed and 2 men wounded. | |
| BRAY | 18th to 19th | 19.15 | The Battalion returned to rest billets in BRAY. | |
| SECTOR A.2. OF TRENCHES | 19th to 26th 23rd | | During this period the weather was variable. The enemy snipers were very active at first, and much quieter. Casualties 2 killed, 3 wounded. | |

Army Form C. 2118.

# WAR DIARY
## or
## INTELLIGENCE SUMMARY.

(Erase heading not required.) 6th (S) Bn Northamptonshire Regt.

MARCH 1916

| Place | Date 1916 | Hour | Summary of Events and Information | Remarks and references to Appendices |
|---|---|---|---|---|
| | MARCH | | | |
| BIENVILLERS SECTOR A.2 OF TRENCHES 21st | 23rd to 29th 24th to | | The Battn. returned to the Intermediate line. Weather fine, snow on 28th. A quiet period except for artillery fire which was chiefly directed against our batteries. Weather fine and warm enabling great improvement to be made in the trenches. The banks of the water were much and much work done in constructing dug-outs and shelters. Casualties – 2 killed, 4 wounded | |

[signature]
O.C. 6th North'n Regt.

6 Northamptons
Army Form C. 2118.
Vol 10

XVIII

# WAR DIARY
# INTELLIGENCE SUMMARY

(Erase heading not required.) 6th (S) Bn. Northamptonshire Regt.

APRIL 1916

| Place | Date | Hour | Summary of Events and Information | Remarks and references to Appendices |
|---|---|---|---|---|
| Section A.2 ¼ mile | 1916 1.4 | | The Battalion completed its tour in the trenches on 2nd April and returned to rest billets in BRAY, being relieved by 4th Bn Bedfords Regt. We had not been killed. | R.V. |
| | 2.4 | | March a mile at 4.30 am on 1st April. 10 casualties during 1st & 2nd April. 1 killed. | |
| BRAY | 2.4 8.4 | | In billets at BRAY. Weather fine. | |
| Section A.2 ¼ mile | 8.4 | | The Battalion marched to the trenches relieving the 4th Bedfords. | |
| | 10 | | At 2 am on the 13th the enemy opened a heavy bombardment on our centre company. Simultaneously two small parties attempted to raid the trench held by our left company. They were quickly driven out, eight of them being killed. They carried off two of our men who were wounded. Captain H. Gilmore and 4 O.R. men were recommended for decoration and eight other for honourable mention. 10 casualties: 2nd Lieut Waite accidentally wounded, 10 killed, 34 wounded, 2 wounded & missing. | R.V. |
| BRONFAY FARM | 14.4 | | The Battalion was relieved by the 4th Bedfords and returned to the intermediate line. Nos B, C, D are 1 company at BRONFAY FARM, 3 companies in BILLON WOOD | R.V. |
| | 20.4 | | Weather wet. | |

Army Form C. 2118.

# WAR DIARY
## or
## INTELLIGENCE SUMMARY.
*(Erase heading not required.)*

APRIL 1916   6(S) for Northamptonshire Regt.

| Place | Date 1916 | Hour | Summary of Events and Information | Remarks and references to Appendices |
|---|---|---|---|---|
| | APRIL | | | |
| Sector A.2 Trenches | 20 to 26 | | Returned to A.2, relieving the 4th Bedfords. A fairly quiet time. Weather fine. Casualties: 2/Lieut H.H.G. White accidentally killed at Brigade Bomb school and 2/Lieut B.B. Horne accidentally wounded at Brigade Bomb school. 1 killed, 2 wounded. The Battalion marched back to BRAY on being relieved by the 4th Bedfords. Weather very hot. | AW |
| BRAY | 26th to 30th | | | |

[signature] Major,
Commanding 6(S) Bn. Northamptonshire Regt.

Instructions regarding War Diaries and Intelligence Summaries are contained in F.S. Regs., Part II. and the Staff Manual respectively. Title pages will be prepared in manuscript.

# WAR DIARY

## INTELLIGENCE SUMMARY.

May 1916.   6th (S) Bn Northamptonshire Regt.

| Place | Date | Hour | Summary of Events and Information | Remarks and references to Appendices |
|---|---|---|---|---|
| BRAY. | 1-5 | | The 18th Division being now in Corps Reserve, the Battalion marched on | |
| LA HOUSSOYE | 1.5 | | May 1st to LA HOUSSOYE from BRAY-SUR-SOMME (13 miles). Weather very hot. | |
| FRÉCHENCOURT | 2.5 | | The Battalion (less D coy) marched the next day 2nd May to FRECHENCOURT | |
| | | | (2 miles). D. coy proceeded to QUERRIEUX (2 miles). All companies were employed | |
| | | | during this period finishing the CONTAY-DAOURS Railway. | |
| | 15.5 | | On 10th May 'D' coy marched to BRAY and were employed burying telephone | |
| | 10.5 | | cable. Captain N. Gatmore proceeded to England on leave and to be invested | |
| | | | with the D.S.O. awarded to him for distinguished conduct on the occasion of the | |
| | | | German attack on the night 12th/13th April. | |
| SAISSEVAL | 15.5 | | On this date 'B' coy marched to BRAY to assist 'D' coy in their work. | |
| BRAY | 16 | | 'A' coy marched to CORBIE to be attached for demonstration purposes to the 18th | |
| LA HOUSSOYE | | | Divl School at LA HOUSSOYE. 2nd Lieut Villiers Price joined Battn from 3rd Bn on 19.5. Genl Ivamier the O.C. the Bn being appointed | |
| | | | Adjutant of the same. 2nd Lieut Villiers Price joined Battn from 3rd Bn on 19.5. | |
| | | | Headquarters & 'B' coy marched to SAISSEVAL (13 miles) Weather wet. | |
| | 24.5 | | Col G.E. RIPLEY returned from England on recovering from his wounds and | |
| | | | took over command of the Battalion from Major W. TWYNDOWE. | |

**Army Form C. 2118.**

# WAR DIARY
## or
## INTELLIGENCE SUMMARY.

*(Erase heading not required.)*

Instructions regarding War Diaries and Intelligence Summaries are contained in F. S. Regs., Part II. and the Staff Manual respectively. Title pages will be prepared in manuscript.

| Place | Date | Hour | Summary of Events and Information | Remarks and references to Appendices |
|---|---|---|---|---|
| SAISSEVAL | 25.5 | | Draft of 38 N.C.O.s vmen joined from an Entrenching Battalion. | |
| | 26.5 | | Two drafts of 50 + 56 respectively joined from Base. | |
| | 30.5 | | Major J.N. Tokarrington, Queen's Officers, 15th Hussars, joined the Regiment and was appointed 2nd in Command. | |

Q Widdy
Colonel,
Commanding 6th (S) Bn. Northamptonshire Regt.

Army Form C. 2

June
XVIII / 6th Northants Vol 12

# WAR DIARY
## or
## INTELLIGENCE SUMMARY.
(Erase heading not required.)

Instructions regarding War Diaries and Intelligence Summaries are contained in F. S. Regs., Part II. and the Staff Manual respectively. Title pages will be prepared in manuscript.

| Place | Date 1916 | Hour | Summary of Events and Information | Remarks and references to Appendices |
|---|---|---|---|---|
| SAISSEVAL | June 1st | | The Battalion was mentioned in Gen. Sir Douglas Haig's despatch for gallant service. | Special Order of the day by Brig-Gen. W.K. Loubridge C.M.G. D.S.O. attached appendix I. |
| " | 4th | | "C" Company marched from BRAY to CORBIE, and joined "D" Company there. | MK. |
| " | 5th | | "C" and "D" companies entrained at CORBIE for PICQUIGNY and marched to SAISSEVAL. | |
| " | 7th | | The following officers joined the Battalion 2nd Lieut. Darrell R, 2nd Lieut. Jackson H.K. 2nd Lieut. Greenwood J. | MK. |
| PICQUIGNY | 11th | | The Battalion - less "A" Company left SAISSEVAL at 5-30 p.m. and marched to PICQUIGNY. "A" Company arrived at PICQUIGNY by train from CORBIE. | MK. |
| " | 12th to 15th | | The Battalion trained in assault on trenches. | MK. |
| " | 16th to 18th | | The Brigade trained in assault on trenches; and was inspected by the Corps and Divisional Commanders. | MK. |
| " | 20th | | The Battalion went on a short route march. | MK. |
| " | 21st | | The Battalion performed a final assault practice over trenches. | MK. |

Army Form C. 2118.

# WAR DIARY
## or
## INTELLIGENCE SUMMARY.
(Erase heading not required.)

Instructions regarding War Diaries and Intelligence Summaries are contained in F. S. Regs., Part II. and the Staff Manual respectively. Title pages will be prepared in manuscript.

2/

| Place | Date 1916 | Hour | Summary of Events and Information | Remarks and references to Appendices |
|---|---|---|---|---|
| PICQUIGNY | JUNE 22nd | | Battalion transport left for HEILLY. | |
| " | 23rd | | Battalion marched from PICQUIGNY at 10.30 a.m. arrived at AILLY at 11-45 a.m. Weather very hot. Train due to leave at 12-18 p.m. did not leave till 4-45 p.m. arrived at HEILLY by train at 6-30 p.m. Marched through MERICOURT, "A" and "B" Coys. to BRAY where they billeted. "C" and "D" Companies and Headquarters to BRONFAY FARM | |
| BRONFAY FARM | 24th and " | | into "dug-outs" - which were not reached till 2-30 a.m. Rain fell during most of afternoon and evening. Artillery bombardment of enemy trenches commenced about 2 a.m. | |
| " | 25th | | Reconnaissance by Officers of "forming up" trenches of battalion for coming attack. Work on "forming up" trenches. | |
| " | 26th | | All officers valises and heavy kits were sent back to 1st Line Transport. | |
| " | 27th | | Rained hard all day and condition of trenches became very bad - forming up trenches completed, wire on our line of advance removed, and all preparations for the attack completed - It was thought that the attack would start tomorrow, | |
| " | 28th | | but, probably owing to the weather - instructions were received that zero hour | |

Army Form C. 2118.

# WAR DIARY
## or
## INTELLIGENCE SUMMARY.

(Erase heading not required.)

3/

| Place | Date 1916 | Hour | Summary of Events and Information | Remarks and references to Appendices |
|---|---|---|---|---|
| BRONFAY FARM | JUNE (CONTD) 29th | | would be postponed for 48 hours. | |
| " | 30th | | Weather cleared and ground began to dry up. See July 1st | |

G Ripley Colonel,
Commdg: 6th (S) Bn: Northamptonshire Regiment.

Appendix

## SPECIAL ORDER OF THE DAY
### by
### Brigadier General T.H.Shoubridge, C.M.G., D.S.O.,
### Commanding 54th. Infantry Brigade.

The Brigade Commander wishes to congratulate sincerely the Officers, N.C.Os and men of the 7th Bn. Bedfordshire Regiment and 6th. Bn. Northamptonshire Regiment on being mentioned as Battalions for gallant service in the Commander-in-Chief's despatch of 20th. May 1916.

He knows that all ranks of other Units in the Brigade will join with him in these congratulations and will fully appreciate the special honour these gallant battalions have gained for the 54th. Infantry Brigade.

H.B.STUTFIELD, Captain.
Staff Captain,
54th. Inf.Bde.

2nd. June 1916.

54th Inf.Bde.
18th Div.

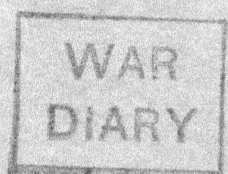

6th BATTN. THE NORTHAMPTONSHIRE REGIMENT.

J U L Y

1 9 1 6

Attached:

Appendices 2, 3, 4 & 5.

**Army Form** C. 2118.

**WAR DIARY**
or
**INTELLIGENCE SUMMARY.**
(Erase heading not required.)

6th S. Bn. Northamptonshire Regt.

| Place | Date | Hour | Summary of Events and Information | Remarks and references to Appendices |
|---|---|---|---|---|
| | 1916 | | | |
| | July 1st | | Operation Orders for the attack and sketch map are attached. | Appendix 2 |
| | | | Narrative of the part taken by the 6th (Service) Battalion, Northamptonshire Regt. in the attack on the German position between MAMETZ and MONTAUBAN. | |
| | | | The 54th Brigade were the left brigade of the 18th Division, which attacked the German position between MAMETZ (exclusive) and MONTAUBAN (inclusive) with three brigades in the front line. The first objective of the 54th Brigade was from the POMMIERS REDOUBT (inclusive) on the right to the junction of BEETLE ALLEY and MAPLE TRENCH (inclusive) on the left. The final objective was a ridge overlooking CATERPILLAR WOOD and WILLOW BROOK, demarcated by a line. The 91st Brigade, 7th Division were on our line on attached map. The 91st Brigade, 7th Division were on our left and the 53rd Brigade, 18th Division on our right. The 11th Royal Fusiliers on the left and the 7th Bedfordshire Regt on the right formed the front line of the 54th Brigade. The 6th Battalion, Northamptonshire Regt. (less six platoons) were the 3rd or supporting battalion and who found one company as "dug-out" |

**Army Form C. 2118.**

**WAR DIARY**
or
**INTELLIGENCE SUMMARY.**
(Erase heading not required.) 1/8 Bn Bedfordshire Regt.

Instructions regarding War Diaries and Intelligence Summaries are contained in F. S. Regs., Part II. and the Staff Manual respectively. Title pages will be prepared in manuscript.

| Place | Date | Hour | Summary of Events and Information | Remarks and references to Appendices |
|---|---|---|---|---|
| (2) (cont.) | 1916 July 1st | | clearing parties, which were attached to the Royal Fusiliers and Bedfords. and cleared the "dug-outs" in the # German trenches. The three remaining platoons acted as carrying parties to the brigade. The 12th Middlesex Regt. was in Brigade Reserve. The Brigade had undergone a week's previous training over ground laid out on the plan of the German trenches to be attacked and were in true fettle when the day arrived. The German trenches and wire entanglement had been battered for seven days by our intense artillery bombardment. On the night preceding the launching of the attack (June 30th – July 1st) the two battalions in the front line were accommodated in our front line trenches. The 6th Northamptonshire Regt. (less six platoons) moved from BRONFAY FARM about 11-30 p.m. on 30th June and occupied their forming-up trenches as follows. A Coy. night Coy. supporting the Bedfordshire Regt. in trenches N. & N.W. of CARNOY. B. Coy. left Coy. supporting the Royal Fusiliers in trenches in | |

# WAR DIARY or INTELLIGENCE SUMMARY

Army Form C. 2118.

| Place | Date | Hour | Summary of Events and Information | Remarks and references to Appendices |
|---|---|---|---|---|
| (3) (cont.) | 1916 July 1 | | CAFTET WOOD - D Coy. (less 2 Platoons) with a portion of Battalion H.qn. was in reserve and were concealed in trenches in the same wood. It was no easy matter for these companies in such a restricted area to debouch from the wood and get into position for the advance as there were many trenches to be negotiated. The terrain however had been carefully reconnoitred by officer and section commanders on previous nights, and trenches had been bridged and wire cut. At half-an-hour after zero hour (8.a.m.) the regiment in lines of half platoons at about 60 paces interval and 150 paces distance found themselves launched to the attack. They had to change direction slightly to the right and often out 7 soon after moving off, but this was successfully accomplished. The Regt Battalion advanced as steadily as if they were on the parade ground, their instructions being, that it was not to halt until the enemy second trench AUSTRIAN SUPPORT was reached. | |

Army Form C. 2118.

WAR DIARY
or
INTELLIGENCE SUMMARY.

(Erase heading not required.) 8.5 2nd Northamptonshire Regt.

| Place | Date | Hour | Summary of Events and Information | Remarks and references to Appendices |
|---|---|---|---|---|
| (4) (cont.) | 1916 July 1st | | All companies came under a heavy artillery barrage before our own trench HYDE ROAD WEST was reached, but they continued to move forward with admirable coolness, A Coy. even checking in "no mans land" to correct their objection. The two leading companies arrived simultaneously at the EMDEN and AUSTRIAN support trenches. A halt of 40 minutes here took place, during which the left Coy. and bombing parties were detached and sent up BLACK ALLEY. At the same time (8.20a.m.) the right platoon of A Coy. had reached BUND TRENCH, and were followed 20 minutes later by the 2nd platoon, who moved to avoid artillery fire. From BUND TRENCH to POMMIER TRENCH both companies came under a heavy artillery fire and suffered considerably, and here Captain Neville commanding B Coy. was wounded. A Coy. on reaching POMMIER TRENCH immediately began making strong point (VI), the three remaining platoons proceeding to POMMIERS REDOUBT and consolidated that on evacuation by the Bedfords. B Coy. moved up at at the same time and started | |

# WAR DIARY or INTELLIGENCE SUMMARY.

| Place | Date | Hour | Summary of Events and Information | Remarks and references to Appendices |
|---|---|---|---|---|
| (5) (cont.) | 1916 July 1st | | to consolidate their allotted strong points as follows:- <br><br> 1 Platoon to No. III Strong Point <br> 1 " " MAPLE TRENCH <br> 1 " " No. IV Strong Point <br> 1 " " No. V " " <br><br> On ascertaining that the 91st Brigade had been held up on our left, which was thus exposed, the officer commanding B Coy. asked for further help and 2 platoons of C Coy., who had been holding dug-outs but had rejoined H.qrs. went out forward and eventually occupied MAPLE TRENCH - D Coy. in reserve had followed B Coy. and detached one platoon to garrison Strong Point (II), placing the remaining platoon in POMMIER TRENCH. This Coy. and part of H.qrs. came in for heavy shell fire and suffered severely. By about 10-15 a.m. all Strong Points in the first objective had been occupied and were being placed in a state of defence, and the task allotted to the Battalion had been accomplished. | |

Army Form C. 2118.

# WAR DIARY
## or
## INTELLIGENCE SUMMARY.

(Erase heading not required.) 5th Buckinghamshire Bn.

| Place | Date | Hour | Summary of Events and Information | Remarks and references to Appendices |
|---|---|---|---|---|
| (6) (cont.) | 1916 July 1 | | The two platoons of C and two of D Coys. who went over with the Royal Fusiliers and Bedfords worked through the 3 front lines of the enemy trenches on a set plan and carried out their work thoroughly & well. - Three sections of D Coy. however suffered very heavily from machine gun fire and were practically wiped out. Liaison was well maintained between the battalion and the companies on its right and left. All company commanders carried out their orders correctly and handled their companies with gallantry & skill. Platoons were well led both by officers and N.C.O.s. - Runners & bearers Signalling was splendidly - 2nd Lt. Price distinguished himself by the excellent and reliable information which he obtained - Bn. Hqrs. was (not) established at PICCADILLY and afterwards moved to a point in BUND TRENCH about 100 yards W of | |

1577 Wt. W10791/1773 500,000 1/15 D. D. & L. A.D.SS./Forms/C. 2118.

Army Form C. 2118.

# WAR DIARY
## or
## INTELLIGENCE SUMMARY.

(Erase heading not required.) 6th (S) Bn Northamptonshire Regt.

| Place | Date | Hour | Summary of Events and Information | Remarks and references to Appendices |
|---|---|---|---|---|
| (b) | 1916 | | | |
| | (cont) July 1st | | The TRIANGLE. | |
| | | | The following casualties occurred on this day. | |
| | | | Officers wounded :- Capt. Neville, Frank Septimus | |
| | | | Lieut. Shankster, George | |
| | | | 2nd Lieut. Hamilton, Noel Crawford. | |
| | | | Shell shock, 1 - | |
| | | | Other ranks :- Killed 29, Wounded 123, Missing 4, Shell shock, 1 - | |
| | | | Total 3 Officers, Other Ranks. 157 | |
| | | | Copies of congratulatory messages received are attached. | Appendix 3. |
| | July 2nd | | Consolidation of position was continued. | |
| | | | Casualties. Other Ranks. Killed 2, Wounded 30, Missing 5. | |
| | July 3rd | | A Coy. relieved the 7th Bedfordshire Regt. in EMDEN TRENCH | |
| | | | B Coy. relieved the 7th " " in BUND TRENCH and No. 2. Strong Post. | |
| | | | C and D. Remained in their old positions | |

**Army Form C. 2118.**

# WAR DIARY
## or
## INTELLIGENCE SUMMARY.

(Erase heading not required.) 6/S.Lin.Northamptonshire Regt

Instructions regarding War Diaries and Intelligence Summaries are contained in F. S. Regs., Part II. and the Staff Manual respectively. Title pages will be prepared in manuscript.

| Place | Date 1916 | Hour | Summary of Events and Information | Remarks and references to Appendices |
|---|---|---|---|---|
| THE LOOP | July 4 | | The work of consolidation was continued. Casualties :- Other Ranks :- Wounded 2. | NK. |
| | " 5 | | | NK. |
| | " 6 | | The battalion moved into bivouacs during the evening to THE LOOP near BRONFAY FARM. | NK. |
| | " 7 | | The C.R.C. wired the following congratulatory message from H.M. The King :- "Please convey to the Army under your command my sincere congratulations on the results achieved in the recent fighting - I am proud of my troops, none could have fought more bravely". | NK. |
| BOIS DE TAILLES | " 9 | | The battalion moved during the evening into camp at BOIS DE TAILLES. | NK. |
| " | " 10 | | Maj. Gen. Morose visited the camp - | NK. |
| | " 11 | | hit | NK. |
| | " 12 | | hit | NK. |

Army Form C. 2118.

# WAR DIARY
## or
## INTELLIGENCE SUMMARY.
(Erase heading not required.)

(1/5) Bn. Bedfordshire Regt.

Instructions regarding War Diaries and Intelligence Summaries are contained in F.S. Regs., Part II. and the Staff Manual respectively. Title pages will be prepared in manuscript.

| Place | Date 1916 | Hour | Summary of Events and Information | Remarks and references to Appendices |
|---|---|---|---|---|
| MAICOURT | July 13 | 6-30 a.m. | The battalion paraded at 6-30 a.m. but did not reach MARICOURT till about 12 noon. Owing to being held up for a long period near BILLON WOOD. The battalion occupied various dug-outs in and around the ruins of the town, which was under rather heavy shell fire - Hqrs. in a cellar in the Chateau stables. Operations resulting in the capture of TRONES WOOD. | For Map. |
| | " | 10-45 p.m. | At 10-45 p.m. orders were received to send two companies (C. & D were sent) to relieve two companies 12th Middlesex Regt. in DulBttn DUBLIN TRENCH. | " Sketch Map. See Appendices 4 & 5 |
| | 14th | 2-45 a.m. | At 2-45 a.m. the remaining two companies (A & B) and Hqrs. were ordered to march to the SUNKEN ROAD, E. of BRIQUETRIE, where they would join up with C. & D companies, who had been moved forward from DUBLIN TRENCH. At the same time Major Thorington received orders to report himself to 54th Bde. Hqrs., where he received the following verbal instructions from the G.O.C. That he was placed in command of the battalion for an attack on TRONES WOOD - Lt. Col. Maxwell V.C. D.S.O. C.S.I. being in command of the whole operation. Our artillery barrage would lift from the wood at 4-30 a.m. The 9" R.W. Kents | |

# WAR DIARY or INTELLIGENCE SUMMARY

Army Form C. 2118.

(B.E.F.) 6th Northamptonshire Regt.

| Place | Date | Hour | Summary of Events and Information | Remarks and references to Appendices |
|---|---|---|---|---|
| | 2/ | | were holding a line from E. to W. across the Southern portion of the wood. The role of the 6th Northants would be that of supporting battalion to the 12th Middlesex, who were to hold the front line. The duties of the battalion were to clear out behind the front line and form a defensive flank on the Eastern edge of the wood. Maj: Charrington was to report himself to Lt. Col. Maxwell, who would be found somewhere in the Southern edge of the wood. Lieut. Ripley was detached at 54th Bde. Hqrs. as liaison officer. Maj: Charrington left Bde. Hqrs at 3.25 a.m. & arrived at BRIQUETRIE about 4-10 a.m. where he found Lt. Col. Maxwell, who informed him that he had been unable to collect all his battalion and had detailed 6th Northants as the attacking line – Orders had been given to Major Clark and the battalion were then moving Eastwards along the SUNKEN ROAD to get into position for the advance on the Southern edge of TRONES WOOD. From Major Clark, the following résumé of the orders he had issued was received. "The Battalion was to move forward to the line held by the 7th R.W. Kent Regt. From there they were to clear the wood of the enemy to its extreme Northern front. A. & B. Companies in the front line line – C. Coy. in support. D. Coy. in reserve. Bn. Hqrs. in centre of SUNKEN ROAD. There was no time to obtain any more detailed information as the two leading Companies were already – 4-25 a.m. – advancing across the open towards the Southern edge of the wood. The advance took place over 1000 yards of open ground which was smothered by an intense barrage of large calibre H.E. shell from the hostile artillery. The Companies advanced through this barrage with the greatest coolness & steadiness and suffered a good many casualties before reaching the wood. | |

# WAR DIARY or INTELLIGENCE SUMMARY

Army Form C. 2118

| Place | Date | Hour | Summary of Events and Information | Remarks and references to Appendices |
|---|---|---|---|---|
| | 3/- | | Lt. & Adjt. Barkham and Bn. Hqrs. except 4 runners, were left in the SUNKEN ROAD, and Major Tharrington accompanied Lt. Col. Maxwell and Maj. Black into the wood to get into touch with O.C. 4th R.W. Kent Regt. and ascertain the situation - The Hqrs. of the 4th R.W.K. was found in a shallow trench in S.W. corner of the wood. From Lt. Col. Fiennes, commanding 4th R.W.K. we learnt that portions of his battalion were holding a line near the light railway, & that he had a detached post holding a Strong Point in the northern edge of the wood - It turned out later that no men of the R.W.K. were found anywhere north of the light railway line that runs E. & W. through centre of wood. 2nd Lt. Price, D Coy., & Lt. Walker, C. Coy. both reported finding R.W.K. in a trench on edge of wood S. of Strong Point A. The latter reported three officers with this party, who said they were short of ammunition, & requested reinforcements to be left with them. 2nd Lt. Price reported that this party at first mistook his men for the enemy, & opened fire on them. Captain Podmore reported that a party of R.W.K. were found lining the light railway running across centre of wood. They were facing South and also mistook his men for the enemy and opened rapid fire on them - It was with the greatest difficulty and not until a compass had been produced that they could be persuaded that they were not facing northwards. No one in the battalion ever reported having found any of the R.W.K. north of this line. | |

Army Form C. 2118.

# WAR DIARY
## or
## INTELLIGENCE SUMMARY.
(Erase heading not required.)

Instructions regarding War Diaries and Intelligence Summaries are contained in F.S. Regs., Part II. and the Staff Manual respectively. Title pages will be prepared in manuscript.

| Place | Date | Hour | Summary of Events and Information | Remarks and references to Appendices |
|---|---|---|---|---|
| | 3a/ | A.M. 4-45 | In addition to the enemy's artillery barrage which was kept on the southern portion of the wood, there were periods of heavy rifle & machine gun fire from a point a little further in the interior. In the meantime Lt. Col. Maxwell went back to the south edge of the wood to collect | |
| | | 4-50 | Message was received from Major Clark that D Coy. was holding the trench running NE & SW towards Strong Point B. German bombers were holding Strong Point about 40 yards to their right - W. Kent officers reports that they are holding N. end of wood - Sent a message to Major Clark that O.C. of R.W.K. confirmed the report that they were holding N. end of wood - | |
| | | 5-10 | Captain Podmore reported that his company were advancing N.E. and bombing up trench running from S.W. corner of the wood, and that he was in touch with portions of B & C Coys. on his right but not with A Coy. He also reported that he was held up by Strong Point B and that he urgently required more bombs. Major Clark killed, Captain Shepherd wounded, only about 100 men of his company left. Major Charrington only had one runner with him at the time so collecting as many bombs as they could carry, he went forward to ascertain the situation. Instructions were left for more bombs to be sent as soon as possible and these were soon afterwards brought up by men of the Middlesex Regt. | |
| | | 6-0 | Men of B & D Coys were found creeping up to the Strong Point through the interior growth, whilst those attempting to get round by the trench were held up owing to lack of bombs. Heavy rifle and machine gun fire was coming from the Strong Point - Captain Shepherd, although wounded in the shoulder, was standing up in the open cheering on his men. In the most gallant manner - On a fresh supply of bombs arriving, the attack was pushed home, and the Strong Point captured about 6-0 a.m. Many dead Germans were found at this short - | |

1577 Wt. W10791/1773 500,000 1/15 D.D. & L. A.D.S.S./Forms/C. 2118.

**Army Form C. 2118**

# WAR DIARY
## or
## INTELLIGENCE SUMMARY
*(Erase heading not required.)*

Instructions regarding War Diaries and Intelligence Summaries are contained in F.S. Regs., Part II. and the Staff Manual respectively. Title Pages will be prepared in manuscript. 4

| Place | Date | Hour A.M. | Summary of Events and Information | Remarks and references to Appendices |
|---|---|---|---|---|
| | | 6-0 | From this time onwards, owing to the impenetrable nature of the wood, heavy losses amongst officers and leaders, units became mixed up and it was difficult to obtain a coherent idea of the situation. | |
| | | 8.05 | Lt. Col. Maxwell proceeded to eastern edge of wood to clear up situation and endeavour to reorganise units. He requested Major Champion to remain where he was until his return. | |
| | | 9-15 | Following message was received from Capt. Podmore (timed 9.0 a.m.) "Have secured all TRONES WOOD. Secured small T head containing about 6 men by Strong Point on GUILLEMONT ROAD. Also about 40 Germans in trench outside wood just S. of same Strong Point. BUFFS are attacking with a Stokes gun. We must have a Stokes gun, if we are to take these two places. Am consolidating E. edge of TRONES WOOD." Above has since been confirmed in a letter from Capt. Podmore (wounded) in which he says:- "I sent Lt. Rickord to work N. through the wood. He did so with great success, clearing the wood up to the W. side up to the North point, & then moving down again the E. side till he joined us by the Strong Point on the GUILLEMONT road." | |
| | | 9-02 | 2nd Lt. Price reported that D Coy. were now occupying main trench running from N. to S. through middle of wood. Enemy were clear of the wood on East & South but snipers still in evidence to the North. | |
| | | 9-25 | 2nd Lt. Redhead reported that his company were holding a position on E. edge of wood N. of Strong Point A. Enemy running away to the East being fired on by 12th Middlesex with machine guns. This was presumably from Strong Point A, which had been captured by 12th Middlesex & 7th Buffs about 9.a.m. From this time till about 11-30 a.m. practically no information was received from the front, but Lt. Col. Maxwell was on the spot re-organising units. | |

# WAR DIARY or INTELLIGENCE SUMMARY

Army Form C. 2118.

1st Bn Northamptonshire Regt

| Place | Date | Hour | Summary of Events and Information | Remarks and references to Appendices |
|---|---|---|---|---|
| | 5/ | A.M. 11-30 | Message received from 2nd Lt. Price. "Have taken over command of B Coy. Strength at present appears to be about 50. Am hanging on to our position lining the East side of wood. Am very thin. Please try & get reinforcements up - Am unfortunately hit in the leg and cannot get along the line very fast." About this time 2nd Lt. Walker arrived & asked for reinforcements for C. Coy. which had suffered many casualties & was also on Eastern edge of wood - An Officer of 11th Royal Fusiliers, who were in support, had just reported to Maj: Harrington with me company, so he was requested to send one platoon to reinforce our Eastern flank, which was done - This platoon was later established in Strong Point A. The other 3 platoons R.F. were being heavily shelled in the wood, & were ordered to fall back to a trench about 400 yards in rear - The only shelter in the Southern part of the wood which was under a continuous artillery barrage, being a shallow trench already etched with wounded) - | |
| | | " | Approximate position of troops as far as can be ascertained at this time is shown in sketch map. The trench shown running parallel to S.E. edge of wood, was formed by 2nd Lt. Walker to be occupied by 3 Officers and a party of 7th R.W. Kent, regained about 6 a.m. They were in a somewhat exhausted condition and were relieved about 9 a.m. Before this time the backbone of the defence enemy's resistance had been broken by the capture of strong Points A & B. The brunt of the fighting had been borne by the 6th Northants, who had suffered severe casualties both in Officers & men. The wood was now clear of the enemy, at any rate, except for snipers - Lt. Col. Tracewell then organised a drive to clear the northern half of wood and broke up any resistance still left | |

**Army Form C. 2118.**

**WAR DIARY**
or
**INTELLIGENCE SUMMARY**
(Erase heading not required.)

6/5 Bn Oxfordshire & Bucks L.I.(?)

| Place | Date | Hour | Summary of Events and Information | Remarks and references to Appendices |
|---|---|---|---|---|
| | 6/ | P.M. | Whilst this drive was in progress the machine guns of 12: Middlesex & 7: Buffs in Strong Point A and 2 Lewis guns of 6: Northants met the COPSE, where given excellent targets, as the enemy fled across the open towards GUILLEMONT, and accounted for many enemy. | |
| | | 1.30 | The news had been received at Adv. Report Centre in S. of TRONES WOOD, of or from Lt. Bat. Maxwell Niv 9.05 a.m. and it was thought that possibly he had become a casualty. | |
| | | 2.30 | Lt. Col. Maxwell returned & gave Major Charrington orders to collect & organise the scattered units of the 6: Northants and as soon as they should be relieved by the 12: Middlesex on the Eastern edge of the wood, to take over the MALTZ HORN TRENCH from the 7: Buffs, keeping one Coy. in support in the back of TRONES WOOD. | |
| | | 3.30 | Units were divided, distributed approximately as shown in sketch — | |
| | | 5.30 | 12: Middlesex commenced relieving 6: Northants from the North. 6: Northants were formed up to West of the COPSE. After Stragglers had been collected the battalion only mustered as follows :— | |

Officers | Other Ranks
A Coy. 2nd Lt. Harris Smith | 54
B Coy. 2nd Lt. Price (wounded in leg, slightly) | 69
C Coy. 2nd Lt. Walker | 46
D Coy. Capt. Podmore (slightly wounded, attached in back) | 45
 | 244

# WAR DIARY or INTELLIGENCE SUMMARY

Army Form C. 2118.

(6/7B) 7th Bn. Northamptonshire Regt.

| Place | Date | Hour | Summary of Events and Information | Remarks and references to Appendices |
|---|---|---|---|---|
| | | P.M. | Total of 3 unwounded officers including Major Charrington, 8 247 other ranks. This was all that remained out of 17 regimental officers, and about 550 other ranks that had left the SUNKEN ROAD and entered TRONES WOOD a few hours previously – Lt. Newbery, the Medical Officer had also been killed, between TRONES and BERNAFAY WOOD, whilst performing his duties in the most gallant manner. The battalion was then moved into the MALTZ HORN TRENCH, except B Coy. under 2nd Lt. Price, who were left in support in the trench previously occupied by the 7th R.W. Kents. | |
| | | 6.0. | On the weak state of the battalion being explained to Lt. Col. Ransome, Commdg. 7th Buffs, & to 54th Bde. Hqrs. it was arranged that the 7th Buffs. should continue to hold the MALTZ HORN line for the night, the 6th Northants remaining in support in the same trenches, in which there were planks of shave room – | |
| | | | Casualties during the day had been as follows:– | |
| | | | Officers – killed – (5)     Officers – wounded – (9) | |
| | | | Major Clark – G.M.C. Coy.    Capt. Thresher – O.D.   A Coy. | |
| | | | 2nd Lt. Lys, F.C.G.B. C "    " Shepherd – S.F.   B " | |
| | | | " Farrell. R. D "    Lt. Arnold – J.F.   D " | |
| | | | " Hamilton. N.C. B "    " Wilcox – F.A.C.   A " | |
| | | | Lt. Newbery. R.F.T. (R.A.M.C.)    2nd Lt. Fawkes – R.B.   D " | |
| | | |     " Redhead – A.H.   D " | |
| | | | Missing – (1)     " Greenwood – J.   B " | |
| | | |     " Price – T.R.   D " | |
| | | | 2nd Lt. Woolfe – C.L. A Coy.    Capt. Podmore – H.   D " | |
| Since returned killed | | | | |

Other Ranks
Killed – 30
Wounded – 198
Missing – 35
Shell shock – 7
    240
Officers – 15.

Army Form C. 2118.

# WAR DIARY
## or
## INTELLIGENCE SUMMARY.

(Erase heading not required.) 6th (S) Bn Northamptonshire Regt

Instructions regarding War Diaries and Intelligence Summaries are contained in F. S. Regs., Part II. and the Staff Manual respectively. Title pages will be prepared in manuscript.

| Place | Date | Hour | Summary of Events and Information | Remarks and references to Appendices |
|---|---|---|---|---|
| | 8/ | | During the night 14/15 July, the following further casualties were reported :- Other Ranks. | |

Killed - 2 - Wounded - 9 - Missing 2 - Shell shock 5 - Total 18.

Making grand total of Officers - 15
                     Other Ranks 288
                     All Ranks 303

Considering the disadvantageous circumstances under which the attack was carried out, the operation resulting in the complete capture and occupation of TRONES WOOD, the capture of which had been attempted and at any rate partially failed on at least three previous occasions, may reflects the greatest credit on all concerned -

The battalion was thrown into the wood in so much haste, that it was impossible to explain in any detail the plan of attack.

After passing through an extremely severe artillery barrage across 1,000 yards of open country the battalion was met, before it had proceeded more than about 150 yards into the wood, by heavy machine gun & rifle fire -

Without the slightest hesitation the attack was immediately launched & pushed home with the greatest vigour. It was inevitable that in the ensuing fighting units should become mixed or to a certain extent lose direction, especially in an attack which had been launched, as this one was, without the opportunity for the least preparation -

There is no doubt that the backbone of the attack resistance to the centre of the wood, was broken entirely by the vigorous initiative taken by the company commanders & other subordinate leaders - It was during the early stages

1577 Wt.W10791/1773 500,000 1/15 D. D. & L. A.D.S.S./Forms/C. 2118.

# WAR DIARY or INTELLIGENCE SUMMARY

Army Form C. 2118

(Erase heading not required.) of (?) Bn. Northamptonshire Regt.

| Place | Date | Hour | Summary of Events and Information | Remarks and references to Appendices |
|---|---|---|---|---|
| | | | that most of the casualties occurred amongst the officers of the battalion. Majors Clark, Captains Shewier, Shepherd & Podmore were all became casualties at very soon after commencement of the attack. The three king killed whilst gallantly reconnoitring in front of his Company. Many subaltern officers were also put out of action at this period — Under these circumstances, it can scarcely be wondered at, that after the fight had been proceeding for about 3 hours, a considerable degree of disorganisation had resulted — A contributary cause was the impenetrableness of the wood, which had been rendered much worse by the heavy artillery bombardment to which it had been subjected from our own & enemy guns, which had laid trees flat in every direction, causing an impassable network of timber and branches. | |
| MALTZ HORN TRENCH | 15th | | Hqs at N. end of HAIRPIN. Reinforcements began to arrive. 2nd Lt. Chatham arrived the previous evening. 2nd Batty early in morning. 2nd Lt. A/Capt. Bastham arrived from SUNKEN ROAD. About 8 a.m. Capt. Swan, Lt. Eldridge, 2 Lt. Keys & Gillett arrived. This allowed Capt. Podmore & 2nd Lt. Price, both of whom had been wounded, on previous day to return to leave their companies, to be relieved — 2nd Lt. Higham also arrived with 60 other ranks, but as the 7th Buffs were still holding the MALTZ HORN TRENCH, these were sent back to FAVIERRE TRENCH until required in front line — | |

**Army Form C. 2118**

# WAR DIARY
## or
## INTELLIGENCE SUMMARY

(Erase heading not required.) (6⁵ᵗʰ) Bn. Northamptonshire Regt

Instructions regarding War Diaries and Intelligence Summaries are contained in F.S. Regs., Part II. and the Staff Manual respectively. Title Pages will be prepared in manuscript.

| Place | Date 1916 | Hour | Summary of Events and Information | Remarks and references to Appendices |
|---|---|---|---|---|
| MALTZ HORN TRENCH | July 15ᵗʰ | 10 | During the evening orders arrived from 54ᵗʰ Bde. Hqrs. for reconstruction of the line holding MALTZ HORN TRENCH. At this time B Coy. had already proceeded under orders from Lt. Col. Muxwell from their support trench in the S.E. edge of TRONES WOOD to the Northern point of the wood. A Coy. was employed transferring bombs & ammunition from TRONES WOOD to a dump in STRONG POINT A. C. Coy. was collecting picks & shovels & carrying them to the same place, & 2 bomb platoons of D Coy. were unloading mules in the valley S. of Strong Point A. Hqrs. had been moved during afternoon from HAIRPIN to a point 1000 yards further N. in MALTZ HORN TRENCH. | |
| | 16ᵗʰ | | The line allotted to the battalion was from the South front of the road in MALTZ HORN TRENCH near point 6550 h. S. 30.c. to an including the COPSE in about centre of Eastern edge of TRONES WOOD. Companies were distributed as follows:- B Coy. from right of our line to Strong Point A exclusive; C Coy. in Strong Point A; D Coy. from Strong Point A exclusive to Northern edge of the COPSE inclusive; A Coy. in support in trench on S.E. edge of TRONES WOOD. Bn. Hqrs. in Northern part of 7ᵗʰ Batto. line, until accommodation could be arranged in Strong Point A. The relief was completed — line taken over about 5 a.m. During afternoon orders were received from Bde. Hqrs. to occupy ARROW HEAD COPSE. | |

# WAR DIARY
## or
## INTELLIGENCE SUMMARY

(Erase heading not required.) O/C for Lt Col Watkins Capt.

Army Form C. 2118

| Place | Date | Hour | Summary of Events and Information | Remarks and references to Appendices |
|---|---|---|---|---|
| | July 1916 11 | | A patrol was at once despatched there to reconnoitre, saw no signs of enemy but was fired on by our own artillery - Artillery were requested not to fire any more," & at 10-30 p.m. ARROW HEAD COPSE was occupied by a detachment of 10 men & a Lewis gun, without opposition - At the same time a patrol proceeded about 300 yards along the trench which runs eastwards from Strong Point A in direction of GUILLEMONT & met with no signs of enemy - | |
| | 14 | | The battalion was relieved by 3 companies, 15th Sherwood Foresters (Bantams). The relief was completed by 4-30 a.m. The battalion arrived at COPSE D. S. of MARICOURT about 6-45 a.m. & went into dug-outs. The account of above operations is unavoidably incomplete & possibly in some particulars inaccurate - It is always difficult to follow the course of events in an operation of this nature, especially so in the present case, when there are only two officers remaining, both very junior, who took part in the attack, from whom any first hand information can be obtained - The whole battalion, both officers, N.C.O.s & men behaved with | & more information has since been obtained by letter from wounded officers. MK |

Army Form C. 2118

# WAR DIARY
or
## INTELLIGENCE SUMMARY
(Erase heading not required.) 8th Bn Northamptonshire Regt

| Place | Date | Hour | Summary of Events and Information | Remarks and references to Appendices |
|---|---|---|---|---|
| | | 12/ | the greatest gallantry. With regard to the Officers, the casualty list speaks for itself.
The medical staff and stretcher bearers, personally directed by their Medical Officer, Lt. R.F.T. Newberry R.A.M.C. carried out their duties with the greatest devotion and suffered many casualties.
It is impossible to speak too highly of the self-sacrifice & fearlessness of Lt. Newberry, who lost his life whilst carrying out his duties to the utmost of his abilities.
The Rev. A.E. Bennet also showed bravery of the highest order in his administration to & assistance of the wounded under heavy shell fire.
The transport & supply arrangements under Lt. Beesley & Lt. Foster was carried out, often in positions of considerable danger with the greatest energy & zeal.
Runners, as usual performed their hazardous & exhausting duties with great courage and devotion to duty.
The report cannot close without a tribute to the memory of Major Clark who was killed in action early on the 14th July.
This officer by his soldierly qualities, his coolness under fire, | |

1875 Wt. W593/826 1,000,000 4/15 J.B.C.& A. A.D.S.S./Forms/C. 2118.

# WAR DIARY
## or
## INTELLIGENCE SUMMARY

(Erase heading not required.) 6 (S) Bn. Northamptonshire Regt.

Army Form C. 2118

| Place | Date | Hour | Summary of Events and Information | Remarks and references to Appendices |
|---|---|---|---|---|
| COPSE D. S. of MARICOURT | 17th (cont.) | | + The interest he always took in the welfare of his men, endeared himself to all ranks. His loss will be keenly felt & his place hard to refill. The names of those who have been brought to notice for special acts of gallantry & devotion to duty have been forwarded to the proper quarter.<br><br>The Battalion rested after having had scarcely any sleep for 96 hours. The following was published in Regimental Orders:— "The C.O.C. in C. has under special authority granted by H.M. The King awarded the "Military Cross" of 1st July 1916 to 3/11054 R.S.M. Fulcher F." | |
| BOIS DE TAILLES | 18th | | The Battalion marched from COPSE D. at 9p.m. and arrived at Camp in BOIS DE TAILLES about midnight — A draft of 300 N.C.O.s & men joined the Battalion. | |
| " | 19th | | C.O. inspected the Battalion. | |
| " | 20th | | The Battalion paraded at 1-30 a.m. & marched to EDGE HILL STATION, arriving about 3-45 a.m. Train suppose to leave at 4p.m. did not depart until 10-30 a.m. | |

Army Form C. 2118

# WAR DIARY
## or
## INTELLIGENCE SUMMARY
(Erase heading not required.)

Instructions regarding War Diaries and Intelligence Summaries are contained in F.S. Regs, Part II. and the Staff Manual respectively. Title Pages will be prepared in manuscript.

| Place | Date 1916 | Hour | Summary of Events and Information | Remarks and references to Appendices |
|---|---|---|---|---|
| CITERNES | July 22nd | | Battalion arrived at LONGPRES at 6-30 a.m. by train, thence by train to WIRY & thence marched about 1½ miles to billets at CITERNES. arriving about 9-45 a.m. | |
| WALLON CAPPEL | 23rd | | Battalion paraded at 5 a.m. and marched back to LONGPRES. arriving at 8-45 a.m., entrained at 9-45 a.m. (rations provided) via ETAPLES & ST. OMAR and arrived at ARQUES at 5 p.m. Left ARQUES at 7-30 p.m. and marched to WALLON CAPPEL arriving (about 9 miles) arriving at 11-0 p.m. Battalion billetted in various farm houses spread out over about 1½ miles. | |
| " | 24th | | Battalion rested | |
| " | 25th | | Work on reorganization of battalion | |
| " | 26th | | The Battalion was inspected by the Divisional Commander at 11-30 a.m. Weather very hot. Company parades - Instruction in bombing - Lewis gun - Drill etc. | |
| " | 27th | | | |
| BAILLEUL | 28th | | Battalion paraded at 9 a.m. & marched with rest of 54th Inf. Bde. to BAILLEUL. Owing to heat & an epidemic of diarrhoea which had broken out yesterday, many men (chiefly of the last draft fell out on the line of march. Arrived at billets in BAILLEUL - ST. JAN CAPPEL road) about 2-30 p.m. | |
| " | 29 | | 2nd Lt. H.E. OSBORNE joined the battalion & was posted to C Coy. | |
| " | 30 | | Company parades - Bombing - Lewis gun - Bayonet fighting - Drill instruction - | |
| " | 31 | | | |

Y. Wigley Colonel
Commdg. 6th (S) Bn Northamptonshire Regt.

A P P E N D I C E S

2, 3, 4 & 5

---

SECRET    OPERATION ORDER No.10.   No 1

by Colonel G.E.Ripley,
Commanding 6th (S) Bn. Northamptonshire Regiment.   22.6.16

Appendix 2

Reference Special Map issued to Company Commanders.

1. GENERAL PLAN.

A decisive battle which the 18th Division will take a prominent part will be fought shortly. The 30th Division (13th Corps) will attack on the right and the 7th Division (15th Corps) on the left of the 18th Division.

Other Corps will attack EASTWARD on our left.

Dividing lines between Units are marked on map thus:- ............... The final objective of the 18th Division is marked "Final Objective". The 55th Brigade will be on the right, 53rd Centre and 54th left of the 18th Division all abreast. The 91st Brigade (7th Division) will be on immediate left of the 54th Bde. The attack will be preceded by a five days bombardment by all calibre of guns and mortars. The days will be designated by letters of the alphabet and the assault will be carried out on "Z" day. The attack will be divided into three phases as shown on map.

   1st Phase ......... Red line.
   2nd Phase ......... ~~Green Line~~ Red & Blue.
   3rd Phase ......... Blue Line.

The ~~Green~~ Line and that portion of the red line included in the frontages of the 18th and 30th Divisions from junction of POMMIERS LANE and POMMIERS TRENCH EASTWARDS must be held at all costs for a prolonged period against counter-attack.

2. TASK OF 54th INFANTRY BRIGADE.

The objectives of the 54th Infantry Brigade will be :-

First Objective. Junction of POMMIERS TRENCH with POPOFF LANE - POMMIERS TRENCH to junction with BLACK ALLEY - BUCKET TRENCH to a point 120 yards west of BLACK ALLEY.

Second Objective. Point (A.1.B.8.1) POMMIERS LANE - JUNCTION OF POMMIERS LANE and MAPLE TRENCH - POMMIERS REDOUBT - MAPLE TRENCH to its junction with BEETLE ALLEY.

Third Objective.

A line from point S.26.A.8.3. through point S.26.A.2.2. to the right of 91st Brigade about point S.25.b.3.0.

In capturing these objectives the following are of vital importance :-

   (a) To secure BLACK ALLEY as a defensive flank to the 18th Div. and should occasion arise to hold it all costs.
   (b) To consolidate and hold the second objective at all costs even if MONTAUBAN and MAMETZ should not be captured.
   (c) To consolidate that portion of BEETLE ALLEY from S.25.d.98.27 to junction with MAPLE TRENCH.

3. TASK OF 6th BN. NORTHAMPTONSHIRE REGIMENT.

The 6th (S) Bn. Northamptonshire Regiment will act as third or supporting Battalion to the Brigade.

Their role is to support the assaulting Battalions if required as far as the line MAPLE TRENCH - POMMIERS REDOUBT. When this line is made good the duty of the Battalion is to put in a state of defence a line Point II (junction of BUND TRENCH and BLACK ALLEY) to junction of BLACK ALLEY and MAPLE TRENCH on the West and on the North from Point 5 (junction of MAPLE TRENCH and BEETLE ALLEY) EASTWARDS to POMMIERS REDOUBT inclusive and from the latter to the Strong Point in POMMIERS ~~TRENCH~~ LANE established by the 53rd Brigade.

4. FLANKS.

The flanks of the Brigade are shown in map.

5. DISPOSITIONS.

During the waiting period the Battalion will be at BRONFAY FARM. Prior to the attack the Battalion will occupy the trench in CARNOY. Bn. Headquarters will be at PICCADILLY.

Contd.

(4)

7. **PLAN OF ATTACK**  Amended from S.O. 18 at o/y 6½

(c) The remaining two platoons of the 3rd Coy, 6th Northants Regt will carry forward small manloads of R.E. Stores. These will be deposited at the TRIANGLE as on arrival at platoons reach that point they will rejoin their battalion. The latter platoons must not be confused with those permanently allotted to A and B dumps.

22. 6. 16.

6. **THE ATTACK.**

At ZERO on "Z" day, "A" and "B" Coys will move forward and occupy GLASGOW ROAD and HIGH ROAD EAST and WEST.

They will move in small "blobs" at irregular intervals and distances.

"A" Coy will be on the right and "B" Coy on the left, the two Companies covering the whole front. "D" Coy will follow in rear of "A" and "B" in the same irregular formation and will cover the whole Brigade front.

"A" and "B" Coys will push forward behind the assaulting Battalions and will enter EMDEN and AUSTRIAN TRENCHES when the assaulting Battalions have vacated them. They will then follow the assaulting Battalions and take over the line MAPLE TRENCH - POMMIERS REDOUBT when the assaulting Battalions have made good BEETLE ALLEY with two Companies and pushed forward their other two Coys to the final objective. Every Commander from Platoon upwards will retain a reserve in his hands for the unexpected.

7. **STRONG POINTS.**

"A" Coy will take over POMMIERS REDOUBT (S.P. VII) with three platoons and Coy Headquarters. The remaining platoon will hold S.P.VI in POMMIERS TRENCH.

"B" Coy will take over the JUNCTION BEETLE ALLEY - MAPLE TRENCH (S.P.V) JUNCTION BLACK ALLEY - BUCKET TRENCH (S.P.IV) JUNCTION BLACK ALLEY - POMMIERS TRENCH (S.P.III). The remaining platoon will hold MAPLE TRENCH between S.P.V. and VII. Coy Headquarters will be at S.P.IV.

"D" Coy will send 1 platoon to hold POMMIERS TRENCH from VI to its JUNCTION with POPOFF LANE whilst two platoons to hold POMMIERS TRENCH from VI to its JUNCTION with BLACK ALLEY. The fourth platoon will take over the CIRCUS (S.P.II). Coy Headquarters will be at VI.2 Battalion Headquarters will be at TRIANGLE.

These strong points will be prepared for allround defence and strengthened with wire. They will be held at any cost. Coys will send Officers or N.C.Os to take over their STRONG POINTS before the assaulting Battalions vacate them.

STRONG POINTS to be constructed by Brigade on our right and left are shown thus - ⊚

8. **DUGOUT CLEARING PARTIES.**

"C" Coy will detail two platoon to report to O.C. 7th ......ds and 1 platoon to report to O.C. 11th Royal Fusiliers. They will ...... used as dugout clearing parties. They will be equipped as shown ... appendix B.

9. **CARRYING PARTIES.**

"C" Coy will detail one platoon to go to "A" Dump and report to Officer in charge and one platoon to report to Officer in charge "B" Dump for carrying.

All these parties will be in position by ZERO.

10. **ROYAL ENGINEERS.**

1 Section Royal Engineers will assist in construction of S.P.II, III, IV and V.

One section R.E. will assist in consolidation of 2nd objective and in construction of S.P.V and VII.

11. **MACHINE GUNS.**

Four Vickers guns will go with the assaulting Battalions. Eight guns will advance in rear and under cover of the 6th Northants Regt. Two of these will go to POMMIERS REDOUBT, two to S.P.V, two to S.P.VI and one each to S.P. II and III.

There will be no Vickers gun in S.P. IV.

12. **STOKES GUNS.**

Twelve guns will be in position in our front line. When S.P.II, III, IV, V, VI, and VII are consolidated one gun will move forward to each. The Hd.Qrs of 54th T.M.B. will be with Hd.Qrs 6th Northants Regt.

Contd.

( 3 )   22.6.16.

13. **BOSCHE COUNTER ATTACK.**
The Bosche delivers small Counter attacks with platoons or Companies immediately hostile troops gain their objectives. These small counter attacks have had far reaching results and must be specially guarded against. To meet these small counter attacks the Reserves in the hands of Platoon and Coy Commanders will be of the greatest value.

14. **RELIEFS.**
All Troops must clearly understand that nor reliefs can be expected until their final objectives have been efficiently consolidated.

15. **DUMPS.**
The supply of all ammunition, Grenades, R.E. material etc., will be worked from a series of Dumps. These are marked on map. Those at "A" and "B" will be considered advanced Dumps, that at "C" advanced Brigade Reserve Dump and that at "D" Brigade Dump. The advanced dumps will move forward by stages. Brigade will keep these Dumps full and Battalion will draw stores from these dumps. Contents are shown in appendix "C".
"A" and "B" Dumps will open at TRIANGLE and CIRCUS respectively as early as possible after first objective is gained. They will move forward to POMMIERS REDOUBT and S.P.IV after the capture of second objective.
Rations and water will not be carried forward till nightfall.

16. **TOOLS.**
50% of "A", "B" and "D" Coys will carry tools in the proportion of two shovels to one pick. Tools will be carried in a vertical position on mans' back. A reserve of tools will be kept at "C" Dump from which Companies may draw to meet their requirements.

17. **AMMUNITION CARRIERS.**
Each Lewis Gun team will be strengthed by four Lewis Reserve gunners to carry S.A.A.

18. **WATER.**
The supply of water during and after the assault will be difficult. All water bottles must be full at ZERO hour and all ranks must practice the greatest restraint in drinking water. The normal supply will be from the Well, CARNOY and pipes in CARNOY. Reserve Storage tanks have been placed in the Russian Saps at "A" and "B" Dumps. 250 petrol tins have also been placed at each of these Dumps.

19. **MEDICAL ARRANGEMENTS.**
The 55th Field Ambulance will collect all wounded in the Division. Advanced dressing stations will be established at the following points :-
(A) In dugouts at West end of BRICK ALLEY, CARNOY for wounded of 53rd and 54th Brigades. (accomodation for 200 S.C.)
(B) In dugouts at BRONFAY FARM for local and walking cases, accomodation 50.
All walking cases will be directed to the Advanced Dressing Station at CARNOY and from there will proceed via CARNOY AVENUE to BRONFAY FARM Dressing station. Regimental aid posts will be established as shown in map. Wounded will be conveyed from these posts to the nearest advanced dressing station by Regimental stretcher bearers.
Wounded cases in enemy trenches will be collected into suitable dugouts by Regimental Medical Officers. These dugouts must be marked and their positions notified to 55th Field Amb.
In addition to Eight stretchers per Battalion 16 R.A.M.C. stretchers will be stored near each Regimental Aid Post and used by both R.A.M.C. and Regimental bearers for bringing in cases.

Contd.

( 4 )                    22. 6. 16.

20. VETERINARY.
The Veterinary Officer in charge of 83rd Brigade R.F.A. is responsible for the 84th Brigade.

21. PRISONERS.
Prisoners will be sent back in batches to the Brigade Dump and thence to the Advanced Divl. collecting station at BILLON FARM. They will be marched <u>across the open</u> and not down communication trenches. Escorts to BILLON Farm will be found by the Battalions which take the prisoners the men rejoining their Units under proper control as soon as possible. The prisoners will be taken in batches of 100 with 10% escort. Slightly wounded men can be used for escort. Prisoners must be disarmed and searched for concealed weapons and documents immediately after capture before being marched off and Officers must be separated from the rank and file <u>immediately</u>.
Prisoners will be searched for documents and examined under Divl. arrangements at Divl. Collecting Station. <u>Immediate information must be sent back concerning the identification of Regiments opposed to us</u>.

22. CAPTURED GUNS.
When hostile guns are captured the following procedure will be adopted.
(a) Report to Bn. Headquarters number and nature of guns captured.
(b) Detail parties to manhandle them to the nearest position where gun teams can be hooked.
(c) Report exact position where teams are required and number of teams necessary.

23. OFFICERS. The following Officers will accompany the Battalion:-
Colonel G.E.Ripley............. In command.
Captain D.L.Evans ............. Adjutant.
Major G.M.Clark ............... O.C. "C" Coy.
Capt. H.Podmore ............... O.C. "D" Coy.
Capt. F.S.Neville ............. O.C. "B" Coy.
Capt O.D. Schreiner ........... O.C. "A" Coy.
Lieut G.G.H.Batty ............. "B" Coy.
"     G.Shankster ............. Lewis Gun Officer.
"     H.M.Eldridge ............ Bombing Officer.
"     J.D.Unwin ................ "D" Coy.
2nd Lt. N.C.Hamilton .......... "B" Coy.
"     G.L.Woulfe ............... "A"  "
"     L.G.Crook ................ "C"  "
"     F.G.B.Lys ................ "C"  "
"     D.M.Heriz-Smith .......... "A"  "
"     C.G.Keys ................. "A"  "
"     J. Greenwood ............. "B"  "
"     A.V.Jackson .............. "C"  "
"     B.C.Gillott .............. O.C. Signals.
"     R.T.Price ................ "D" Coy.

Major S.H.Charrington will be employed as Liason Officer at Bde.H.Qrs and will be accomodated in a dugout at BRONFAY FARM. The Left group R.A. will arrange for his Messing.
The following Officers will be with 1st Line Transport :-
Capt S.F.Shepherd ............. 2nd -in-C "B" Coy.
Lieut J.F.Arnold .............. ditto  "D"  "
Lieut J.N.Beasley ............. Transport Officer.
Lieut W.H.Fowler .............. Quartermaster.
2nd Lt.Redhead, 2nd Lt.H.M.Margoliouth ...... Assist Qr.Mr.
The following Officers are at Schools :-
2nd Lieut R.B.Fawkes
2nd Lieut G.K.Chatham
2nd Lieut F.D.S.Walker.

( 5 )  22.6.16

The following will be with the 1st Line Transport.
- Capt. Shepherd S.F.
- Lieut Arnold J.F.
- 2nd Lt. Margoliouth H.M.
- " " Redhead H.A.
- " " Higham P.H.
- " " Hayward H.W.
- " " Farrell R.
- Lieut Fowler W.H.
- " Beasley J.N.

The following will be at Schools :-
- Lieut Wilcox F.A.C. Divl.
- 2nd Lt Walker F.D.S. "
- " " Chatham G.K. "
- " " Fawkes R.B. Army.

24. COLLECTION OF INTELLIGENCE.
Two men will be attached to each assaulting Battalion to collect documents etc., in enemy trenches. They will each carry a sack with a red white and blue bullseye on each side of it.

25. STRAGGLERS.
Regimental Police will control traffic in trenches and will check stragglers moving to the rear. They will take numbers, names and Units of all stragglers and march them back in parties to their Units. Their duties will be detailed by Brigade.

26. RATIONS.
Normal system of supply will be continued throughout operations.
Rations will be delivered to 1st Line Transport, GROVE-TOWN, who will convey same to BRONFAY FARM where they will be transferred to Tramline.
Reserve rations are dumped in "A" and "B" Dumps and in CARNOY to meet any unforeseen contingency. These will only be issued under Bde Orders.

27. COMMUNICATION TRENCHES.
The Main UP trench will be XXXXX PIONEER AVENUE commencing at BRONFAY FARM.
The Main DOWN Trench (evacuation) trench will be MAIDSTONE-CARNOY AVENUE.

28. ARTILLERY FLAGS.
Every Platoon will carry two red and yellow Artillery flags. These will be waved to and fro for a short period by the leading line to show our Artillery how far the attack has progressed. On no account will any flag be stuck in the ground.
These flags will not be waved at any position in advance of POMMIERS REDOUBT.

29. EQUIPMENT TO BE CARRIED ON THE MAN.
Every man will carry :-
Rifle and equipment (less pack) one bandolier in addition to his equipment ammunition, 170 rounds in all.
One day's ration and one iron ration.
One waterproof sheet, two sandbags, one white enamel disc hung on the back or yellow patch. Two smoke helmets.
NOTE. The haversack will be carried on back.
Grenadiers will carry 50 rounds S.A.A. only.

30. CASUALTIES.
Casualties will be reported to Bn.Hd.Qrs as soon as possible. They should be reported under the heading of Officers, Other ranks. Numbers only are required for these frequent estimates, but at 2 p.m. each day the correct names of casualties should be sent in correct as far as possible. The day will be reckoned from 12 noon to 12 noon. Attention is called to S.C.113 issued to Coy Commanders.

Contd.

( 6 )  22. 6. 16.

31. **COMMUNICATIONS.**

(a). <u>Telephonic</u>. Brigade Telephone Stations will be established at Hd.Qrs of the two assaulting Battalions and the 3rd Battalion in our own Trenches. These will be Signal Offices worked by Bde operators. There will be a permanent exchange at CARNOY. Communication with Artillery can be obtained through CARNOY EXCHANGE or through Battalion Hd.Qrs. The 6th Northants Regt. will take over the Signal Office at the TRIANGLE from the 7th Beds Regt. when the Hd.Qrs move there. When the second objective is captured the Bde Signals will open at Bde Signal Station at TRIANGLE they will move forward to POMMIERS REDOUBT when circumstances admit. If telephonic communication breaks down between stations messages will be sent back by runner to the nearest exchange that is in communication with Bde.Hd.Qrs and telephone from there.

(b) <u>Visual</u>. A Divl.Reading station will be established at A.19 b.3.9. from this the German lines up to POMMIERS TRENCH are under observation and Signallers will be on the lookout day and night. The ground beyond POMMIERS TRENCH is not visible from this station.

Signallers with Coy and Bn.Hd.Qrs will carry discs and a few flags will be taken forward by Battn.Hd.Qrs. All messages will be sent "DD" and repeated twice. They should therefore be as sgort as possible. The 6th Northants will establish a Visual Station at the TRIANGLE as soon as they reach there and will provide a visual station at VI S.P. POMMIERS TRENCH as soon as the second objective is captured. Messages coming back by runner and from assaulting battalions may be sent from the last named station by visual.

As many Signallers as possible to carry electric torches by night.

(c) <u>Contact Aeroplane Patrols.</u>

Every man will carry one red flare. One special Signalling panel and one ground sheet will be carried by Bn.Hd.Qr. Signallers.

The ground sheet will be put out as soon as Hd.Qrs reach a new position but should only be unfolded when one of our own aeroplanes is over the line.

XIIIth and XVth Corps aeroplanes will be of type B.E.2.C. will have a broad black band and on each lower plane. The method of communication with aeroplanes will be that already practised.

(d) <u>Runners.</u>

Bde will send Runners to CIRCUE and TRIANGLE and a Bde Runner Post will be established at TRIANGLE when second objective is captured.

Permanent Brigade Runner Posts will be established at Signal Office, CARNOY at PICADILLY and at Bde.Hd.Qrs. All important messages must be sent by Runners in pairs.

(e) <u>General</u>. The Bn.Signal Officer will ascertain all details from Bde Signal Officer.

All Signaller and runners will be under the Battn.Signal Officer.

Officers should always speak on telephone themselves if possible or else write down messages and sign them. Signallers are ordered not to accept messages unless signed by an Officer, or N.C.O. or man commanding a Unit. All messages must have time and place on them and should be as short as possible. Constant communication must be kept up with the assaulting Bns. and the Bns. on the right and left of the Bde. All information should be sent back to Bn.Hd.Qrs. immediately

Contd.

( 7 ).   22. 6. 16.

32. MISCELLANEOUS.
No maps showing our own trenches or important papers will be carried by Officers and men taking part in the attack.

Headquarters.
The Hd.Qrs 6th Northants Regt will open at TRIANGLE when that Bn. takes over the second objective and S.P. I to VII from assaulting Battalions.

Wire.
All our wire in front and behind our Front line will be cleared by 7th Beds and 11th Royal Fusiliers.


(Sgd) D.L.Evans, Capt & Actg Adjt.
6th (S) Bn. Northamptonshire Regiment.


Copies Issued to :-

1. C.O.
2. Brigade.
3. O.C. "A" Coy.
4. O.C. "B"  "
5. O.C. "C"  "
6. O.C. "D"  "
7. Signals Officer.

APPENDIX "A"   Position of Units 54th Inf.Bde
immediately before ZERO hour.

| UNIT | POSITION | FRONTAGE | BATTN.H.Q. | REMARKS. |
|------|----------|----------|------------|----------|
| 11th R.F. (also 2 Vickers Guns & 2 Stokes Mortars). | Forming up trenches Left assaulting Battn. | Chester St. (exclusive) F.12.C.20.90 to Trench Junction (inclusive) F.12.C.8590 | LONDON ROAD & BROWN STREET JUNCTN. | Each Assaultg Bn. is on 2 Coy front. 1st Trnch - 4 pltns 2nd " - 4 " 3rd " - 1 Coy(& 1 pltn N'hants as dug-out Clearing party 4th Trnch - 1 Coy. |
| 7th Beds. as 11th R.F. | ditto | Trench Junctn. (exclusive) F.12.C.85.90 to YORK Road (exclusive) A.7.d.54.82. | NEW CUT. | ditto |
| 6th N'hants (less 4 platoons). | In old Trenches just W of CARNOY. | -------------- | PICCADILLY | As in attached Orders. |
| 12th Bn. Midd'x R. | In dug-outs in CARNOY | -------------- | A.2 Hd.Qrs, CARNOY. | Reserve Battalion. |

( 1 )

| Unit. | POSITION | HEADQUARTERS. | REMARKS. |
|-------|----------|---------------|----------|
| 54th M.G.C. | 2 guns in Tunnelled saps 2 guns with 11th R.F. 2 guns with 7th Beds. 4 guns with 6th N'hants. 6 guns in CAFTET WOOD. | A.2 Hd.Qrs. CARNOY. | |
| 54th T.M.B. & 1 sectn 26th T.M.B. | 2 mortars with 11th R.F. 2 mortars with 7th Beds. 8 mortars in position for bombardment. | ditto | |
| 2 secths R.E. | CARNOY. | | |
| 2 Pltns Suss Pioneers. | CARNOY. | | |
| 54th Bde H.Q. | At Bde Battle Hd.Qrs at F.24.C.55 near BILLON FARM. | | |

No._____    ACQUITTANCE ROLL (ALL ARMS).    Army Form N 1513.

_____ {Squadron / Battery / Company} of the _____

Imprest a/c No. _____

| Regl. No. | RANK AND NAME. | *Adapt if necessary. | Cash Payment. Francs | Centimes | Sterling Equivalent (To be completed in Fixed centre Pay Office). s. | d. | Receipt of Soldier. |
|---|---|---|---|---|---|---|---|
|  |  |  |  |  |  |  |  |
|  |  |  |  |  |  |  |  |
|  |  |  |  |  |  |  |  |
|  |  |  |  |  |  |  |  |
|  |  |  |  |  |  |  |  |
|  |  |  |  |  |  |  |  |
|  |  |  |  |  |  |  |  |
|  |  |  |  |  |  |  |  |
|  |  |  |  |  |  |  |  |
|  |  |  |  |  |  |  |  |
|  |  |  |  |  |  |  |  |
|  |  |  |  |  |  |  |  |
|  |  |  |  |  |  |  |  |
|  |  | Total |  |  |  |  |  |

The undermentioned (1) and (2) to be completed by Paymaster i/c Clearing House—

To be inserted by Paying Officer. Total, in words—

(1) Rate of Exchange—5 = s./d.

(2) Total Sterling equivalent, in words—

Francs_____ _____Pounds,

Centimes_____ _____Shgs., and_____Pence.

Signature of the Officer making the Payments_____

Date of Payment_____ 19 .    Officer Commanding_____Coy.,

_____Regt.

Certified that the above amounts have been charged in the ledger accounts of the men concerned.

Date_____ 19 .    _____Paymaster_____

APPENDIX "B"    G R E N A D E S.

| ALL BATTALIONS. | HOW CARRIED. | WHERE STORED BEFORE THE ATTACK. | WHEN TO BE DRAWN. | REMARKS. |
|---|---|---|---|---|
| Each Pltn Bombg section of 8 men. | 10 gdes on each man. | Carried on the man. | Now in possession of Battns. | |
| Rifle Gdes. 10 per Pltn. Bombg section. | On N.C.O i/c Pltn. Bombg Section. | At Coy Hd.Qrs in Forming up trenches. | When forming up. | 3rd & 4th Bns. will draw 160 rifle gdes each from A.2 Sub-sector H.Q. CARNOY before moving fwd. |
| THE TWO ASSAULTING BNS ONLY. One per Platoon Bombg Sec. each carryg a bucket containg 15 MILLS Gdes. | In Bucket. | At Coy H.Qrs. in forming up trenches. | When formg up. | Two assaulting Battalions only. |
| 50% strength of the 2 pltns of 3rd Bn.employed as dug-out clearg parties (say 20 men per pltn) each carryg a bucket containing 18 MILLS Gdes. | In Bucket. | "C" Dump. | From "C" Dump when forming up. | Two Platoons. |

"B" Dumped at the hour of assault.

"A" DUMP ........................ 2,490 MILLS Grenades.
                                  390 Rifle    "

"B" DUMP ........................ 2,490 MILLS Grenades.
                                  390 Rifle    "

"C" (Advanced Bde) DUMP ........ 4,280 MILLS Grenades
                                 & 240 Rifle  "

"D" (Bde Reserve) DUMP ........ N I L.

Mobile Reserve on limbered wagon with 1st Line Transport at 768 MILLS Grenades per Battalion ................... 3,072 MILLS.

Total ....
          13,352

No._____  ACQUITTANCE ROLL (ALL ARMS).          Army Form N. 1513.

{Squadron}
{Battery } of the _____
{Company }

Imprest a/c No. _____

| Regl. No. | RANK AND NAME. | *Adapt if necessary. | Cash Payment. | | Sterling Equivalent (To be completed in Fixed-centre Pay Office). | | Receipt of Soldier. |
|---|---|---|---|---|---|---|---|
| | | | Francs | Centimes | s. | d. | |
| | | | | | | | |

Total

To be inserted by Paying Officer. Total, in words—

Francs _____

Centimes _____

The undermentioned (1) and (2) to be completed by Paymaster i/c Clearing House—
(1) Rate of Exchange—5 = s./d.
(2) Total Sterling equivalent, in words—
_____ Pounds,
_____ Shgs., and _____ Pence.

Signature of the Officer making the Payments _____

Date of Payment _____ 19 .   Officer Commanding _____ Coy.,
_____ Regt.

Certified that the above amounts have been charged in the ledger accounts of the men concerned.

Date _____ 19 .   _____ Paymaster _____

APPENDIX "C"     D U M P S.

---

| OFFICER IN CHARGE. | CONTENTS | REMARKS. |

---

**"A"**

Lieut Tilton,           950 MILLS GRENADES.            (At present at A.2
7th Bedford Regt.      1540 MILLS      "                Grenade Store).
                        390 Rifle      "
                        100 Boxes  S.A.A.
                         40 Boxes  S.A.A. (Reserve
                              for LEWIS GUNS).
                        250 Petrol tins of water.
                            Water tanks.
                        560 rounds STOKES ammn.
                       2000 Rations.
                            Material for rapid wiring.

---

**"B"**

Lieut Rendle.
11th R.Fus.             Same as "A" Dump.

---

**"C"**

Lieut Covell           4280 Mills Grenades.
7th Bedford Regt.       240 Rifle      "
                       4000 Rations.
                            Picks.
                            Shovels.
                            R.E.Material.
                         80 Boxes S.A.A.(Reserve
                              for LEWIS GUNS).

---

**"D"**
(Brigade Dump).

Lieut Whiteman.         170 Boxes S.A.A. (Div.Res)
11th R. Fus.             62  "    S.A.A. (Div.Res)
                                    for M.G.Coy.
                       8000 Rations.
                       1000 Reserve Smoke Helmets.

No._____ ACQUITTANCE ROLL (ALL ARMS). Army Form N 1513.

{ Squadron }
{ Battery } of the _____
{ Company }

Imprest a/c No. _____

| Regl. No. | RANK AND NAME. | *Adapt if necessary. | Cash Payment. Francs | Cash Payment. Centimes | Sterling Equivalent (To be completed in Fixed-centre Pay Office). s. | Sterling Equivalent d. | Receipt of Soldier. |
|---|---|---|---|---|---|---|---|
| | | | | | | | |

Total

To be inserted by Paying Officer. Total, in words—

Francs _____

Centimes _____

The undermentioned (1) and (2) to be completed by Paymaster i/c Clearing House—

(1) Rate of Exchange—5   =   s./d.

(2) Total Sterling equivalent, in words—

_____ Pounds,

_____ Shgs., and _____ Pence.

Signature of the Officer making the Payments _____

Date of Payment _____ 19   .   Officer Commanding _____ Coy.,

_____ Regt.

Certified that the above amounts have been charged in the ledger accounts of the men concerned.

Date _____ 19   .   _____ Paymaster _____

Wt. W. 16927—270.  80,000.  2/16.  H. W. & V. Ld.  Books /6/3.

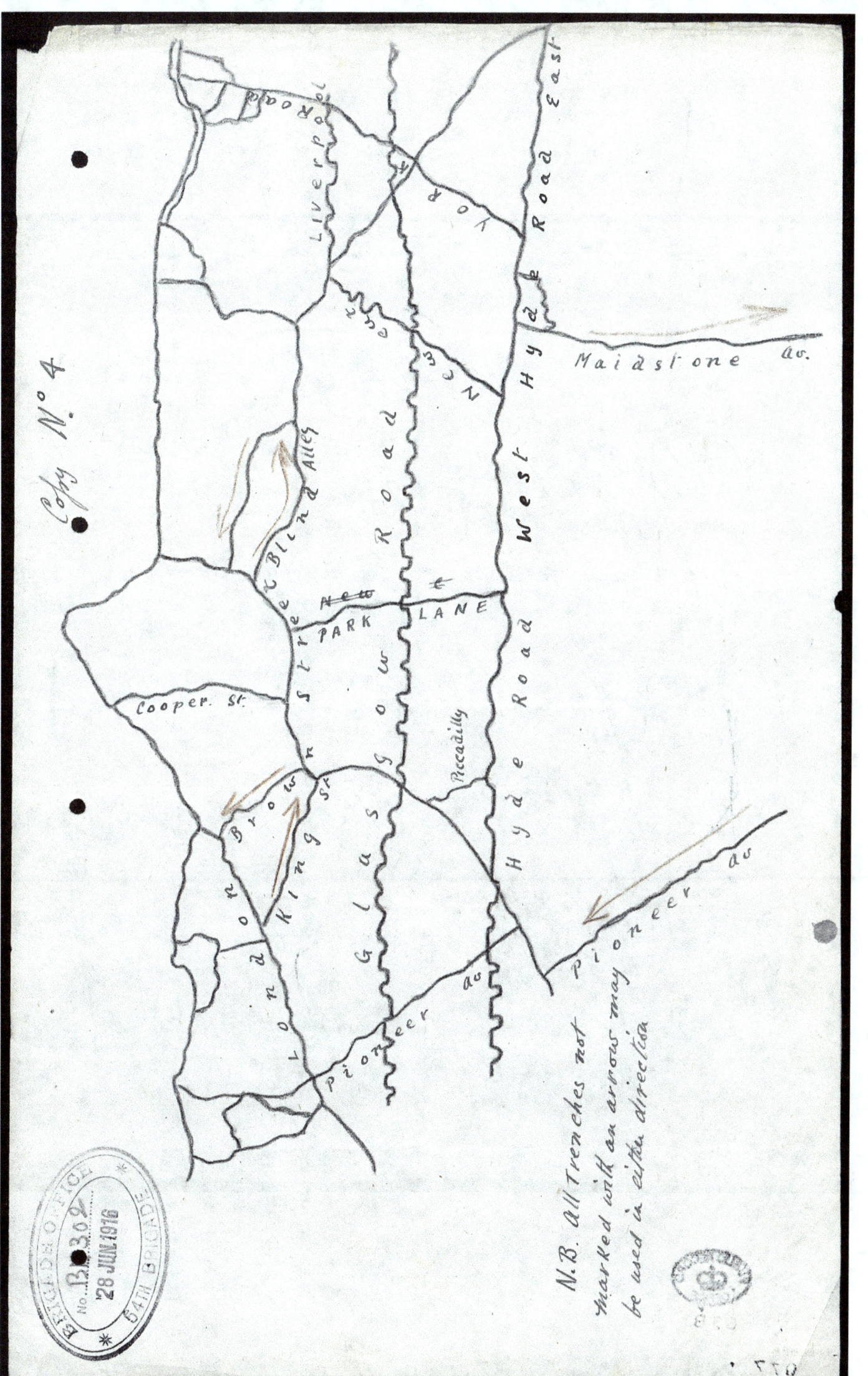

APPENDIX D

COPY

SECRET  EXTRACT FROM O.O.18 of 24.6.16

1. INFORMATION.

(a) Enemy.
The XII Div, VI German Corps is holding the line from the RIVER SOMME to FRICOURT.

The 62nd Inf. Regt. holds from the MARICOURT-HARDECOURT to the CARNOY-MONTAUBAN ROAD.

The 23rd Inf. Regt. holds from the latter Road to FRICOURT.

(b) Our own Troops.
Following further information regarding the objective of the Fourth Army as a whole are published.

After the capture and consolidation of the objective laid down for the first days operations preparations have been made for a further advance to the line MONTAUBAN-BAZENTIN le GRAND-MARTINPUICH. This advance will be effected by the 15th and 3rd Corps passing across the front of the 18th Division.

In order that that operation may be successfully carried out, it will be necessary for the 18th Division to hold the line to its furtherest objective for at least three days without being relieved.

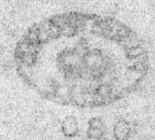

2.  24.6.16

The positions of neighbouring Corps and Divisions on the flanks of the 18th Division remain as described in Operation Order No 17.

The 9th Division is in XIII Corps Reserve.

THE FOLLOWING MESSAGES ARE TO ALL CONCERNED.

Appendix B.

1. General CONGREVE wires please convey to all ranks my intense appreciation of their splendid fighting which has attained all asked of them and resulted in heavy losses to the enemy nearly 1000 prisoners have already passed through the cage aaa Ends.

2. General SIR H. RAWLINSON aaa Please convey to 18th. Div. my best congratulations and thanks for their dashing attack yesterday aaa They have done excellent work and I desire to thank them most heartily aaa.

3. General MAXSE to 18th. Div. aaa Well done its what I expected, now hold on to what you have gained so splendidly.

4. The COMMANDING OFFICER desires to congratulate the Regiment on the above complimentary messages from the Divisional, Corps and Army Commanders. At the same time he desires to thank all ranks for the splendid way in which they carried out their role in the attack. A task in which most of them were required to face a heavy shell fire without the excitement of getting at close quarters with their enemy. This entails the highest courage and discipline which the Regiment most fully displayed.

           (sd)    W.BARKHAM, Lieut. & Adjutant.
                     6th.(S) Bn. Northamptonshire Regiment.

In the Field
   1 - 7 - 16.

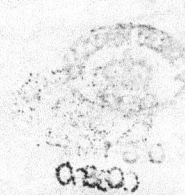

Appendix IV

OPERATIONS IN TRONES WOOD

Approximate position of troops at 11 am (not underlined).

Approximate position of troops at 3-30 p.m. underlined in blue.

Mixed Line of Mx & Nn driving Wood to N.

A party of R.W.K. found here facing S.

Taken by 6th Nn about 6 am.

Report Centre 18th Mx

Adv. Report Centre 6th Nn

Appendix 4.

10 men & 2nd Lieut Platoon Mx

A Coy Nn

A Coy Mx

B Coys Nn

C Coy Nn

LINE OF BOSCH RETREAT

2 Lewis Guns Nn

Copse

QSP

D Coy Nn

D Coy Mx

B Coy 6 Nn

RWK Coy

C Coy Mx

D Coy Mx

Strong Point A

Captured by Mx & Buffs about 9 a.m.

3 Officers & party of RWK till about 9 am.

6th (S) Bn The

Northamptonshire

Regt

Vol IV

Army Form C. 2118.

# WAR DIARY
## or
## INTELLIGENCE SUMMARY.
*(Erase heading not required.)*

Instructions regarding War Diaries and Intelligence Summaries are contained in F. S. Regs., Part II. and the Staff Manual respectively. Title pages will be prepared in manuscript.

| Place | Date 1916 | Hour | Summary of Events and Information | Remarks and references to Appendices |
|---|---|---|---|---|
| | August | | | |
| N.W. of BAILLEUL | 1st | | Company Training. | |
| | 2nd | | 2nd Lt. A. BATES joined the battalion on 31-7-16, and was posted to D Coy. Lecture on Trench Warfare - Instruction in bombing & Lewis gun - Coy. drill and bayonet fighting. | |
| | 3rd | | Battalion route march. Battalion sports in afternoon. | |
| | 4th | | Lecture and instruction in gas helmets by Divl. Gas Expert. Baths at BAILLEUL. 2nd Lieut. H.W. STONE joined the battalion in the 2nd instt. & was posted to B Coy. Lieut. C.G. KEMP (R.A.M.C.) appointed M.O. vice Capt. D. MACFARLANE (R.A.M.C.) | |
| RUE MARLE ARMENTIERES | 5th | | The Battalion marched from BAILLEUL at 5.15 p.m. and marched to RUE MARLE ARMENTIERES, where it arrived about 10 p.m. & went into billets. | |
| | 6th | | The Battalion took over various Strong Points in the "Subsidiary line", to be occupied in case of emergency. | |
| | 7th to 10th | | Training in bombing, Lewis gun, wiring, rapid loading, firing rifle exercises. | |
| | 10th | | C.O., 2nd in command and Adjutant inspected left sector of 54th Brigade trench line. | |
| | 11th | | The Battalion left RUE MARLE by platoons at 7.30 a.m. and formed up at BAC ST. MAUR; left there at 9.30 a.m. and marched to camp at near | |

# WAR DIARY or INTELLIGENCE SUMMARY

Army Form C. 2118

| Place | Date 1916 | Hour | Summary of Events and Information | Remarks and references to Appendices |
|---|---|---|---|---|
| CAMP near LA MOTTE | Aug 11th | | LA MOTTE, arriving about 8-15 p.m. Distance about 19 miles. A very hot & fatiguing march. | |
| LA MOTTE | | | The following officers joined the battalion on 8th inst & were posted as follows :- 2nd Lt. W.H. GODDARD to B Coy. 2nd Lt. L.G. BAILEY to C Coy. One man was killed & one man wounded by shell fire in RUE MARLE on 9th inst. | |
| | 12th | | Morning & afternoon, Practice in wood fighting in BOIS DES VACHES by platoons. Night practice by the battalion. | |
| | 13th | | Practice in the attack on a wood in the BOIS DES VACHES inspected by Lt. Gen Godley Commdg. 2nd ANZAC & G.O.C. 54th Inf Bde. Night practice, firing very trough wood by companies & platoons. | |
| | 14th | | Morning. Battalion attack practice in wood. Afternoon. Inspection of kits, arms & accoutrements | |
| RUE MARLE | 15th | | Battalion left camp near LA MOTTE in motor buses & lorries at 5-30 a.m. for ERQUINGHAM; marched from there & arrived in its billets at RUE MARLE about 6-15 a.m. | |
| B.2 Sector II Army | 16th | | The Battalion relieved the 4th Bedford Regt. in B.2 Sector. The relief was carried out rapidly & without incident and was completed by 10-30 p.m. Coys were distributed as follows :- B Coy. Relief. Sec on right, A Coy in centre, C Coy on left of the line. D Coy in reserve near "The Orchard" | Orders for Relief. See Appendix 6 |
| | 18th | | The following three officers joined the Battalion & were posted as follows :- 2nd Lt. R.A. WEBB - D Coy. " " H.P. FREND - A Coy. " " L. NENDICK - B Coy. | |

Army Form C. 2118.

# WAR DIARY
## or
## INTELLIGENCE SUMMARY.
(Erase heading not required.)

| Place | Date | Hour | Summary of Events and Information | Remarks and references to Appendices |
|---|---|---|---|---|
|  | 19/2/22 |  | Nothing of importance occurred – A considerable amount of work was done in rebuilding traverses & knocked & putting up wire in front of our front & support line trenches – Several officers patrols went out each night to examine ground in "No mans land" & also to listen for enemy officers. Enemy appeared very nervous in sectors on our right, especially on night of 19/20. On night of 22/23, enemy put a few large trench mortar shells into left of our line, but did scarcely any damage. Our artillery retaliated with 144 rounds 18ft. on his front line trenches, causing casualties in one of his working parties. The weather was fine on the whole, though a little rain fell on 18th & 19th. |  |
|  | 23rd |  | During night of 23/24 the Battalion was relieved by 20th Bn Northumberland Fusiliers. The relief was not completed till 11-55 p.m. Total casualties during 8 days in trenches 4 O.Rs wounded (1 subsequently bullet went into billets, the last Platoon arriving in billets about 2 a.m. | Order for relief see Appendix 6A |
| ERQUINGHAM | 24th |  | The Battalion marched by Platoons from B 2 Sub-Sector |  |
|  | 25th |  | Marched from ERQUINGHAM at 5 p.m. Arrived at BAILLEUL Station at 6 p.m. Left by train at 10-30 p.m. |  |

Army Form C. 2118.

# WAR DIARY
## or
## INTELLIGENCE SUMMARY.

(Erase heading not required.)

Instructions regarding War Diaries and Intelligence Summaries are contained in F. S. Regs., Part II and the Staff Manual respectively. Title pages will be prepared in manuscript.

| Place | Date 1916 | Hour | Summary of Events and Information | Remarks and references to Appendices |
|---|---|---|---|---|
| BAILLEUL AUX CORNAILLES | Aug. 26 | | Arrived at ST. POL Station about 3 a.m. Marched at 4.15 a.m. arriving at BAILLEUL AUX-CORNAILLES about 7 a.m. & went into billets. C.O. & 2nd-in-command attended a Bde. Conference at ORLENCOURT at 4 p.m. | For programme of training. See Appendix 4. |
| | 27 to 30th | | Company & Battalion training in the MONCHY BRETON training area and near billets. | |
| | 31st | | C.O., 2nd-in-command, & Adjt. attended Bde. Conference at Bde. Hqrs. Brigade training scheme for the attack. | |

M. Harrington Maj.
Commanding 6' (S.) Bn. Northamptonshire Regt.

SECRET.         OPERATION ORDERS No.1.
                   by Colonel G.E.Ripley,
         Commdg. 6th (S) Bn. Northamptonshire Regiment.    15.8.16

*Appendix 6*

1. INTENTION.  Ref. Map Sheet 36 N.W. Edition 6B 1/20,000.
   The 6th (S) Bn. Northants Regt will relieve the 7th Beds Regt in B.2 Sector on the night 16th/17th Aug.1916

2. ORDER AND TIMES OF RELIEF.
   "C" Coy will parade in time so that its leading platoon arrives at the Level Crossing LA CHAPPELLE ARMENTIARES I.8.Central at 9.15 p.m. and will relieve "C" Coy 7th Bn. Beds Regt in the Left Sub-sector.
   "A" Coy will parade in time so that its leading platoons arrives at the Level crossing LA CHAPPELLE ARMENTIARES I.8 Central at 9.35 p.m. and will relieve "B" Coy 7th Beds Regt in the Centre Sub-sector.
   "B" Coy will parade in time so that its leading platoon arrives at xxx I.14.d.4.8. at 9.20 p.m. and will relieve "A" Coy 7th Beds in the Right sub-sector.
   "D" Coy will parade in time so that the leading platoon arrives at I.14.d.4.8. at 9.40 p.m. and relieve "D" Coy 7th Beds. in reserve at the ORCHARD.
   LEWIS GUNNERS, SIGNALLERS, SNIPERS, will parade in time so that the first named arrives at LA CHAPPELLE ARMENTIARES I.8.Central at 5 p.m. and the others at 15 minutes interval.
   Bn.H.Qrs will parade at 8.15 p.m.

3. INTERVAL.  Platoons will move to their positions at 8 minutes interval and will march off with Right of their Coy leading i.e. "A" Coy No.1 platoon.

4. GUIDES.  Guides will meet each platoon at the above times and places stated.

5. MESS CART.  The Mess Cart will call at Coy Messes at the following times :-
   "A" Coy. 8.30 p.m.,  H.Qrs. 8.40 p.m.  "B" Coy. 8.50 p.m.
   "C" Coy. 8.55 p.m., "D" Coy 9 p.m.

6. OFFICERS' KITS.  A limbered wagon will call at Coys for Officers' Kits, commencing at "A" Coy at 8.30 p.m.

7. TRENCH STORES.  Os.C.Coys will forward a list to Bn.H.Qrs of all Trench Stores taken over.

8. COOKING.  All Cooking will be done in the Trenches the greatest care being taken that no unnecessary smoke is made from the kitchens.

9. WATER.  Water can be obtained from the wells at CHARDS FARM and the ORCHARD.

10. RATION DUMP.
    The Rations will be dumped at the Northern end of WINE AVENUE.

11. COMPLETION OF RELIEF.
    Os.C.Coys will report in writing to Bn.H.Qrs I.14.c.99 when they have completed the Relief.


                (Sgd) W.Barkham, Lieut & Adjt.
                6th (S) Bn. Northamptonshire Regiment.

12. OFFICERS' KITS.
    Officers kits not required in the trenches will be collected at 36m Bay.

Appendix 6A    WAR DIARY

S E C R E T.    OPERATION ORDERS      No. 2.
by Colonel G.E. Ripley,        22. 8. 16
Commanding 6th (S) Bn. Northamptonshire Regiment.

Reference Map France, 1/40,000 Sheet 36.

1. **INTENTION.**

   The 6th (S) Bn. Northants Regt. will be relieved by 20th Bn. Northumberland Fusiliers in B.2 Sub-sector on the night 23rd/24th inst.

2. **TIME.**

   The hour of commencement of relief will be about 9 pm. The first platoon of 20th Northumberland Fusiliers will pass the level crossing I.8 Central at LA CHAPPELLE d'ARMENTIARES at 8.45 p.m.

3. **GUIDES.**

   One guide per platoon and one from Headquarters will report to the Adjutant at Bn.Hd.Qrs at 7.30 p.m on the evening of the 23rd inst.

   O.C. "D" Coy will detail one Officer to take charge of this party of guides. He will report at Bn.H.Qrs at 7.30 pm. 23rd inst.

   Os.C. Coys will be responsible that each guide thoroughly understands the nearest way to lead the incoming platoons to the trenches.

4. **ORDER OF RELIEF.**
   1st. "B" Coy, Right Sub-s.    2nd "A" Coy Centre Sub-s.
   3rd "C" " Left " "    4th "D" " Res. ORCHARD.
   5th Headquarters.

5. **SPECIALISTS.** ( Lewis Gunners, Snipers, Signallers etc.)
   Will be relieved about 8.30 p.m.

6. **ADVANCED PARTIES - 20th NORTHUMBERLAND FUSILIERS.**

   Advanced parties of the relieving battalion to take over Trench Stores will be at the level crossing I.8.Central at 5 p.m. One Guide per coy to be detailed.

7. **TRENCH STORES.**

   Three Trench Store Lists per Coy are issued herewith. All three will be made out by Coys and signed by the Officers who take over and hand over and will be distributed as follows :- One to Adjutant immediately on completion of relief, One handed to the Officer taking over and the other retained by Officer handing over.

   All Battalion property will be taken out of the trenches such as Verey Pistols, Wire cutters, Wiring gloves etc. Maps, plans, aeroplane photographs and trench log-books will be handed over on relief.

8. **COMPLETION OF RELIEF.**

   On completion of relief the 6th (S) Bn. Northants Regt will proceed by platoons to ERQUINGHEM via CHAPPELLE d'ARMENTIERES - RUE MARLE-EMERGENCY ROAD A.3 (near old Bn.H.Qrs ).

9. **KITS.**

   All Stores, Officers' kits, cooking utensils etc. will be dumped at the Coy ration Dumps by 7 p.m. the 23rd inst ready for loading. Each Coy and Bn.H.Qrs will detail a loading party of 1 N.C.O. and two men to load the limbers. These parties will travel with the kits.

   All spare kit that is not required should be sent down by the Ration limber tonight, 22nd inst.

Contd.

S E C R E T.    OPERATION    ORDERS. (Contd)         No. 2.
                                                     22. 8. 16.

10. BILLETING PARTY.
    2nd Lieut Walker and one senior N.C.O. of each Coy will
parade in time so that they arrive at ERQUINGHEM CHURCH to take
xxxxbilletxxx by 2 p.m. to take over Billets, to report to the
Adjutant before marching off.
    The Sergt. Cook and one cook per Company will be sent
forward to prepare hot tea for the men when they arrive in
billets. The necessary cooking utensils will be sent down
tonight the 22nd inst.

11. TRANSPORT.
    O.C. Transport will arrange for one limber per Coy and one
for Headquarters to be at the Coy Ration Dumps at 8.45 p.m.
the 23rd inst. The First Line Transport will remain in its
present position until the Brigade marches out of ERQUINGHEM.

12. REPORT"
    Os.C.Coys will report in the following manner on completion
of relief (by phone) :-
    "D" Coy 1010, meaning "D" Coy relieved at 10.10 p.m.

13. CLEANLINESS OF TRENCHES AND LINES.
    Os.C.Coys are reminded that their cookhouse, latrines
and trenches are handed over thoroughly clean.


                        (Sgd) W. Barkham, Lieut & Adjt.
                        6th (S) Bn. Northamptonshire Regiment.

Subject:- WAR ... SECRET

From,
    Officer Commanding,
        6th.(S) Bn.Northamptonshire Regiment.

To,
    Headquarters,
        54th. Infantry Brigade.

54/78

Herewith War Diary for September 1916.

Please acknowledge.

In the Field,        *A.W.Channing*    Major,
    5th. October 1916.    Commdg:6th.(S)Bn.Northamptonshire R.

Army Form C. 2118

# WAR DIARY
## or
## INTELLIGENCE SUMMARY
(Erase heading not required.)

Instructions regarding War Diaries and Intelligence Summaries are contained in F.S. Regs., Part II. and the Staff Manual respectively. Title Pages will be prepared in manuscript.

| Place | Date 1916 | Hour | Summary of Events and Information | Remarks and references to Appendices |
|---|---|---|---|---|
| BAILLEUL AUX CORNAILLES | Sept. 1 | | In morning Tactical training in MONCHY BRETON training area. In afternoon - Coy. training in bayonet fighting, bombing, physical training, rapid loading & instruction & lecture on bayonet fighting & physical training by expert. | |
| | 2" | | All Coys attended baths at TINQUES. C.O. & Batt. Bands departed to England on leave. | |
| | 3" | | Church Parade at 11.30 a.m. Lt MARGOLIOUTH departed to England on leave. | |
| | 4" | | Brigade Tactical Scheme - Practice in attack on woods & rearguard action in MONCHY BRETON training area. Demonstration in constructing "dug-outs" & intensive digging. 1st & 2nd prizes in Intensive Digging Competition won by No. 11, Platoon, C. Coy. 1 Platoon from each Battalion in the Brigade competing. | |
| | 5" | | In morning - training, men billets under Coy. Commanders. In afternoon, bombing, & rapid firing on rifle range in training area. | |
| | 6" | | In morning Practice in intensive digging, following an artillery barrage, in training area. C.O. Adjt. & O.C.'s Coys attended demonstration in construction of tunnelled dug-outs in afternoon. Battalion paraded at 30 a.m. and carried out tactical scheme in forming up in the dark & an attack on a position at dawn. | |
| | 7" | | In afternoon - Practice in following an artillery barrage & construction of tunnelled dug-outs on training ground. | |
| | 8" | | In morning - (ditto) In afternoon - Rapid firing on rifle range in A.1. area. | |

Army Form C. 2118.

# WAR DIARY
## or
## INTELLIGENCE SUMMARY.
(Erase heading not required.)

Instructions regarding War Diaries and Intelligence Summaries are contained in F. S. Regs., Part II. and the Staff Manual respectively. Title pages will be prepared in manuscript.

| Place | Date 1916 | Hour | Summary of Events and Information | Remarks and references to Appendices |
|---|---|---|---|---|
| BUNEVILLE | Sept. 9th | | The battalion marched from BAILLEUL AUX CORNAILLES with the rest of the 54th Inf. Bde. at 9-30 a.m. and arrived at BUNEVILLE at 12 noon and went into billets. | |
| SUS ST LEGER | 10th | | The battalion left BUNEVILLE at 10-30 a.m. and marched with the 54th Inf. Bde. to SUS ST LEGER, arriving at 1-45 p.m. Colonel Ridley and Capt. Evans returned from leave about 10-30 p.m. | |
| ARQUEVES | 11th | | The battalion left SUS ST LEGER and marched with 54th Inf. Bde. at 7-30 a.m. to HALLOY arriving there at 11 a.m. At 12 noon the battalion with 12th Middlesex Regt. & 54th T.M. Battery left in buses & motor lorries for ARQUEVES arriving at 1-45 p.m. & went into billets. The battalion joined the II Corps of the Reserve Army, and has during last 3½ months been in every Army, except the 1st. During the march from BAILLEUL AUX CORNAILLES only one man fell out. On 10th inst. fourteen N.C.O.'s & men of the battalion were awarded the Military Medal for acts of gallantry performed on 13th & 14th July 1916. | See Appendix 13. |

Army Form C. 2118.

# WAR DIARY
## or
## INTELLIGENCE SUMMARY.
(Erase heading not required.)

Instructions regarding War Diaries and Intelligence Summaries are contained in F. S. Regs., Part II. and the Staff Manual respectively. Title pages will be prepared in manuscript.

| Place | Date 1916 | Hour | Summary of Events and Information | Remarks and references to Appendices |
|---|---|---|---|---|
| ARQUÈVES | Sept. 12" | | The C.O. & 2nd in Command Viewed the lines around THIEPVAL from various Observation Posts. Coy. Training in bayonet fighting, rapid loading, physical training, advancing behind barrage etc. 2nd Lt Margotiouth returned from leave. | |
| " | 13" | | Coy. Training. Same as yesterday. 2nd Lt. Margotiouth returned from leave. Battalion route march. Ten 1 platoon per company, who practised construction of "funnelled" dug-outs. | |
| " | 14" | | 2nd Lt. W.C. CLOSE joined the battalion on 12th inst. & was posted to D. Coy. A draft of 10 N.C.O.s & men joined the battalion. | |
| " | 15" | | Coy. training. Most of the battalion attended baths at near VAUCHELLES. Battalion tactical scheme - (Outposts) in morning. In afternoon the C.O. presented | Appendix 13. |
| " | 16" | | the ribbon of the MILITARY MEDAL to those N.C.Os & men to whom the medal had been awarded. | |
| " | 17" | | The Battalion paraded for Divine Service at 10 a.m. | |
| " | 18" | | Coy. training. Certain Officers, N.C.O.s & men attended a Stokes Mortar demonstration at RAINCHEVAL. C.O., 2nd in command, Adjutant, Coy. Commanders & 2nd in Commanders & Coy. attended a Brigade conference at RAINCHEVAL at 2 p.m. In morning the Battalion went on a route march. All Officers attended a Battalion conference in afternoon. | |

Army Form C. 2118

# WAR DIARY
## or
## INTELLIGENCE SUMMARY.

(Erase heading not required.)

Instructions regarding War Diaries and Intelligence Summaries are contained in F.S. Regs., Part II. and the Staff Manual respectively. Title pages will be prepared in manuscript.

| Place | Date 1916 | Hour | Summary of Events and Information | Remarks and references to Appendices |
|---|---|---|---|---|
| ARQUÈVES | Sept. 19 | | For conspicuous gallantry & devotion to duty the following decorations were awarded :— Capt. O.D SHREINER - Military Cross, Capt. S. le FLEMING SHERER - Military Cross, No. 16734 Sgt. C.S.M H. R PEET - D.C.M., No. 15940 Pte F.J.D RUSSELL - D.C.M. | |
| " | " 20 | | Coy. training in morning - All companies practiced attack formation - One Platoon per Coy gave demonstration in intensive digging under Bn. instructors. In afternoon inspection of the battalion by C.O. | |
| " | " 21 | | In morning, Coy. training - The afternoon was devoted to interior economy. "turn-out" - inspection of clothing, equipment etc. The Medal of St George, 4th class was awarded to No. 15940 Pte F.J.D RUSSELL. 2nd Lt. N.R. HUNTING joined the battalion on 19th Sept & was posted to C. Coy. | |
| " | 22d | | Coy. training in morning. The battalion practised the attack in afternoon. | |
| HÉDAUVILLE | 23d | | Physical training in early morning - Bn. left at 9:15 a.m. & marched to HEDAUVILLE where it camped. | |
| S. BLUFF | 25th | | The battalion paraded at 4.15 a.m. & marched to S. BLUFF arriving about 10-30 a.m. | See Appendix 14. |
| AUTHUILLE | | | C.O. & 2nd i.c command attended a Bde. conference at PASSERELLE DE MAGENTA at 11 a.m. & received instructions for the attack on THIEPVAL on the morrow. | Operation Order No. 29. |

# WAR DIARY
## or
## INTELLIGENCE SUMMARY.
*(Erase heading not required.)*

Army Form C

Instructions regarding War Diaries and Intelligence Summaries are contained in F.S. Regs., Part II. and the Staff Manual respectively. Title pages will be prepared in manuscript.

| Place | Date 1916 | Hour | Summary of Events and Information | Appendix |
|---|---|---|---|---|
| | Sept. | | | See Appendix 15. |
| THIEPVAL | 26 | | Assault on and capture of THIEPVAL – | |
| S. BLUFF | 27 | | The battalion having been relieved in THIEPVAL by the 4th Bedfords, returned at 8 a.m. returned to dug-outs at S. BLUFF by about 10 a.m. | |
| " | 28 | | Re-organisation of companies was commenced. Officers were placed in temporary command of companies as follows:- A Coy. 2nd Lt. D.M. HERTZ-SMITH, B Coy. 2nd Lt. C.R. CHATHAM, C Coy. 2nd Lt. F.D.S. WALKER, D Coy. 2nd Lt. WEBB. Inspections of arms, equipment, ammunition etc. | |
| MAILLY MAILLET WOOD | 29 | | The battalion left S. BLUFF about 9 p.m. and marched to MAILLY MAILLET WOOD arriving about 10.30 p.m., where the whole battalion was most hospitably entertained by the 12th Middlesex before turning in. | |
| " | 30 | | The battalion was visited and congratulated by the C.O. on the glorious part it had played in the capture of THIEPVAL. The strongest enemy position on the whole of the Western Front. Numerous congratulatory telegrams were received | See Appendix 16. |

6th (S) Bn Northamptonshire Regiment.

## SUMMARY OF CASUALTIES.

| | | |
|---|---|---|
| 2nd Lt STONE, WILLIAM HENRY. | Killed in Action. | 26.9.16. |
| " " HAYWARD, HERBERT WILLIAM. | " " | " |
| CAPTAIN EVANS, DOUGLAS LANE. | Died of Wounds. | 27.9.16. |
| " BATTY" GEOFFREY GEORGE HORN | " " | " |
| COLONEL RIPLEY, GEORGE EUSTACE. | Wounded in Action. | 26.9.16. |
| Lt & Adj BARKHAM, WILLIAM HENRY. | " " | " |
| CAPTAIN STOKES, EVAN FRASER. | " " | " |
| 2nd Lt. GODDARD "HAROLD WILLIAM. | " " | " |
| " NENDICK, LAURENCE. | " " | " |
| " KEYS, CLEMENT GEOFFREY. | " " | " |
| " FREND, HUGH PALLISER. | " " | " |
| " SMYTH" NUGENT. | " " | " |
| " BAILEY, LESLIE CHARLES. | " " | " |

### The following are other Ranks.

Killed........................... 24
Wounded..........................105
Missing..........................  17
Suffering from Shell Shock.......   5
Wounded and Missing..............   3
Missing believed Killed..........   2

Major.

Commdg. 6th (S) Bn Northamptonshire Regiment.

In the Field.
2/10/16.

APPENDIX A. Distribution of 54th Bde immediately before ZERO hour

| UNIT | POSITION | H.Q. (BATTN) |
|---|---|---|
| 12" Midd'x Regt.<br>also - ½ sect. (2 guns) 54th M.G. Coy<br>½ " (2 mortars) 54th T.M.B.<br>1 Coy 11 R. Fus. (dug-out clearing party) | Forming up trenches included in the Rectangle R.31.b.2.5 - a.6.6.- a.4.0. - c.6.9 - d.2.6 (less the actual trench running from R.31.a.6.6. to R.31.a.4.8. | H.Q. 12" Midd'x in dug-outs immediately South of R.31.a.4.2. |
| 2 Coys 11th R. Fusiliers.<br>also ½ sec. (2 guns) 54th M.G. Coy<br>½ " (2 mortars) 54th T.M.B. | In trench R.31.a.6.6 - a.4.8 and new communication trench from old British front line leading to old German front line N. of Point R.31.a.5.5. | |
| 11th R. Fus. (less 2 coys)<br>also - 1 sec. 54th M.G. Coy. | in LEMBERG TRENCH and QUARRY. | H.Q. 11th R. Fus. in dugouts at R.31.c.6.8. |

2.

| UNIT. | POSITION. | BATTN. H. QRS. |
|---|---|---|
| 2 Secs. 80th F. Coy. R.E. | In tunnel West of R.31.a.5.3. | |
| 6th BN. NORTHANTS. | | |
| 1 Company. | In old German trench between X.1.b.1.8. – X.1.a.3.8. and old British front line South of that trench. | H.Q. 6th Northants in CAMPBELLS POST Q.36.d.2-2 |
| 1 Company | In CAMPBELL AVENUE | |
| 2 coys | In dug outs SOUTH BLUFF. | |
| 4th BEDS ROT | | |
| 2 Companies | In dug-outs NORTH BLUFF | H.Q. 4th Beds |
| 2 Companies | In PAISLEY AV (THIEPVAL WOOD). | in NORTH BLUFF. |

3.

| UNIT | POSITION | BATTN. H.Q.RS. |
|---|---|---|
| 2 Secs 80th F. Coy R.E. } 1 Sec 54th M.G. Coy } | In PAISLEY AV. (THIEPVAL WOOD) | |
| 1 Sec 54th M.G. Coy. | In trenches on HAMEL-MESNIL Ridge (to bring direct overhead fire during attack) | |
| H.Q. 54th M.G. Coy } 54th T.M.B. (less 1 Sec.) } | In NORTH BLUFF | |

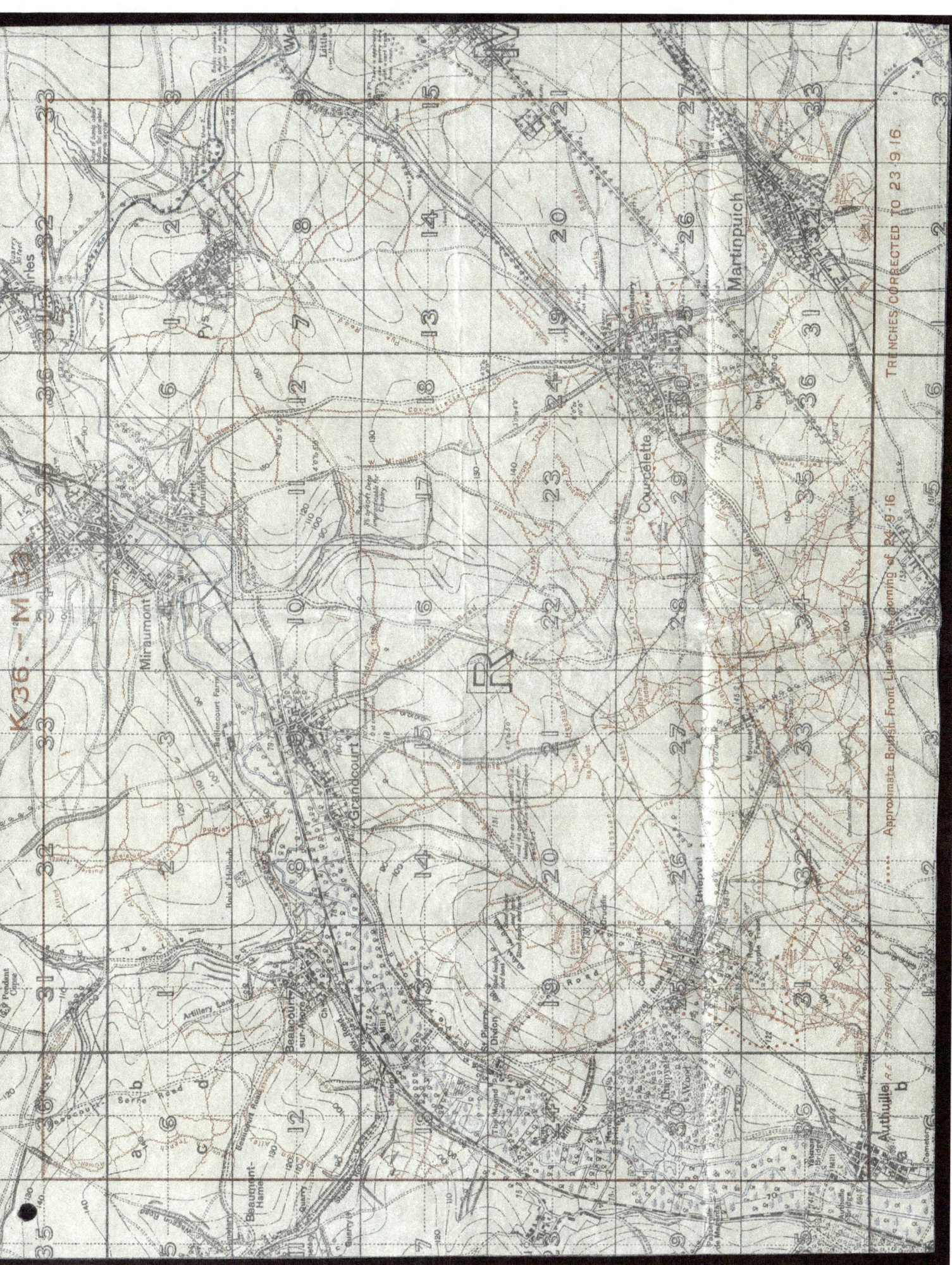

Plan showing approximate position of 54th Inf. Bde. on night of 26/27th Sept. 1916.

Tracing from German Map of Thiepval
(Captured at Wonder Work 14/9/16)

6th (S.) Bn. Northamptonshire Regt.

SECRET

## Preliminary Instructions for Attack.

Ref. Map Sheet. 57 d. S.E. 1/20,000         25th Sept 1916.

1. The Reserve Army is about to make a general attack on the ridge which runs from N.W. of COURCELETTE to the SCHWABEN REDOUBT.
   The 18th Div. is the left Div. in the attack with the 11th Div. on its right.
   The dividing line between formations is shown on the special map thus
   The objectives of the 18th Div are marked on the special map:-
      First Objective ..... Blue line.
      Second   "    ...... Green Line
      Final    "    ...... Red Line.
   The main line to be consolidated in rear of the final objective is shown on the map thus :-
   The 18th Div. will attack with the 53rd Bde on the right and the 54th Bde on the Left. The 55th Bde will be in Div. Reserve.
   The 146th Inf Bde (47th Div) will continue to hold its present line.

2. TASK OF 54th INF. BDE.
   The task of the 54th Bde is to capture and hold the final objective and take every opportunity of exploiting success by pushing forward patrols and Lewis Guns to inflict casualties on retiring enemy.

3. DISTRIBUTION OF BDE AT ZERO HOUR.
   ( see appendix "A" attached).

4. ROLE OF BATTALIONS.
   12th Midd'x Regt. will act as the assaulting Battn. and fight its way through to the final objective. It will first consolidate the line shown on the special map.

5. 11th Royal Fusiliers.
   The special task of the 11th R.Fusiliers is to capture the Bosche front line from R.31.a.5.9. to R.25.a.9.1. and clear all dugouts South of the trench running from R.25.b.7.3. to 25.b.3.4. To ensure that the 12th Midd'x Regt is neither attacked in flank from the Bosche front line or the trench named or from the rear by any enemy that may come out of dug-outs after the assaulting Battalion has passed.
   Battalion will be distributed as follows :-
   One Coy detailed for special task of clearing the present Bosche front line trench from R.31.a.5.9. to R.25.a.9.1. At the latter point it will establish a block.
   One Coy attached to 12th Midd'x as dug-out clearing parties. This Coy will be responsible for clearing all dugouts south of the enemy trench running from R.25.b.7.3. to R.25.b.3.4. and will not proceed beyond the trench named.. It will be allotted definite objectives for dug-out clearing by the O.C. 12th Midd'x.
   One Coy for attachment to 12th Midd'x Regt for dug-out clearing and other special purposes during the advance from the second to the final objective. This Coy will reach the first objective in sufficient time to take part in the advance of the 12th Midd'x on its final objective.
   One Coy Battn. Reserve for use in support of the remaining Coys of the Battn.

Contd.

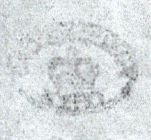

**6th Northants Regt.**

Will act as supports to the 12th Midd'x Regt and will be prepared to support that Battn. in its advance from the second to the final objective. It will also find two platoons for carrying from the Dump referred to in para 9.

**7th Beds.Regt.**

In Bde Reserve.

5. **STRONG POINTS.**

Strong points will be established at the points shown on special map. Those in the final objective will be made and garrisoned by the 12th Midd'x Rgt. That in the second objective by the 11th R.Fus.

The 86th Field Coy will assist in the supervision and construction of these strong points. Strong points will be capable of accommodating and garrisoning one platoon and will be provided with Vickers guns and Stokes Mortars as stated in paras 7 and 8

6. **BARRAGES.**

Details regarding Barrages have not been received but it is understood that the form of barrage to be adopted will be a "creeping one" and it is essential that assaulting waves should follow it as closely as possible throughout the attack.

7. **MACHINE GUN COY.**

Distribution of this Coy will be as follows :-
2 guns each to 11th R.Fus. and 12th Midd'x Rgt respectively.
1 gun from LEIPZIG QUARRY in Bde Reserve to be detailed to proceed to Strong Point R.25.b.3.5.
Remaining guns in LEIPZIG QUARRY in Bde Reserve.
1 section from THIEPVAL WOOD to proceed to final objective as soon as it is consolidated. 2 guns of this section to be earmarked for strong points R.25.c.1.5. and R.19.c.5.8.
1 section covering fire from High ground just south of HAMEL.

8. **84th TRENCH MORTAR BATTERY.**

Distribution of this Battery will be as follows :-
2 mortars each to accompany 11th R.Fus. and 12th Midd'x in the attack.
Remainder of Battery in Bde Reserve.
2 mortars to be earmarked for strong points R.25.d.1.9 and R.19.c.4.5.

9. **DUMPS.**

All Dumps will be under the control of the Bde Bombing Officer.
Forward dumps will be established at R.31.a.4.5. and in PAISLEY AVENUE (THIEPVAL WOOD). Carrying Parties will be provided as follows :-
For that in THIEPVAL WOOD,.. Special parties detailed from all Battns.
For that at R.31.a.4.5. D... By two platoons of 6th Northants Regt.

10. **TANKS.**

Two tanks are to be allotted to 54th Inf.Bde. Instructions regarding their use have not been issued from Divl.H.Qrs. but all ranks should be informed that they will take part in the attack.

11. **SPECIAL COMMUNICATIONS.**

As soon as the second objective is occupied a special communication trench will be constructed from our present front line trench R.25.c.3.4. to R.25.c.7.4.

Contd.

2.

12. **TOOLS, S.A.A.**
Will be carried on the scale laid down for the attack on July 1st. Those required in excess of those already in possession will be drawn from LANCASHIRE DUMP.

13. **MEDICAL ARRANGEMENTS.**
Will be in accordance with 12th Div.Q.M. No of 23rd inst.

14. **PRISONERS OF WAR.**
Prisoners of War will be dealt with in accordance with 18th Div.Q.S.It of 24th Sept. All prisoners will as far as possible be handed over to 11th R.Fus. Where this is not possible Battalion capturing prisoners will conduct them to Divl. cage. A written receipt should be obtained for all prisoners handed in at Divl. cage. These receipts should be forwarded to Bde H.Qrs.

15. **STRAGGLERS.**
Police Posts for the collection of Stragglers will be established as under, Bde arrangements, at BLACK HORSE BRIDGE, W end of CAMPBELL AVENUE, AUTHUILLE BRIDGE, SOUTH CAUSEWAY.

16. **PACK DUMPS.**
Will be selected by Battns. as follows :-
11th R.Fus., in neighbourhood of QUARRY, R.31.c.3.4.
7th Beds. at N.BLUFF.
6th Northants S.BLUFF.
12th Midd'x Regt. under Battn. arrangements.
Battalions will leave two men in charge of their pack Dumps.

17. **RATIONS.**
Arrangements will be in accordance with 18th Div.Q.R.12 of 23rd inst except that para 2 (b) is altered as follows :-
" 1st L/Ams Transport will deliver rations at LANCASHIRE DUMP Q.35.d.3.5. by day as early as possible. Rations will then be transferred to tramline and conveyed to AUTHUILLE whence they will be carried by hand under Battn. arrangement.

18. **GRENADES.**
Instructions regarding number of grenades to be carried have been issued in S.C. 692 of 24th inst.

19. **COMMUNICATIONS.**
Telephone. Every effort will be made to keep lines going to Battn.Hd Qrs. through the Bde Exchanges at CAMPBELLS POST and NORTH BLUFF. These Exchanges will always be kept open.

20. **VISUAL.**
Battn.H.Qrs will take forward French Signalling lamps as well as ordinary visual kit.
Divl.Reading Station is at Q.35.a.3.5. - call AV - and in full view from West side of THIEPVAL RIDGE.
D.D. messages repeated three times to be sent to this station.

**RUNNERS.**
Rnners returning from front should come via CAMPBELLS POST or NORTH BLUFF or PAISLEY DUMP DUMP at all of which places messages can be wired on to Bde.
Bde Runner Posts will be at CAMPBELLS POST and the BLUFF.

OPERATION ORDERS No.44.

by Colonel C.H.Ripley,　　　　　In the Field.
Commanding 6th (S) Bn. Northamptonshire Regiment.　　25.9.16.

Ref. Maps.
ST. PIERRE DIVION　} 1/5000
THIEPVAL
57 D. S.E.　　　　　1/20,000
& Special maps issued

1. **PRELIMINARY INSTRUCTIONS.**
　(1) Orders with regard to the following dispositions and objectives.

　(2) TASK - ON 54th INF. BDE.
　　　(3) Distribution of Bde at Zero hour.
　　　(4) Role of Battalions.
　　　(5) Strong Points.
　　　(6) Barrage.
　　　(7) Machine Gun Coy.
　　　(8) 54th T.M. Battery.
　　　(9) Dumps.
　　　(10) Tanks.
　　　(11) Special Communication.
　　　(12) Tools and S.A.A.
　　　(13) MEDICAL ARRANGEMENTS.
　　　(14) Prisoners of War.
　　　(15) Stragglers.
　　　(16) Past Maps.
　　　(17) Rations.
　　　(18) Grenades.
　　　(19) Communications.
　　Have already been issued in the form of Preliminary Instructions.

　CORRIGENDA.
　　Para (1) for "between formations on the special map thus" read "by track running through R.31.a.b., 25.d.c., 19.b. 20.c."
　　Para (1) for "Final objective is shown on Special Map thus" read "by red dotted line."

2. **ZERO HOUR.**
　The time for Zero hour will be notified as soon as known.

3. **DISTRIBUTION AT ZERO HOUR.**
　One hour before Zero hour "B" Coy will be formed up in CAMPBELL AVENUE, "C" Coy will be formed up in the old German front line trench which faces South in R.1.a. and will move into this trench via BURY STREET and CROWHURST STREET., "A" Coy ( with 2 platoons of "D" Coy attached) will remain in dug-outs in South Bluff till receipt of further orders. Two platoons of "D" Coy will be employed at the Dump at R.31.a.5.3. under the orders of the Bde Dumping Officer. Orders will be issued later as to the time this party will report themselves to the Dump.

　　　　　　　　Contd.

2.                                                    28.9.16.

4. ROLE OF 6th Bn. NORTHANTS REGT.
The role of the 6th Bn. Northants Regt. will be that of the Supporting Battalion to 12th Bn. Midd'x Regt.
"B" and "C" Coys must be in such a position that they can reinforce the 12th Bn. Midd'x Regt. as quickly as possible if required. To ensure this they must keep close in rear of the fourth Coy of the 11th Bn. R. Fusiliers who will be acting in co-operation with the 12th Bn. Midd'x Regt (vide para 4 Preliminary Instructions) unless required in support of the 12th Bn. Midd'x Regt. Neither Coys will proceed North of Track running east and west, South of THIEPVAL and shown on special map in red dotted line. Either or both Coys will act in Support of the 12th Bn. Midd'x Regt in receiving a written order from O.C. 12th Bn. Midd'x Regt and will act under his orders.     "B" Coy will advance first in rear of fourth Coy R. Fusiliers, its route will be from CAMPBELL AVENUE along old German front line to "forming up" trench in R.31.a.8.6. - 7.5 - 9.4. and thence to R.25.c.5.6. to D-1.2.
"C" Coy will advance in rear of "B" Coy, its route will be from its "forming up" trench via CABBAGE STREET to the "forming up" trench in R.a.5.5. - 6.5. - 9.4. and thence to R.25.c.5.4. to R.31.D.5.0.
In the event of the 12th Bn. Midd'x Regt being unable to advance to the attack on the final objective the 6th Bn. Northants may be called upon to undertake this attack. In this case a re-bombardment will be ordered and the new operation will be inaugurated by him under the command of O.C. 6th Bn. Northants Regt. An hour for re-bombardment will be given and Zero hour will commence half an hour after the hour notified.

5. LIAISON.
The strictest Liaison must be maintained between "B" and "C" Coys and also between "B" Coy and 4th Coy 11th R. Fusiliers

6. FLARES, S.O.S. SIGNALS & COMMUNICATIONS WITH AEROPLANES.
Instructions have been issued.

7. WATER.
Water bottles must be full at ZERO hour and all ranks must be made to understand that the water in their bottles will have to last them till Nightfall. A small supply of water only will be obtainable at CAMPBELL POST and PAISLEY AVENUE (THIEPVAL WOOD).

8. RATIONS.
One day's rations and one day's iron rations will be carried.

9. HEADQUARTERS.
6th Bn. Northants Regt Hd.Qrs. will be at Zero hour at CAMPBELL POST and will move to R.31.a.7.2. about one hour later. 12th Bn. Midd'x Regt Hd.Qrs at Zero hour at R.31.a.7.2. and will move to first objective about one hour later.
11th Bn. R. Fusiliers will be at ZERO hour at R.31.a.6.5. and will move to near first objective about one hour later.

10. INFORMATION.
No effort must be spared to send back information to Bn.H.Qrs.
When sending back a report of a situation not obtained by by personal observation the source of information must always be clearly stated.

11. BARRAGE.
Should any Coy of the 6th Bn. Northants Regt be in the front line all ranks must remember to keep within 40 to 50 yards of our barrage. When the Barrage stops they stop. When it moves on again they move on also

Contd.

12. **MEDICAL ARRANGEMENTS.**
Stretcherbearers will remain with their Coys and will take orders from their Coy Commanders.
All Sanitary men will be in Reserve and will report to the M.O. at Bn.Hd.Qrs.
Walking wounded will make their way to Advanced Dressing Station at BLACK HORSE BRIDGE.
As the Advance proceeds other Advanced Dressing Stations will be opened. Information concerning these will be sent to Coys as fresh stations are opened.
When final objective is reached Regtl.Aid Post will be opened near Bn.Hd.Qrs.

13. **WATCHES.**
Os.C.Coys will synchronize their watches at Battn.Hd.Qrs before leaving their present position.

14. **SMALL ENTRENCHING TOOLS & DUG-OUT FRAMES.**
These will be sent up as opportunity permits by O.C. Dumps.


(Sgd) W.Burnham, Lieut & Adjt.
6th (S) Bn. Northamptonshire Regiment.


Copy No. 1   "A" Coy
        2   "B"  "
        3   "C"  "
        4   "D"  "
        5   Bde.
        6   Hd.Qrs.
        7   War Diary.

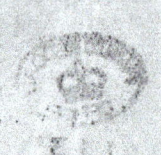

SECRET.

## OPERATION ORDERS No. 40

by Colonel G.E. Ripley,
Commanding 6th (S) Bn. Northamptonshire Regiment.

In the Field
26.9.16.

1. **ZERO HOUR.**

   Zero hour will be at 12.35 p.m. today, 26th inst.
   All Units are to be in position by 10.30 a.m. instead of as stated in Operation Order No.30, para 3.

2. **STRONG POINTS.**

   The Strong Point in the Final Objective at R.20.d.1.5. will now be garrisoned by the 53rd Inf.Bde instead of as stated in Preliminary Instructions, para 5.

3. **DUMPS.**

   The forward Dumps at R.31.a.4.5. and Q.30.d.6.1. will be moved forward to R.25.c.9.4. and R.25.b.4.9. respectively as soon as circumstances permit.

4. **TANKS.**

   One "TANK" will emerge from the small copse at Q.30.d.3..0 at Zero hour and proceed in the direction of THIEPVAL Chateau. It should arrive at the Chateau ruins at approximately the same time as the leading infantry. This "TANK" will be followed by a second "TANK". These two tanks will remain in THIEPVAL to assist the Infantry in clearing the village. As soon as the Infantry advance on the final objective the two "TANKS" will accompany them. Their objective will be th SCHWABEN REDOUBT.

5. **FLARES.**

   The leading line of Infantry will light flares at the following times :-
   (a) Forty eight minutes after ZERO.
   (b) Two hours, fifteen minutes after ZERO.
   (c) Three hours, thirty minutes after ZERO.
   or at any time on demand being made from Contact Aeroplanes sound Klaxon horns or dropping white Verey lights.

6. **DISTINGUISHING FLAG.**

   The leading wave of the 12th Midd'x Rgt. will carry a large yellow and red flag in order to show the Infantry in rear and the "tanks" their position.

7. **EQUIPMENT.**

   In addition to normal fighting equipment the following will be carried :-
   One bandolier in addition to equipment ammunition.(170 rounds in all).
   One waterproof sheet.
   All men will wear one Smoke helmet in the 'alert' position.

8. **TIME IN POSITION.**

   All Coys will inform Bn.H.Qrs immediately they are in position.

9. **PRISONERS OF WAR.**

   Reference "Preliminary Instructions, para 14 Prisoners of War". Receipts obtained on delivery of prisoners at Divl.cages should be handed to any of the Bde. Police at Stragglers Posts.

Contd.

2.                                                          26.9.16.

10. WATER SUPPLY.

There will be a water supply in THIEPVAL WOOD at ROSS CASTLE XX Q.30.b.6.1. by the afternoon. There will also be a supply of water at JOHNSTONE POST, Q.30.d.8.2. Filled petrol tins will be taken forward to Dumps.

11. CARRYING PARTIES FOR DUMPS.

The two platoons of "D" Coy mentioned in Operation Order No.39, para 3. will report to the Bde Bombing Officer at the Dump at R.31.a.5.3. at 10.30 a.m.

12. PACK DUMPS.

All packs will be dumped by 9 a.m. near East end of BLACK HORSE STREET.

13. SECRECY OF ORDERS.

Complete copies of orders and instructions or maps of our Trenches must not be taken into action, only sufficient notes made from them should be carried in writing as are necessary for reference.

Os.C.Coys will retain return their copies of orders to Bn. H.Qrs before moving up to Front Line trenches.


                    (Sgd) W.Barkham, Lieut & Adjt.
                         6th (S) Bn. Northants Regt.


               Copies No.1 "A" Coy
                      2. "B"  "
                      3. "C"  "
                      4. "D"  "
                      5. Bde.
                      6. Hd.Qrs.
                      7. War Diary.

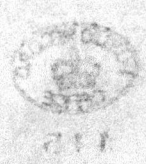

Narrative of the part played by the 6th S. Bn.
Northamptonshire Regiment in the capture of
THIEPVAL on the 26th September 1916.

Copies of preliminary instructions, Operation Orders
and Sketch maps are attached.

At 9-15 a.m. "B" Company left their dug-outs in SOUTH BLUFF
to move into their "Forming up" Trench in CAMPBELL AVENUE.
"C" Company followed a few minutes later, and proceeded
to their "Forming-up" Trench in R.31.c.6.6. to X.1.A.6.8.
At 9-30 a.m. Battalion Headquarters left South BLUFF and
proceeded to their First Battle Headquarters at CAMPBELL POST
arriving there at 10 a.m.
At 10 a.m. two platoons "D" Company left SOUTH BLUFF under
2nd Lieuts HIGHAM and SCOTT-TAGGART and reported themselves
to Officer Commanding Dump at CAMPBELL POST as Carrying parties
At 10-15 a.m. and 10-30 a.m. "B" and "C" Companies had respectively taken up their positions in their "Forming-up" Trenches.
At 11-25 a.m. 2.Lt Goddard "B" Company, reported that he was in
touch with the rear Company of 11th Royal Fusiliers, who were
then moving up from LEMBERG TRENCH via PRINCE STREET.
At 11-35 a.m. "B" Company arrived at FIRTH AVENUE.
At 1 p.m. "C" Company left their "Forming-up" Trench and began
to move forward. By this time an extremely heavy Enemy
Barrage was being put on all communication trenches leading
up to the Front Line and Battalion Headquarters at CAMPBELL
POST was being shelled by heavy H.E. shells - one shell burst
in trench three yards from Headquarter Dug-out, blowing to
pieces the three men in next dug-out.
At 1-23 p.m. a message was received from "C" Company stating
that Captain Evans, and 2 Lt Bailey had become casualties.
At 1-40 p.m. "B" Company arrived in Trench just SOUTH of the
CHATEAU, though news of their arrival there was not received
until 3-30 p.m. At this time Battalion Headquarters - although
no news had been received from 12th Middlesex Regt that their
Headquarters at R.31.c.66. had been vacated - decided to
transfer their Headquarters there. Owing to the extremely
heavy Barrage, a considerable amount of disorganization took
place during this move, and many units of Headquarters became
cut off by the Barrage, or owing to most trenches being
obliterated by shell fire, lost their direction.
On arrival at INVERARY TRENCH just East of R.31.A.4.2. one H.E.
shell wounded Colonel Ripley badly in the arm and Lieut and Adjutant
Barkham in the leg and arm. The former was put into a dug-out
and shortly afterwards attended to by the Medical Officer.
Just before leaving CAMPBELL POST, under instructions received
from Brigade Headquarters, "A" Company and "D" Company (less
two platoons) had been sent orders by 2 Lieut Frend to proceed
immediately to the Road SOUTH of the CHATEAU, and reinforce
the 12th Middlesex.
At 2-45 p.m. I proceeded with 2 Lieut Walker and four runners,
the only Headquarters personnel which could be collected, to
take up my Headquarters in R.31.c.6.6., and take over command
of the Battalion.
At 2-30 p.m. "A" Company and "D" Company (less two platoons)
had left SOUTH BLUFF and commenced their advance to the Road
SOUTH of the CHATEAU.
On arrival at R.31.c.6.6. I found that the dug-out lately
occupied by 12th Middlesex Headquarters was choked with wounded.
A Brigade Report Centre was established there, but all Telephone
wires had been cut and the only possible communication was by
runners or pigeons.

At 3-30 p.m. my Signalling Officer, 2 Lt Margoliouth arrived with about six Signallers.

It was about this time that "C" Company arrived in trench just SOUTH of the CHATEAU.

2nd Lt. Hayward being the only Officer left with the Company, this Officer very shortly afterwards became a casualty, and as the Sergeant Major had also been put out of action earlier, the command of the Company devolved on Sergeant Pullen who carried out his duties with the greatest courage and coolness. This Company under orders from O.C. 12th Middlesex Regiment were sent to reinforce the 11th Royal Fusiliers who were held up on the left of the line N.W. of the CHATEAU. During the ensuing night they were used to hold a portion of the line on this flank.

"B" Company in the meantime had moved forward to support the 12th Middlesex Regt., in the centre of the line near Second Objective.

Immediately on leaving the CHATEAU, Machine-gun fire and fire from Snipers hidden in shell holes was very deadly especially on the Left Flank.

It was whilst advancing from the CHATEAU that Capt Batty, gallantly leading his men, was severely wounded, and 2nd Lt Stone killed. 2nd Lieuts Goddard and Wendick having been previously wounded, this Company was in a similar plight to "C" Company, and was without any Officers. The Acting-Sergt Major, Sergt Partridge, then assumed command of the Company and carried on with the greatest gallantry.

At 4 p.m., half an hour after "B" and "C" Companies had gone forward from the CHATEAU, "A" Company and two platoons of "D" Company arrived on the scene and immediately advanced to the support of the Front Line on the centre and right of the second Objective.

Captain Stokes, commanding "A" Company was wounded before arriving at the CHATEAU, 2nd Lieut Keys was wounded by rifle-fire whilst leading the Company across the open to the North of the CHATEAU and 2nd Lieut Frend had also been put out of action.

The situation with regard to Officers of the 8th S. Bn. Northamptonshire Regiment in the Front Line was therefore as follows:-

"B" Company - No Officers, Sgt Partridge in Command
"C"    "    -    "     "    Sgt Pullen in Command
"A"    "    - One Officer, 2nd Lieut Gotch in Command
"D" Company (less 2 platoons) 2nd Lieut Bates in Command.

At 4-30 p.m., Lieut Ashmole 11th Royal Fusiliers, 54th Infantry Brigade Liason Officer arrived at my Headquarters and I gave him the situation as far as I had learnt it, from two messages for Brigade Headquarters just received from Lieut Col Maxwell, from the CHATEAU, and which had been forwarded one by runner and one by pigeon.

As I had now been informed that my last two remaining Companies had arrived at the CHATEAU, I decided to move my Headquarters there, leaving 2nd Lieut Margoliouth and his Signallers at the Report Centre to try and obtain communication.

Accompanied by 2nd Lieut Walker and four Runners only, as I did not know if there would be accomodation for my Headquarters Staff, as well as that of 12th Middlesex Regiment, at the CHATEAU. I arrived there about 5-15 p.m. - Here I found Lieut-Col. Maxwell and his Headquarters Staff.

After being informed of the situation in front as far as it was known, Lieut-Col. Maxwell directed me to proceed to the Front Line to clear up the situation, and take command of the Front Line on the Right and Centre. A considerable amount of Sniping and Machine Gun Fire was still coming from the enemy on our left flank, which continued until night-fall. After getting into touch with Lieut Odhams 12th Middlesex Regt, and 2nd Lt. Bates and Gotch of my Battalion, I managed to visit most of that part of the line before dusk, and found to ranges shown on accompanying sketch.

3.

6th. Northamptonshire Regiment and 11th Middlesex Regiment were somewhat mixed up, whilst a few Royal Fusiliers were on the Right of the Line which was in touch with the 10th Essex.
Owing to the lateness of the hour and the near approach of dusk, I decided that it was not feasable to straighten out the line, but preferable to consolidate the line already held.
I accordingly sorted out Battalions as well as possible, filled up all gaps, withdrew a few small isolated detachments that were too far advanced and liable to be cut off or come under our own fire and commenced to consolidate the line.
Several Bombing Posts and Blocks were also established in Communication Trenches, which led towards the enemy.
Lieut Odgers with two Subalterns was in command of the Right of the Line, and I placed 2nd Lt Gotch in Command of the Right half Battalion 6th Northants, and 2nd Lieut Bates in Command of Left half of Battalion, in the Centre of the Line. The latter informed me that he was in touch with the 11th Royal Fusiliers on his left and so, as I knew there was a Captain of the 11th Royal Fusiliers on that part of the Line, I did not visit it.
It was not until about 11-30 p.m. that I was able to send Lieut Col Maxwell a Report of the situation, at which time I had managed to establish my Headquarters in a dug-out in the Front Line near R.25.B.4.8.
Except for a certain amount of promiscuous shelling between our Line and the CHATEAU" the night passed fairly quietly. At 5-30 a.m. two companies of the 7th Bedfords passed through our lines to take the German Front Line on our left flank.
At the same time the personnel of an Enemy Dressing Station consisting of one officer and about twenty other ranks came over to us and gave themselves up as prisoners. They were all spotlessly clean and it did not appear as though they had been attending to the duties of their profession.
At 8 a.m. "A" Company 7th Bedfords arrived, and I informed Lieut Odgers that he could withdraw his Battalion. As soon as he was clear I withdrew my Battalion, except "C" Company, who were on the left of the line and were withdrawn under orders direct by Lieut Col. Maxwell.
The withdrawal was carried out with practically no casualties in spite of a certain amount of hostile shelling.

4.

I wish to bring to notice the names of the following Officers N.C.O-s and men for special acts of gallantry or devotion to duty during the above operations.

    2nd Lt. F.D.S. Walker
    Capt K.A.Bennet   C.to P.
    2.Lt. A.C.Bates
    2.Lt. D.I.Gotch
    Lieut C.G.Kemp  R.A.M.C.
    ---------------

No. 10478 Sgt. (Actg C.S.M.) Partridge J.W.
  18527  "  F.C.Pullen
  17986  "  W.L.Miles
  7865  "  F. Rowlands
  14561  "  H.T.Scriven
  14006 Pte W.G.Cox
  10914 L/Cpl A.F.Simmons
  15310 Sgt. A.C.Bury
  15687 L.Cpl T. Thompson
  14302 Pte. G. Byrne
  31879 Pte I.Tebbatt
  13464 L.Cpl F. Whipton
  28113 Pte J.Walsh
  11631 L.Cpl F. Hill
  15986 Cpl. Scott. W.A.


Appendices attached:-

 A. Preliminary Instructions for Attack

 B. Operation Orders No. 38

 C. Do    Do    No. 40

 D. Sketch Map

 E. Report by Signal Officer


        Major
    Commdg 6th S. Bn. Northamptonshire Regt.

Appendix 4.

6th (S) Bn. Northamptonshire Regiment.

PROGRAMME OF WORK.

27th August to 2nd September 1916.

| Date | Time | Area | Nature of work. |
|---|---|---|---|
| Aug. 27th. | | | See Programme already issued. |
| Aug. 28th. | 7.45 am | Near Billets. | Companies at disposal of Os.C.Coys for Bombing, Physical Training, Bayonet Fighting Rapid Loading etc. |
| " | 1.30 pm. | D | (a) Coys to carry out Tactical Exercises in Close Country.<br>(b) Battn. to carry out a Tactical Exercise in Close Country. |
| Aug. 29th. | 7.45 am. | A.2. | (a) Coys will carry out Tactical Exercises in open Country.<br>(b) Battalion will carry out a Tactical Exercise in Open Country. |
| | 6 p.m. | Bn. H.Q. | Conference with all Officers on work done and proposed for tomorrow. |
| Aug. 29/30th | 3 a.m. | A.1. | *(not carried out, owing to rain)*<br>(By arrangement). ~~Forming up by night and attack on position at dawn.~~ |
| Aug. 30th. | 9.30 am. | Near billets. | Physical Training, Bayonet Fighting, Rapid loading, Bombing, etc. |
| | 1.30 p.m | B.1. | (a) Coys to carry out Tactical Exercises in the Open, preparing for attack on trenches, Various methods of attacking single line of trenches.<br>(b) Battalion ditto. |
| Aug. 31st. | | B & C. | BRIGADE TRAINING. |
| | 6.30 pm. | Bn. H.Q. | Conference with all Officers. |
| Sept. 1st. | 7.45 am | C.1. | (a) Coys to carry out Tactical Exercises in the Open.<br>(b) Battalion to carry out Tactical Exercises in the Open. |
| | 2 p.m. | Near Billets. | Coys at disposal of Os.C.for Bayonet Fightg, Physical Training, Rapid Loading etc. |

Contd.

( 2 ).

| Date | Time | Area | Nature of Work. |
|---|---|---|---|
| Sept. 2nd. | 7.45 am | Near Billets. | Coys at disposal of Os.C.Coys for Bombing practice, Physical Training, Bayonet Fightg, rapid Loading, etc. |
|  | 2 p.m. | D, | Marching on Compass bearing in Close Country. |
|  | 7 p.m. | Bn. H.Qrs. | Conference with all Officers. |

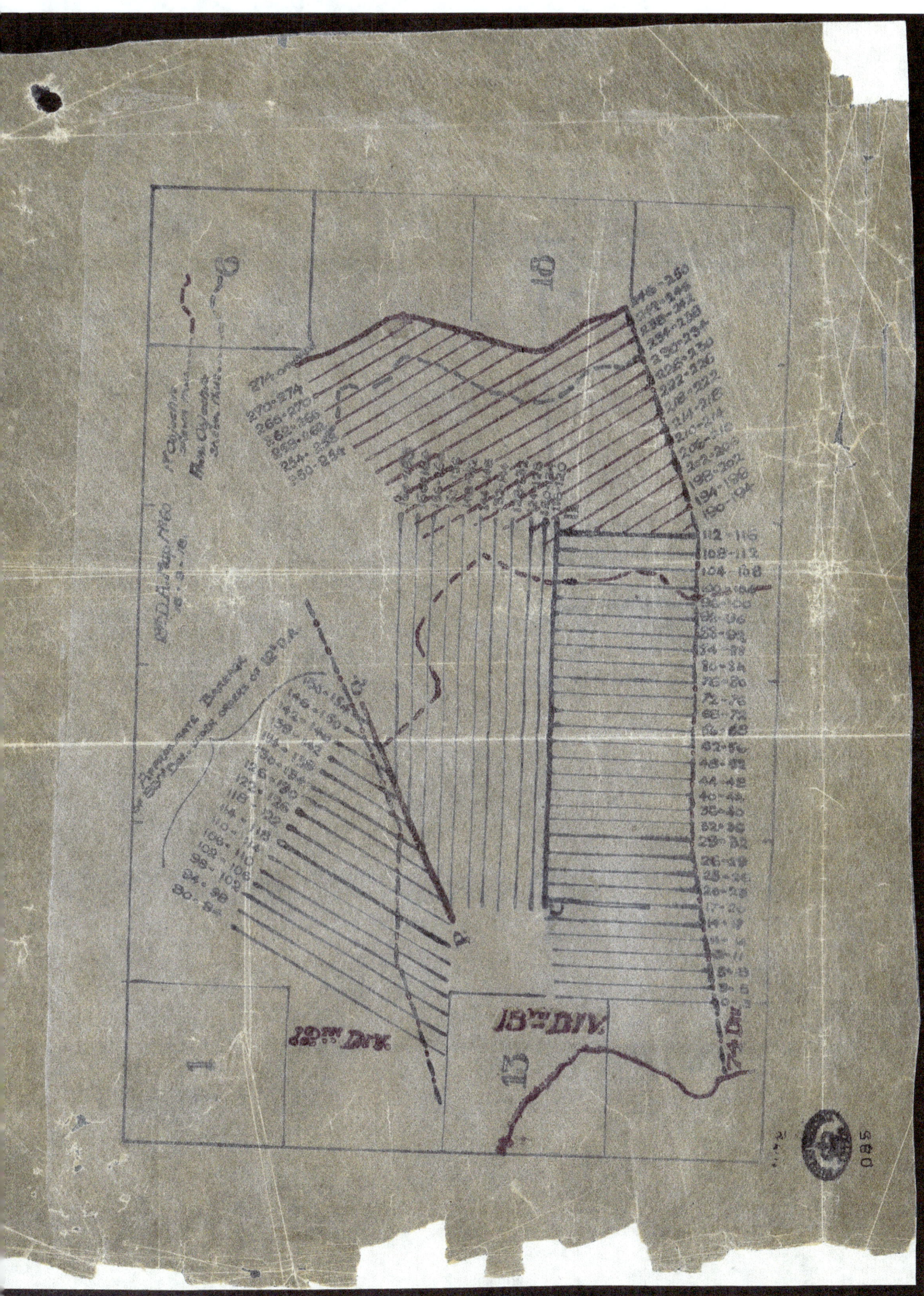

## 6th (S) Bn. Northamptonshire Regiment. Appendix 13

The folowing is a list of N.C.Os. and Men awarded the MILITARY MEDAL, as per Divisional Routine Order No.147, d/10.9.16:-

| | | | | | | | |
|---|---|---|---|---|---|---|---|
| 8239 Cpl. Stapleton | M. | "D" Coy. | | 8277 Sgt. Sullivan | W. | "C" Coy. |
| 13104 Sgt. Tack | E.W. | "C" " | | 12766 Cpl. Alleway | E. | "B" " |
| 3/10888 Pte. Blunt | H. | "C" " | | 13396 Pte. Stevens | S. | "D" " |
| 14856 " Adams | G. | "D" " | | 13945 " Sanders | G.H. | "B" " |
| 13138 " Walker | W.H. | "B" " | | 14495 Cpl. Radley | L. | "A" " |
| 13968 Sgt. Freeman | J. | "D" " | | 15592 L/C. Roberts | L.J. | "D" " |
| 13908 Pte. Golding | G. | "C" " | | 13830 Pte. Shrive | C. | "A" " |

Appendix 14

S E C R E T.    OPERATION    ORDERS  No.38
                    by Colonel G.E.Ripley,                    24.9.16
            Commanding 6th (S) Bn. Northamptonshire Regiment.
            ─────────────────────────────────────
                    S.S.
            Reference Map Sheet 57 D. 1/20,000


1. MOVE.
    The Battalion will move to Dug-outs in South Bluff and AUTHUILLE.

   ROUTE.
    BOUZINCOURT, W.7.Central., W.2.b.8.0., South end of MARTIN-SART WOOD, W.9.b.8.0. through C in CEMETERY (in W.18.b.) W.5.a.4.0. BLACK HORSE ROAD.

   STARTING POINT AND TIME.
    Heads of Column will be at Cross roads P.24.c.8.3. at 7.15 am. in the following order:-  Headquarters, "D", "A", "B", "C", Coy Cookers, Mess Carts, Water carts, Maltese cart and Baggage Wagon.

   INTERVAL.
    After BOUZINCOURT Coys will march to their destination at ten minutes interval.

   ADVANCED PARTY.
    2nd Lieut F.D.S.Walker, 4 C.Q.M.Ss and Sergt.Jakes will report to the Staff Captain at the West end of BLACK HORSE ROAD (W.5.a.4.0.) at 8.30 a.m.

   OFFICERS' VALISES.
    Officers' Valises will be Dumped near Bn.H.Qrs. before marching off.

   OFFICERS' MESS CARTS.
    Officers' Mess carts will be packed by 6.30 a.m.

   WATER.
    All Water bottles will be filled tonight.

   LEWIS GUN CARTS.
    Lewis Gun Carts will travel in rear of their respective Coys

   CLEANLINESS OF BILLETS.
    All Billets will be left thoroughly clean, Os.C.Coys reporting to the Adjutant that this order has been carried out.

   OFFICERS' KITS.
    Officers' Kits that are required for the trenches must be ready by 6 a.m.


            (Sgd) W.Barkham, Lieut & Adjt.
            6th (S) Bn. Northamptonshire Regiment.

Appendix 15.

(1) Map Sheet 57 D. S.E. Square R.

(2) Plan of THIEPVAL, showing approximate line held by 6" Northants Regt., 12" Middlesex Regt. & 11" R. Fusiliers on night of Sept. 26/27.

(3) Sketch Map of THIEPVAL, showing objectives.

(4) Preliminary Instructions for the attack.

(5) Operation Order No. 39.

(6) " " No. 40.

(7) Narrative of the part played by the 6" (S.) Bn. Northamptonshire Regt. in the capture of THIEPVAL, including list of those mentioned for conspicuous gallantry & summary of casualties.

Appendix 18.

## 18th. DIVISION.

Copies of Congratulatory Messages received by the Division on the successful operations resulting in the Capture of THIEPVAL on September 26th 1916 and of SCHWABEN REDOUBT on September 28th, 1916.

---

(1) Telegrams from Lieutenant General C.W. JACOB, C.B. Commanding IInd. Army Corps.

"TO:- 18th. Division.

G.1881.            26th.

Corps Commander wishes to thank you and all Ranks of your Division for their admirable work today AAA THIEPVAL has withstood all attacks upon it for exactly two years and it is a great honour to your Division to have captured the whole of this strongly fortified village at their first attempt AAA Hearty congratulations to you all.

FROM:- IInd. Corps.
9.10 p.m.

"TO:- 18th. Division.

G.1998.            28th.
              Commander
The Corps/again thanks and congratulates all ranks of 18th. Division on further gallant and successful work today. AAA He specially commends the good organisation, training and Staff Work displayed and the methodical and determined manner in which all orders and plans have been carried out and all prearranged objectives reached and consolidated.

FROM:- IInd. Corps.
11/12 p.m.

(2) Telegram from General Sir. H. de la P. GOUGH, K.C.B. Commanding Reserve Army.

"TO:- Maj.Gen.MAXSE.                28.9.16.
       18th. Division.

Congratulate you very heartily on success of to-days attack as well as of previous operations AAA Reflects greatest credit on you and your troops.

FROM:- General Gough.

P.T.O.

( 2 )

(3) Telegram from General Sir. HERBERT C.O.PLUMER, G.C.M.G.,K.C.B. Commanding Second Army.

"TO:- Eighteenth DIVISION.

G.930.        28th.

Many congratulations to you and your Division from Commander and Staff Second Army.

FROM:- Second Army.
5-45 p.m."

(4) Personal congratulations of GENERAL SIR. DOUGLAS HAIG, G.C.B.,G.C.V.O.,K.C.I.E. Commander-in-Chief British Armies in France.

"TO:- 53rd, 54th, and 55th Infantry Brigades.

G.221.        Sept. 27th.

The Commander-in-Chief personally called to-day on General MAXSE to congratulate the Division on its success at THIEPVAL.

FROM:- 18th. Division.
4-30 p.m.

E.V.RIDDELL, Lt.Colonel,
A.A. & Q.M.G., 18th. Division.
29th. September 1916.

# WAR DIARY
## or
## INTELLIGENCE SUMMARY

6th Northamptonshire Regt

Oct 16

| Place | Date | Hour | Summary of Events and Information | Remarks and references to Appendices |
|---|---|---|---|---|
| MAILLY-MAILLET | 1916 OCT 1 | | Return to winter time. At Church parade which was held in conjunction with the 11th Royal Fusiliers Brigadier-General STOUBRIDGE congratulated the Brigade on the work at THIEPVAL. All companies attended (later) at HEDAUVILLE. A draft of 100 men joined the Battalion at night. | Appx I Thiepval |
| | 2 | | Company training. | |
| | 3 | | The Battalion entrained (H.Q. two companies and the new draft at BELLE EGLISE two companies at ACHEUX) and proceeded to CANDAS, whence they marched to BERNEUIL, arriving at 9 p.m. | |
| BERNEUIL | 4 | | Company training from 10 a.m. to 12 noon and from 2 p.m. to 4 p.m. | |
| | 5 | | Company training as above | |
| | 6 | | Company training 7-7.30 am  9 a.m. to 12.30 p.m.  2 p.m. to 4 p.m. 2Lt SCOTT-TAGGART & Hee Nau nacka proceeded to a Lewis Gun Course at LE TOUQUET  2Lt WALKER proceeded on leave to ENGLAND. | |
| | 7 | | Major H. POSNORE D.S.O. rejoined Battalion & was appointed acting 2nd in Command Church Parade at 11 am  Corps Commander's proposed inspection in the afternoon was cancelled owing to inclement weather. | |
| | 8 | | 2Lt BOULTON & 2Lt BATHURST joined the battalion | |

# WAR DIARY
## or
## INTELLIGENCE SUMMARY.
*(Erase heading not required.)*

Army Form C. 2118

| Place | Date 1916 OCT | Hour | Summary of Events and Information | Remarks and references to Appendices |
|---|---|---|---|---|
| BERTEUIL | 9 | | Company Training + C.O.'s inspection in the morning. 3 hour route march in the afternoon | App. 15 Training Programme for week ending 14/15 |
| | 10 | | Lt PRICE rejoined the Battalion. | |
| | | | At PRICE rejoined the Battalion. 2 Lt CRICK joined the Battalion | |
| | | | A draft of 7 other ranks arrived (15 being former members of the Battalion) | |
| | 11 | | Company Training. Major General MAXSE visited Headquarters. Lt Col CARRINGTON went to lecture | |
| | 12 | | Company Training in the morning. Company football match in the afternoon | |
| | 13 | | Lt PRICE was appointed acting Adjutant | |
| | 14 | | Preparation for move | |
| BEAUVAL | 15 | | Battalion moved with rest of 9 Infy Bde (but independently) to BEAUVAL (billets) | |
| WARLOY | 16 | | Brigade moved into billets in CONTAY area. The Battalion into billets at WARLOY | |
| BOUZINCOURT | 17 | | Brigade moved into billets at BOUZINCOURT | |
| | 18 | | Battalion practised attack in the afternoon | |
| | | | Battalion practised attack. C.O. Adjutant & Coy. Commanders went on a reconnoitre on line in front of AUCHONVILLERS | |
| | 19 | | Brigade moved into billets at HEBUTERNE | |
| | 20 | | Battalion practised the attack | |
| | 21 | | Lt Col CARRINGTON returned from leave. Battalion practised attack | |

# WAR DIARY
## INTELLIGENCE SUMMARY.
*(Erase heading not required.)*

Army Form C. 2118.

| Place | Date | Hour | Summary of Events and Information | Remarks and references to Appendices |
|---|---|---|---|---|
| ALBERT | OCT 22 | | C.O. Adjt & several officers & N.C.O.'s carried out a future reconnaissance of ground to-day near WARLOY-SIETTE. | |
| | 23 | | Company parades in the morning and conference of Officers & Platoon Commanders. In the afternoon Battalion attack-practice. | |
| | 24 | | Preparation for move into Trenches. | |
| | 25 | | Battalion relieved 7th Bedfordshire Regiment in Trenches N. of COURCELETTE. A and C Coys in REGINA TRENCH, D in support area in VANCOUVER and HESSIAN TRENCHES, B Coy in Reserve in LOWER TRENCH. H.Q. at R.29 central near Brigade H.Q. 6 casualties in the relief. | |
| TRENCHES | 26 | | Weather fairly fine. The enemy was shelling of REGINA and VANCOUVER trenches specially on left of REGINA which was constantly being blown in 3 splints of S.9 guns from direction of LOUPART WOOD. About 1 a.m. two Germans came up to our parapet and gave themselves up. Casualties 8. | |
| | 27 | | A Coy HQ in REGINA TRENCH was twice blown in in the early morning. D Company relieved A Company in the left sector of REGINA trench. Relief only | |

# WAR DIARY
## or
## INTELLIGENCE SUMMARY.

Army Form C. 2118.

| Place | Date | Hour | Summary of Events and Information | Remarks and references to Appendices |
|---|---|---|---|---|
| | OCT 27 | | Two platoons in front line of REGINA Trench which we were now holding. Casualties 14. | |
| | 28 | | Continued shelling of our front and support lines by hostile fire from the direction of LOUPART WOOD. Casualties 9. | |
| ALBERT | 29 | | Battalion was relieved in the morning by the 8th Suffolk Regiment by 11 am and history two men cold, the last state of trench relief to finish on the top of daylight. 1st platoon under MUSSET shot up on the enemy showed no activity in front, but the continuous artillery shelling of trenches which contained few troops and no dug-outs made this a very trying tour in the trenches. Total casualties 52, including 7 missing – Many standing fast and not in front of our line posted in the dark on the first day they were had but they lay in on the next nights and entered the German lines. 6 officers joined Battalion in arrival in billets | |

Lt T.S UNWIN & the men commanded by J and 2Lieuts COWPER
"     McWHA                                A      WINKWORTH
"     CADDEN                               B      WELFORD

# WAR DIARY
## or
## INTELLIGENCE SUMMARY

(Erase heading not required.)

Army Form C. 2118.

| Place | Date | Hour | Summary of Events and Information | Remarks and references to Appendices |
|---|---|---|---|---|
| | OCT. | | | |
| ALBERT | 30 | | C.O. presented the MILITARY MEDAL ribbon to those NCO's + men still with the Battalion to whom the decoration has been awarded for gallantry at THIEPVAL. There were 19 awards in all. The Battalion had letters. | |
| WARLOY | 31 | | Battalion moved in the morning to billets at WARLOY | |

M.H. Hannington Lt. Col.
Commdg. 6th North Lancs Regt.

Subject. Operations.

From. Officer Commanding
    6th. S. Bn. Northamptonshire Regt.

To. Headquarters,
    54th Brigade.

Reference my N.R.A. 606 of yesterday, I should like to add the following names to those appearing on page 4 of my Narrative,-

2 Lt Keys C.G.
No. 13094 Pte Grace H.C.
No. 18910  "   Hayes. S.

Appendice F. is also forwarded to be attached.

Major
Commdg. 6th. S.Bn. Northamptonshire Regt.

In the Field
 2.10.16.

6th.(S) Bn. Northamptonshire Regiment.

## TRAINING PROGRAMME.

| DATE | HOUR | COY | NATURE OF WORK. |
|---|---|---|---|
| Mon. Oct. 9th. | 7 a.m. to 7-30 a.m. | All Coys. | Physical Training. |
| | 8 a.m. to 9-45 a.m. | do. | Company Drill. |
| | 9-45a.m. to 11 a.m. | do. | Company in attack with special reference to barrages. |
| | 11-15a.m. to 12 noon | do. | Ceremonial parade by Companies |
| | 12 noon to 12-45 p.m. | do. | Battalion Ceremonial parade. |
| | 2 p.m. to 5 p.m. | do. | Route march. FIENVILLERS - BERNAVILLE - BERNEUIL. Rifle Range allotted to Snipers. |
| Tues. Oct. 10th. | 7 a.m. to 7-30 a.m. | All Coys. | Physical Training. |
| | 8 a.m. to 8-45 a.m. | do. | Company Drill. |
| | 9 a.m. to 9-45 a.m. | "A" Coy. | Lewis Gunners on range. |
| | 10 a.m. to12-30 p.m. | "A" " | (i) On rifle range. |
| | 10 a.m. to12-30 p.m. | "B" " | (ii) Live Bombing Ground. |
| | 10 a.m. to12-30 p.m. | "C" " | (iii) Digging Ground (intensive). |
| | 10 a.m. to12-30 p.m. | "D" " | (iv) Smoke Helmet drill, rapid loading, bayonet fighting, attack from trenches with special reference to barrages. |
| | 2 p.m. to 4-30 p.m. | "B" " | (i) |
| | 2 p.m. to 4-30 p.m. | "C" " | (ii) |
| | 2 p.m. to 4-30 p.m. | "D" " | (iii) |
| | 2 p.m. to 4-30 p.m. | "A" " | (iv) |
| Wed. Oct. 11th. | 7 a.m. to 7-30 a.m. | All Coys. | Physical Training. |
| | 8 a.m. to 8-45 a.m. | do. | Company Drill. |
| | 9 a.m. to 9-45 a.m. | "B" Coy. | Lewis Gunners on range. |
| | 10 a.m. to12-30 p.m. | "C" " | (i) |
| | 10 a.m. to12-30 p.m. | "D" " | (ii) |
| | 10 a.m. to12-30 p.m. | "A" " | (iii) |
| | 10 a.m. to12-30 p.m. | "B" " | (iv) |
| | 2 p.m. to 4-30 p.m. | "D" " | (i) |
| | 2 p.m. to 4-30 p.m. | "A" " | (ii) |
| | 2 p.m. to 4-30 p.m. | "B" " | (iii) |
| | 2 p.m. to 4-30 p.m. | "C" " | (iv) |
| Thus. Oct. 12th. | 7 a.m. to 7-30 a.m. | All Coys. | Physical Training. |
| | 8 a.m. to 8-45 a.m. | do. | Company Drill. |
| | 9 a.m. to 9-45 a.m. | "C" Coy. | Lewis Gunners on range. |
| | 10 a.m. to12-30 p.m. | "A" " | (i) |
| | 10 a.m. to12-30 p.m. | "B" " | (ii) |
| | 10 a.m. to12-30 p.m. | "C" " | (iii) |
| | 10 a.m. to12-30 p.m. | "D" " | (iv) |
| | 2 p.m. to 4-30 p.m. | "B" " | (i) |
| | 2 p.m. to 4-30 p.m. | "C" " | (ii) |
| | 2 p.m. to 4-30 p.m. | "D" " | (iii) |
| | 2 p.m. to 4-30 p.m. | "A" " | (iv) |

Continued.

( 2 )

| DATE | TIME | COY | NATURE OF WORK. |
|------|------|-----|-----------------|
| Fri. Oct. 13th. | 7 a.m. to 7-30 a.m. | All Coys. | Physical Training. |
| | 8 a.m. to 8-45 a.m. | do. | Company Drill. |
| | 9 a.m. to 9-45 a.m. | "A" Coy. | Lewis Gunners on range. |
| | 10 a.m. to 10-45 a.m. | "B" " (i) | |
| | 10 a.m. to 10-45 a.m. | "B" " (ii) | |
| | 10 a.m. to 10-45 a.m. | "B" " (iii) | |
| | 10 a.m. to 10-45 a.m. | "B" " (iv) | |
| | 2 p.m. to 2-45 p.m. | "C" " (i) | |
| | 2 p.m. to 2-45 p.m. | "C" " (ii) | |
| | 2 p.m. to 2-45 p.m. | "C" " (iii) | |
| | 2 p.m. to 2-45 p.m. | "C" " (iv) | |
| Sat. Oct. 14th. | 7 a.m. to 7-30 a.m. | All Coys. | Physical Training. |
| | 8 a.m. to 8-45 a.m. | do. | Company Drill. |
| | 10 a.m. to 12-30 p.m. | do. | Battalion practice in the drill of attack on trenches and following a barrage. |
| | In the afternoon. | - | Athletic Sports. |
| Sun. Oct. 15th. | Baths(if they can be arranged) | | |
| | 7 p.m. | All Coys. | Tactical Scheme with night outposts. |

NOTES:-   (1)   N.C.Os. to be trained in message writing and map reading during the evening or other available times.
(2)   The Snipers to be trained under Sergt. Jukes and the Signallers under Sergt. Bingham.
(3)   The Lewis Gunners are trained entirely under Company arrangements.

TRAINING GROUNDS (Reference Map LENS 11. 1/100,000)

BATTALION PARADE GROUND just NORTH of word BERGUEIL.

BATTALION AREA FOR TACTICAL SCHEMES bounded by BOMART - ST.HILAIRE - BERGUEIL - DRESSIS roads.

BATTALION RIFLE RANGE on BERGUEIL - LANCHES road 700 yards WEST of BERGUEIL.
BATTALION DIGGING GROUND just WEST of Rifle Range on SOUTH side of road.

BATTALION LIVE BOMBING GROUNDS.
(1)   Borrowed from 2nd. Canadian School LANCHES.
(2)   Just WEST of Rifle Range on NORTH side of road.

COMPANY TRAINING GROUNDS on NORTH, SOUTH and EAST edges of BERGUEIL.


9th. October 1916.                    (sd) S.H.Charrington, Lieut-Colonel,
                    Commdg:6th.(S) Bn.Northamptonshire Regiment.

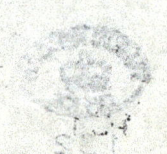

Army Form C. 2118

WAR DIARY or INTELLIGENCE SUMMARY

6th Bn. Northants.

Vol 17

| Place | Date | Hour | Summary of Events and Information | Remarks and references to Appendices |
|---|---|---|---|---|
| WARLOY | Nov 1916 1 | | Morning: cleaning up and company drill. Afternoon inspection by C.O. | |
| | 2 | | Battalion handed in the afternoon to late MIDDLESEX REGT and 2 battalions of 55th Bde. Major General MAXSE presented to officers and men decorations awarded since July 1. and congratulated the parade on the work done by the 18th Division since that date. | |
| | 3 | | Battalion practised the attack as front battalion and as three battalion in the vicinity of WARLOY & HENINCOURT. | |
| ALBERT | 4. | | Battalion moved to billets in ALBERT. | |
| | 5. | | Preparations for move into trenches for offensive operations | |
| TRENCHES | 6. | | Battalion relieved the Bedfordshire Regt in same sector as before. Trenches & right VANCOUVER much less shelling than before. Casualties 2. | |
| | 7. | | in front another ? B and C companies in front the A very wet day, sidings trolley to mud and water. no communication trouble with front line kept at night. Casualties 3. | |
| | 8. | | O but bright. let off very little hostile shelling, much shelling as there has not been held guns in front and not the previous heavy gun in flank fire Casualties 1 | |

# WAR DIARY
or
## INTELLIGENCE SUMMARY

Army Form C. 2118

| Place | Date | Hour | Summary of Events and Information | Remarks and references to Appendices |
|---|---|---|---|---|
| TRENCHES | Nov 9 | | A fine day. At 9.30 p.m. enemy opened heavy fire with gas and tear shells, chiefly on MOUQUET ROAD (Bn. H.Q.) and ZOLLERN TRENCH. This lasted with intervals till 2 a.m. There was a slight wind blowing back towards the enemy, and the gas reached our front line, was 1000 yds. in front, but not in quantities necessitating putting on smoke helmets. No casualties from the gas.  Casualties 4. | |
| | 10 | | A fine day. About 10 a.m. an explosion (presumably started by a heavy trench mortar) occurred among (what is left of) artillery regiment in a shallow communicating trench dug-out. 2 men were killed and 5 wounded - all H.Q. personnel.  Casualties 18. The Battn. was relieved by the 8th Suffolk Regiment, and proceeded to new huts in NASH VALLEY near OVILLERS. The last man left in what. 2 a.m. | |
| OVILLERS HUTS | | | | |
| | 11 | | The Battn. moved via AVELUY and BOUZINCOURT to WARLOY. 1st Battn. arrived at WARLOY with very few in a very bad condition. H.- the Battn. arrived at WARLOY with very few casualties (12) - a very creditable performance after the incessant wet, and heavy cannonade. The Trenches were manned in part in the daytime. | |
| WARLOY | | | | |

# WAR DIARY or INTELLIGENCE SUMMARY

Army Form C. 2118

| Place | Date | Hour | Summary of Events and Information | Remarks and references to Appendices |
|---|---|---|---|---|
| WARLOY | Nov 12 | | Clearing & lifting. Brig Gen SHUTTLEBRIDGE presently brought the news of an immediate return to ALBERT - the long-expected attack being fixed at last: beginning N. of the ANCRE on Monday 13th. | |
| ALBERT | 13 | | B⁰ moved to ALBERT via HENENCOURT - MILLENCOURT: in blub. ready to move at ½ hours notice | |
| OVILLERS HUTS | 14 | | B⁰ moved to OVILLERS HUTS in the afternoon: where were 12th/AUS Essex Regt and 2 Battalions of 55th Brigade | |
| | 15 | | 5th Bn. first in attack my (with 6th CANADIANS. 6th NORTHAMPTONSHIRE and 12th MIDDLESEX were attached to 55th Brigade. Fine cool weather: B⁰ occupied in making patrols & sandbagging huts. | |
| | 16 | | Fine and cold: Ground very hard + dry. General MAXSE held an officers' conference explaining the operations N of the ANCRE & the part to be played by 18th Division. Morning: by ground reconnoitred ways up to 55th Bde front. | |
| | 17 | | 1.30 a.m. orders received that B⁰ was to go up in support to 55th Bde. Wished four battalions attacking two objectives. | |
| TRENCHES | 18 | | Early morning B⁰ moved up. 3 companies to FABECK TRENCH, one company (D) to GRAVEL PIT near MOUQUET FARM (55th Bde HQ) | |

1875 Wt. W593/886 1,000,000 4/15 J.B.C. & A. A.D.S.S./Forms/C. 2118.

| Place | Date | Hour | Summary of Events and Information | Remarks and references to Appendices |
|---|---|---|---|---|
| TRENCHES | 18 | | 2cno at 6.10. 55th Bde attack successful — Bn trying to support left (blue) communication difficult, and A and C Coys 6th N'n were ordered to carry out the consolidation allotted to them. Org ordered rest of Bn in PABSCH for the night & the 18th with advanced HQ. Returned to orders for Bn to go forward to dg. HQ into D and B Coy (less 50 men employed in tramway) returned to OVILLERS HUTS. Men employed in tramway returned to Trenches early in the evening and turned to further trg. One Sheet taken (hardly room to work). Found (heavy day) heavy rain at night. A and C Coys in PABSCH TRENCH. | |
| | 19 | | Moved 6 p.m. D Coy ordered to relieve A and C Coys in OVILLERS HUTS, when the other of the Bde was. | |
| OVILLERS HUTS | 20 | | Preparations for move took to billets. One company + 50 men drill in other. (6 NORTHUMBERLANDS started from each area & 6 NORTHAMPTONSHIRE started from WARLOY. | |
| | 21 | | 5th Bde began march to billets in the afternoon and went into billets at WARLOY. OVILLERS HUTS in the afternoon and went into T.E.S. at WARLOY. I Company relieved in turn to 10pm (P.B.) . The 50 men on Tramways arrived | |
| WARLOY | | | a few hours late. | |

Army Form C. 2118

# WAR DIARY
## or
## INTELLIGENCE SUMMARY
*(Erase heading not required.)*

Instructions regarding War Diaries and Intelligence Summaries are contained in F.S. Regs., Part II. and the Staff Manual respectively. Title Pages will be prepared in manuscript.

| Place | Date | Hour | Summary of Events and Information | Remarks and references to Appendices |
|---|---|---|---|---|
| | Nov | | | |
| HERISSART | 22 | | Continued march to back area WARLOY to KRAWART - fine weather and good marching | |
| SOUHENS | 23 | | Continued march to SOULENS - a long day but a fine day. Battalion marched splendidly. Came into billets very well - | |
| BERNEUIL | 24 | | Continued march to BERNEUIL - weather worsening - occasional showers | |
| DOMQUEUR & Le PLOY | 25 | | Continued march to DOMQUEUR and Le PLOY - a short march but in-accurate run - billets poor but very scattered | |
| ONEUX | 26 | | Continued march to ONEUX - another short stage - weather improved. In the afternoon officers went over to see permanent billets at NEUF MOULIN. | |
| NEUF MOULIN | 27 | | Final stage of march to NEUF MOULIN. - 3 Companies in the village - mostly poor billets - Hd/y. Hters. at the Chateau in BOIS DE L'ABBAYE nearly a mile away; v.g. billet. | |
| | 28 | | Refitting and drill near billets. | |
| | 29 | | Lt Col CHARRINGTON went on leave. Battalion on F area - company training. | |
| | 30 | | Battalion in F area. Company training - bayonet fighting, class at drill and improving influence. Major Palmer Coy 6th Northamptonshire Regt | |

1875 Wt. W593/826 1,000,000 4/15 J.B.C. & A. A.D.S.S./Forms/C. 2118.

# WAR DIARY
## INTELLIGENCE SUMMARY

Army Form C. 2118.

6 North'ants R
Vol 18

| Place | Date 1916 | Hour | Summary of Events and Information | Remarks and references to Appendices |
|---|---|---|---|---|
| NEUF MOULIN | Dec 1 | | Company Training in Areas | |
| | 2 | | Battalion digging trenches for Brigade Attack Scheme | |
| | 3 | | Lt MARGOLIOUTH temporarily attached to 5/R. Bde. | |
| | 4 | | Church parade in the Chateau grounds | |
| | 5 | | Battalion digging trenches for Brigade Attack Scheme | |
| | 5.30 | | Battalion practice the 1st & 3rd Batt'n in Bde Attack | |
| | 6 | | Capt V.P. NOBBS joined battalion | |
| | 6 | | Battalion practised first battalion in attack | |
| | 7 | | Company training in areas | |
| | 8 | | Battalion practised 4th battalion in attack | |
| | 9 | | Bde practised attack. 6th Northamptonshire 4/= Battalion | |
| | 10 | | Church parade in the village in conjunction with artillery | |
| | 11 | | Bde practised attack. 6 Northamptonshire right covering Battalion | |
| | 12 | | first day prevented attack carried - presence of 2nd Corps Commander of Northampton | |
| | 13 | | Bde practised attack in presence of | |
| | | | Shire Regiment 4/= Battalion | |
| CANCHY | 14 | | Battalion moved to CANCHY. Bde. School of Bombing, Signalling, | |
| | | | Trench Mortars established. | |

Army Form C. 2118

WAR DIARY
or
INTELLIGENCE SUMMARY
(Erase heading not required.)

| Place | Date | Hour | Summary of Events and Information | Remarks and references to Appendices |
|---|---|---|---|---|
| CANCHY | Dec 15 | | Company Training - last two days drilling under R.S.M. and special instructors | |
| | 16 | | Company Training. Range finally completed into gallery, for firing 2/Lt LLOYD, joined on the 15th, posted to A Coy. | |
| | 17 | | Church parade on football ground. Military Cross awarded to 2/Lts HIGHAM, BATES and BOTCH | |
| | 18 | | Company Training: Junior N.C.Os class under C.S.M's | |
| | 19 | | Company Training: Junior N.C.Os class under C.S.M's. a/Capt ONWIN proceeds to 5th Army School Bayonet Fighting Course for Senior N.C.Os ended a Staff Sergt. Major for 6 days | |
| | 20 | | Company Training - | |
| | 21 | | Company Training | |
| | 22 | | Inspection of Division at training by 5th Army Commander. 6th Northamptonshire Regiment not visited | |
| | 23 | | Company Training. | |

# WAR DIARY or INTELLIGENCE SUMMARY

Army Form C. 2118

| Place | Date | Hour | Summary of Events and Information | Remarks and references to Appendices |
|---|---|---|---|---|
| CAN CHY | Dec 24 | | No church parade: Munitory service | |
| | 25 | | Christmas Dinners in the villages. ATMS at 12 noon. Carol D at 2.30 p.m. | |
| | 26 | | Church parade at 9.45 | |
| | 27 | | Battalion marched over to BUIGNY for Divisional Symphonia. Sp.F. Bde demonstration attack before G.O.C. 5th Army and Divn and Bde Staffs of 2nd Corps: 6th Northamptonshire Regt. Left Battalion. | |
| | 28 | | Company Training. | |
| | 29 | | Company Training. Information received that Director of Artillery — has office his Htrs than German Machine Guns as informed 3 to 6 Northamptonshire Regt. | |
| | 30. | | Company Training. | |
| | 31. | | Church Parade at 10.30 a.m. | |

M. Harrington Lt Col
Commanding 6th Northamptonshire Regt.

6th Northants
Jany Dec
1917

VOLUME No.

# BRITISH SALONIKA FORCE

# WAR DIARY.

12th Corps.

| VOL. No. | UNIT | PERIOD FROM | TO |
|---|---|---|---|
| 28. | Chief Engineer | 1.8.18 | 31.8.18 |
| 34. | "M" Signal Co. R.E. | " | " |
| 11. | 140th Army Troops Co. R.E. | 1.8.18 | 31.8.18 |

Army Form C. 2118

# WAR DIARY
## or
## INTELLIGENCE SUMMARY
*(Erase heading not required.)*

Instructions regarding War Diaries and Intelligence Summaries are contained in F. S. Regs, Part II. and the Staff Manual respectively. Title Pages will be prepared in manuscript.

L. K Montaña

J. E. 19

| Place | Date | Hour | Summary of Events and Information | Remarks and references to Appendices |
|---|---|---|---|---|
| CANCHY | JAN 1. | | Company training | |
| | 2. | | Company training. Short Bn parade at 12.45 pm to am drill etc messages wishing Bn good luck in coming year received from 1st, 2nd, 5th & 7th Bns. | |
| | 3. | | Bn route march. | |
| | 4. | | Company training. Increase in establishment of Lewis Gunners commenced. | |
| | 5. | | Company training. Bn had baths. | |
| | 6. | | The Bn was fitted with the new Box Respirator. Bde Cross Country Race won by Sgt. BRADBURY. | |
| | 7. | | Church parade 11 am. Received Gazette with New Year Honours. D.S.O. Lt. Col. S. N. Charrington. mentioned in Despatches. Ripley. 2/Lt. Gritton Cpl. C.E. Charrington. Capt. (Temp. Maj.) S. N. Re-adj. Off. Nos. Bodmore Temp. Maj. A. A.S.O. Neville Temp. Capt. J.S. Beasley Temp. Lt. J.H. Bales Temp. 2/Lt. A.C. Cotch Temp. 2/Lt. A.J. Bowker Sents Qmr. Hon. Rt. W.H. Carter No 13166 Coy. QmSgt. R.J. Bradbury No 14455 Sgt. C. Clutterbuck No 14625 Sgt. J.R. | |

# WAR DIARY or INTELLIGENCE SUMMARY

Army Form C. 2118

| Place | Date | Hour | Summary of Events and Information | Remarks and references to Appendices |
|---|---|---|---|---|
| CANCHY | Jan 8. | | Company training | |
| | 9. | | Company training. At 10.0 a.m. Major General hease said goodbye to the Bde at Bde HQ. There was no formal parade but each Bn was represented by those officers who had served with the Bde longest. Renault the Divisional Commander best. At the same time General hease presented decorations to all those who had had them awarded but had not been presented with them. | |
| | 10. | | Kit inspection and cleaning up in preparation for move. | |
| | 11. | | The Bde commenced its march into Ivsand area. The Bn moved to billets in DOMQUEUR. | |
| DOMQUEUR | 12. | | march continued. Bn moved to billets in FIENVILLERS. | |
| FIENVILLERS | 13. | | Day spent in resting. | |
| | 14. | | march continued. Bn moved to billets in RUBEMPRE. A trying march over bad roads. On several occasions the Bn had to march in single file. | |
| | 15. | | Advance party went from RUBEMPRE to the line to The Bn took over line from 2/8th Bn R.War.R. in right sector of Rde how 1/20,000 Bn front extended from W MIRAUMONT RD on night to about R.16.c.65. 57 D S.E. | |
| 2nd LINE | 16. | | The Bn left RUBEMPRE in bus at 9.30am and arrived at AVELUY at 2.03m where the men had dinners. Relief was complete about midnight. Frost getting more severe. A quiet day practically no shelling. | |

Army Form C. 2118

# WAR DIARY or INTELLIGENCE SUMMARY
(Erase heading not required.)

Instructions regarding War Diaries and Intelligence Summaries are contained in F.S. Regs., Part II. and the Staff Manual respectively. Title Pages will be prepared in manuscript.

| Place | Date | Hour | Summary of Events and Information | Remarks and references to Appendices |
|---|---|---|---|---|
| Pt Kichu | 17. | | The formation adopted by 2/8th RWarR was not considered satisfactory and the following dispositions were substituted. A Coy on night. B Coy on right in front line (DESIRE). This line to be held by a succession of posts, there is no continuous trench. Each of these Coys has two supporting platoons in REGINA TRENCH. C Coy in HESSIAN TRENCH as counter attack Coy and D Coy in ZOLLERN trench as reserve Coy. This rearrangement was carried out at night without incident. 2Lt Brigham went out on patrol and gained useful information regarding enemy defences. | |
| | 18 | | Very quiet all day. Snow getting more severe. Three slight casualties. | |
| | 19. | | Very quiet all day. On morning of 20th C.O., 2nd in Command & two front line Coy Commanders carried out a reconnaissance with a view to moving some of the posts into more advantageous positions. | |
| | 20 | | The Bn was relieved by the 11th Bn Royal Fusiliers. The relief was reported all complete by 10.30pm. The Bn took over WARWICK HUTS vacated by 11th Royal Fusiliers. Snow very intense and duckboards untill 16 officers coming out. C Coy left in line attached to 11th Royal Fusiliers. | |
| | 21. | | Inspections of Rifles etc & cleaning up huts. | |
| | 22. | | The Bn resting in huts. All Coys doing physical drill in the morning. The Lewis Gun Officer gave lectures in the huts. | |
| | 23. | | " " " " | |
| | 24 | | Preparations for move back into line. At night the Bn relieved the 11th Royal Fusiliers in the same sector. Relief reported complete by 8.30pm. in spite of very slippery duck boards. Dispositions D Coy on right, C Coy on left in front line. B Coy Counter attack Coy and A Coy Reserve Coy. Great care had to be taken. Consolidation was available during the night. | |
| | 25. | | Shelling (below normal). Snow very severe. 2Lt Higham went out in patrol at night but was forced within owing to his own shells dropping short. R.E. material dumps established with front line Coys. | |
| | 26. | | Shelling (below normal) but very severe. New R.E. material dump formed in REGINA TRENCH. B Coy reclaimed part of REGINA TRENCH and established line positions. Two casualties owing to a man hitting a dud shell with a pick. | |

| Date | Hour | Summary of Events and Information | Remarks and references to Appendices |
|---|---|---|---|
| 27. | | A quiet day. The Bn was relieved at night by 8th Bn Suffolk Regt. Relief reported all complete by 8.15pm. The ducktboards were very slippery but the men all had sandbags round their feet. The Bn took over MACKENZIE HUTS in W.10.C | 1/26000 57D SE. |
| 28 | | Rested in huts. Very cold. | |
| 29. | | One and a half Coys on working party under R.E. ½ Coy working for Bde. ½ Coy clearing up camp. Remainder cutting wood for the Bn in AUTHUILE WOOD for burning purposes. Very little coke being issued. Unkwned draft withdrawn from Corps and issued under Bn arrangements. | |
| 30 | | Working parties as yesterday. More wood cut. Training of draft continued. Bde Conference for CO. 2nd in Command & adjt at Bde Hq Plans for proposed attacks discussed. Baths for one Coy. | |
| 31 | | Working parties as yesterday. Baths for one Coy. | |

6/Northamptonshire

Feb 1917

# WAR DIARY or INTELLIGENCE SUMMARY

Army Form C. 2118

1st Northants

Nov 20

| Place | Date 1917 | Hour | Summary of Events and Information | Remarks and references to Appendices |
|---|---|---|---|---|
| MKENZIE HUTS | FEB 1 | | Working parties and baths. Practice in forming up, advancing, & digging in on reverse slope. | |
| | 2 | | Same as on 1st. Lt Col CITHERINGTON left the battalion to take command of C Battn. Heavy Branch, Machine Gun Corps. | |
| | 3 | | Lt Col A.J.F. MEYRICK (9th Bn 11th Royal Fusiliers) assumed command. Working parties & practice attacks. | |
| | 4 | | Working parties by night r day | |
| | 5 | | As for Feb 4 | |
| | 6 | | Three companies practiced forming up, advancing & digging in on reverse slope. | |
| | 7 | | 4 Companies working on new divisional tramway. OVERALLS: groins frozen two feet down. Took away 5 lbs. | |
| | 8 | | As for Feb 7 | |
| | 9 | | As for Feb 8. Companies went up in full order. Packs brought up by transport to WARWICK HUTS, where the battalion moved in the afternoon. | |
| WARWICK HUTS | 10 | | Two companies on working parties, remainder coy organisation. | |
| | 11 | | As for Feb 10 | |
| | 12 | | 4 companies working on new divisional tramway to RIFLE DUMP 7.30 to 12. relieved 3 2 coys 13th Middlesex & 2 coys 11th Royal Fusiliers. Battalion moved to SLOSITRA HUTS in the afternoon | |

Army Form C. 2118

# WAR DIARY
## or
## INTELLIGENCE SUMMARY
*(Erase heading not required.)*

Instructions regarding War Diaries and Intelligence Summaries are contained in F. S. Regs., Part II. and the Staff Manual respectively. Title Pages will be prepared in manuscript.

| Place | Date | Hour | Summary of Events and Information | Remarks and references to Appendices |
|---|---|---|---|---|
| GLOSTER WARRIOR HUTS | 1917 Feb 13 | | Work in tramway: two companies 8.15 a.m. to 12.30 p.m.: two companies 12.30 p.m. to 4.45 p.m. | |
| | 14 | | As for Feb 13 + baths in afternoon. | |
| TRENCHES | 15. | | Battalion took over its battle front from the 8th Bn East Surrey Regt. v. Appendix | |
| | 16 | | Preparations for battle: forming up positions marked out by 12 midnight. First company reached GULLY at 1 a.m. | |
| | 17 | | Battle forming up completed by 5 a.m. v. Appendix  R Turner Lt Col | |
| MARLBORO' HUTS | 18. | | Battalion relieved by company of 8th East Surrey Regt: return to MARLBOROUGH HUTS. | |
| BOUZINCOURT | 19. | | Battalion moved to Billets in BOUZINCOURT. Brigadier on the recent operations - and then of holiday to reputation of the Sheffield Bat. | |
| | 20. | | Baths and refitting | |
| | 21. | | Messages of congratulation to the Division from the left of the Army Commanders - | |
| | 22. | | Organization Drill on ground N. of BOUZINCOURT. Congratulations from C. in C. | |
| | 23. | | One coy working on ENGLEBELMER road: remainder training | |
| | 24 | | Two coys working on SUCRERIE - MESNIL road: remainder training - with special instruction in bar refixations. | |

# WAR DIARY
## INTELLIGENCE SUMMARY

Army Form C. 2118

| Place | Date | Hour | Summary of Events and Information | Remarks and references to Appendices |
|---|---|---|---|---|
| BOUZINCOURT | Feb. 25 | | Church Parade in the CINEMA at 11 a.m. No working parties. Sgt. Major T.A. Price proceeded on a fortnight's special leave | |
| | 26. | | Coy. parades for Gunnery - musketry etc in Group N.9 BOUZINCOURT. | |
| | 27. | | Coy. parades as on 26. In the afternoon battalion had a form-up to demonstrate the efficiency of gas-respirators & properly fitted. One subject - country (Capt. Evans) badly failing mark. | |
| | 28. | | Coy parades for Gunnery - musketry & Physical Drill - Standard order. | |

R. Turner Lt Colonel

Narrative of the part played by the 6th Northamptonshire Regiment in the operations against S. MIRAUMONT TRENCH Feb: 17. 1917

On the night of Feb.15 the Battalion took over its battle front from the 8th East Surrey Regiment. This front was held by one company; the others being situated as shown in Appendix.

The ground was carefully reconnoitred for forming-up lines, but no actual marks were put in on the night of the 15th. At about 5 a.m. the enemy opened a fairly heavy barrage on the line of the GULLY & 80 yards north of it. This was most useful – enabling us to adjust our forming up positions & close them up; so as to have all lines well clear of the GULLY where it seemed his barrage would come.

On the night of the 16th 2Lt. BOULTON (O.C. B Company, holding the line) & 2Lt HIGHAM (Intelligence Officer) assisted by Officers & N.C.O.s of the assaulting companies got the lines for forming up taped out & otherwise marked, & our own wire sufficiently cut, by 12 midnight. They accomplished this in spite of great difficulties owing to the extreme darkness of the night, & although a heavy enemy barrage was opened on them about 9 p.m.

Orders had been received that all troops were to be in position by 4.45 a.m. i.e. an hour before the time fixed for zero hour.

At 1 a.m. the leading platoon of C Company (the left assaulting company) reached the GULLY, and was at once taken out to its position by guides. There was some congestion on the way up at this time, and the rest of the company with its attached dug-out clearing parties was not in position till nearly 2.30. However by 3.30 the whole of A Company, the centre company, was also in position with its dug-out clearing parties: by 4.15 the leading 3 platoons of the right company (D) were also in position; just before 4.30 however as the last platoon with Coy H.Q. & Lewis Guns was being taken out into position the enemy sent up yellow & green light sprays & a heavy barrage was immediately

(Opened

opened on the line of the GULLY & a line running about 80 yards N. of it. This last platoon of D Company suffered heavy casualties from these shells — the whole of one Lewis Gun team becoming casualties & the O.C. Company. Capt. Unwin being slightly wounded & suffering a serious concussion. The acting Sergeant Major however showed splendid coolness : got the platoon together again & placed them in their forming-up positions.

The shelling while the 4th company was moving into its position N.E. of the GULLY about 4.45 a.m. was extremely heavy & there were a certain amount of casualties : too high praise cannot be given to 2 Lt BOULTON & C.S.M. CUTHBERT for their courage & coolness in directing the move under these trying circumstances.

The whole battalion was in position by 4.50 a.m. The enemy shelling continued heavy till 5.30 a.m. & then slackened a little. It was afterwards discovered that the enemy had received information of the attack 6 hours previously from some deserters (or prisoners) from the Division on the right, who had told them everything except that they put the zero hour at 5.15 instead of 5.45. The barrage was certainly much heavier than on the previous morning, & was on this occasion accompanied by S.O.S. Signals in great profusion.

The morning was extremely dark (heavy clouds obscuring the moon which should have risen about 4.20 a.m), the ground was very soft & slippery — the thaw after nearly a month's hard frost having just commenced, & altogether conditions could not have been more unfavourable to forming up for an attack absolutely without trenches. The greatest credit is due to 2 Lts BOULTON & HIGHAM for the success of the forming up, and to all ranks for the absolute quiet & order with which the forming up was carried out & the calm courage with which they lay on the mud (some of them for 3 or 4 hours) whilst this heavy hostile shelling upon them. Actual casualties among the lines actually formed up & lying down were extremely few; but the test of discipline was extremely severe.

At 5.45 a.m. our barrage opened & the enemy at once sent up showers of yellow spray lights & some green lights as well. His answering barrage was however very short-lived & it would seem that our counter-battery work on this morning was excellent.

Our men had no difficulty in following our barrage up to GRANDCOURT TRENCH — though the light was very poor until after 6 a.m. But on arrival at the wire they found in many cases that it had not been cut. Only a few very narrow passages were to be found & the delay in finding these gave the enemy time to get into position again both in GRANDCOURT TRENCH & also on both sides of the BOOM RAVINE. This movement along the wire to find gaps was also largely responsible for the loss of direction & mixing up of companies which took place. In the case of the left company (C) the first two waves & those behind were held up by machine gun & rifle fire in GRAND-COURT TRENCH, which delayed them at least half an hour & caused heavy casualties. The O.C. Company Lt WINKWORTH & another officer 2Lt COOPER both became casualties before getting over GRANDCOURT TRENCH.

The first two waves of the centre company (A) got over GRANDCOURT TRENCH with little opposition, but were then met by heavy machine gun & trench mortar fire from their left, a large body of Germans holding the tongue in the BOOM RAVINE about R 11 C.5.3. It was necessary to clear this point before advancing: during this operation A/CAPT. McWHA & Lt HERTZ-SMITH became casualties. The rear waves of the centre company met with considerable opposition in GRANDCOURT TRENCH. It is not clear whether this opposition was present when the first two waves went
(through

through" or not; but the 4th have encountered machine guns in the line of GRANDCOURT TRENCH.

The right company D was the only one which was able to advance from BOOM RAVINE in anything like time down to barrage – that is to say half an hour after entering it. The left & centre companies were occupied for a good hour in clearing GRANDCOURT trench and the RAVINE: no actual time is available – only one company officer authors surviving crossed the RAVINE – but it seems quite certain that none of the left or centre company started out of the RAVINE till a clear half hour after the barrage had lifted from its first halt. Of the right company a certain number – chiefly those who – losing directions – had moved NW so as to clear BOOM RAVINE just on its left did, after finding their mistakes & regaining directions, start up the hill in R.11.0. on the W. of the West MIRAUMONT road. But even these only arrived in time to see the barrage leaving the top of the hill, & by the time they came in view of SOUTH MIRAUMONT trench, the barrage was on the N side of it & Germans already re-appearing in the trench. The 2nd Division on our right had established themselves in portions of S. MIRAUMONT trench: our men found only very few gaps cut in the wire & were forced in the majority of cases to lie down just on our side of the wire & try to cut it. A few or few parties one under 2/Lt HIGHAM M.C. & the Miss. another Lt PRICE did enter the trench W. of W. MIRAUMONT road and establish a footing. But on the whole the total number of 18th Divisional troops in SOUTH MIRAUMONT trench was small. Whereas the trench E. of W. MIRAUMONT road was fairly thickly occupied by British troops.

It was at this time – apparently about 8.30 am that is to say when our Barrage was behind the 3rd (Objective)

objective – that a strong German counter-attack was delivered from PETIT MIRAUMONT & the GULLY in R.5.d. This appears to have been the main attack, though parties also advanced from the bank in R.5.c (on the GRANDCOURT – MIRAUMONT road). It appears from captured German orders & statements of prisoners, that these were specially trained counter-attack troops, who had been brought up as soon as the information of our coming attack reached them on the preceding night. They consisted largely of riflemen & machine gunners. The fire was extremely accurate, while in the majority of cases, the British rifles & Lewis & Vickers guns had become clogged almost from the start – owing to the lying in the mud in the dark before the attack & the bad ground traversed during the advance.

Whatever the exact cause, the British line seeing no appreciable effect produced by their fire on the advancing Germans began to fall back chiefly on the right & then all along the line. It was at this point that Lt PRICE (Adjutant of the 1st Northamptonshires) displayed most conspicuous gallantry. He moved to & fro along the line – steadying the retiring & then perceiving that our right was being left in the air & attacking our left comparatively safer, he formed the whole Northampton body of survivors into a defensive flank on the W. MIRAUMONT road. This was done & I personally under heavy rifle & machine gun fire & done most successfully. In this position they stayed from about 9' to 9.30 : at this time fire began to be opened on them from their left rear i.e. from S. MIRAUMONT trench – with both machine guns & light trench

Madam. After suffering long cruelties for years the Prince decided to sing back to Europe for his eyesight fact. In the two cannot act under five + of about 10 are the Baby was carrying a boy that 100 years old of Born privine.

She justified her conducted felt by system — than in compartin with ... eighty Egyptian the lied in public formed almost to the word of the hill + crossper of a sum of ... wife + machine gun last.

That that we landed as C. Ferth of our Lord ... in it ... a count of Bishop Dumin of ... of a catholic mortars. After suffering heavy casualties for some time Lt PRICE decided to swing back his line & face his original front: this also was carried out under heavy fire & at about 10 a.m. the Battⁿ was occupying a line about 100 yds N of BOOM RAVINE.

This position was maintained till the afternoon — when in conjunction with the 11th Royal Fusiliers the line was pushed forward almost to the crest of the hill + occupied by a series of rifle & machine gun posts.

This line was handed over to the 8th East Surrey Regiment on the evening of Feb 18.

A summary of casualties is attached.

H. Bodmin Major

April 5.

# WAR DIARY
## or
## INTELLIGENCE SUMMARY
*(Erase heading not required.)*

Army Form C. 2118

Month: March 1917

| Place | Date | Hour | Summary of Events and Information | Remarks and references to Appendices |
|---|---|---|---|---|
| BEAUMONT | 1 | | Company parades for musketry, bombing, and Rifle Range – Major R. Turner D.S.O. assumed command of the Battalion. | |
| THIEPVAL WOOD | 2 | | Battalion moved to dug-outs and tents in THIEPVAL WOOD | |
| | 3 | | Coy. handing inspection by Commanding Officer | |
| | 4 | | 250 men working parties on SPEEDCART – MIRAUMONT road; remainder Batt. musketry training. Lewis Gun classes | |
| | 5 | | Working parties as on 4th. Parades no longer for remainder. | |
| | 6 | | Working parties, hand by N.C.O's under Army Supervision to districts N of MIRAUMONT. N.C.O's under Army Supervision in instructs on | |
| | 7 | | Two Companies working half, remainder firing on ranges + live rivalry on THIEPVAL. N.C.O's urged Army Gym to Intercoy training was Working parties as before Lt EOPL W.H. Fowler left for Inflerne. | |
| | 8 | | Working parties, paraders as before. Lt R.Y.H. Stretcher in Galaxy Draft of 50 and 92 men to join at Batt H.Q. at S H.Q as instructed | |
| | 9 | | Training Working parties as before | |
| | 10 | | Training + working parties as before. Award of 13 Military Medal + 4 Bars to Military Medals for N.C.O's men for the actions against SAILLAUMONT TRENCH | |

# WAR DIARY or INTELLIGENCE SUMMARY

Army Form C. 2118

| Place | Date March | Hour | Summary of Events and Information | Remarks and references to Appendices |
|---|---|---|---|---|
| THIEPVAL (WOOD) | 11 | | Practice attack against ACHIET-LOUPART line in ground near AUTHUILLE. Battn in reserve. | |
| | 12 | | Battn relieved units of the 53rd Infantry Brigade. Taking over the front to be ACHIET-LOUPART attack. Very long business (relief) owing to (intrica-) nature of ground, & necessary to relieve 3 different units by 4 Coys. | |
| | 13 | | ACHIET-LOUPART line reported abandoned on our front. Patrols under Sgt FRIND (Bombers) and Cpl(?) WALSH examined that area. B & C Companies advanced through ACHIET-LOUPART line to on to a line running from about Q.22.a.6.3 to Q.22.c.81 with 12th Middlesex on right and 7 Bedfords on left. ACHIET LE PETIT still occupied. A Coy in ACHIET PUIS advanced  (?) through ACHIET line. IRLES, & forward of B line. Heavy enemy shelling on ACHIET line. Battn HQ in GROVILLERS TRENCH. ACHIET line, but very few casualties. | |
| | 14 | | Battn relieved in front line & holds support line. A Coy in S.MAUMONT Trench. B Coy in GRANDCOURT line and IRLES. Confereries (?) in ACHIET line. Btn HQ at P45. | |
| PUISIEUX(?) | 15 | | No movement. ACHIET LE PETIT still occupied. | |

# WAR DIARY or INTELLIGENCE SUMMARY

Army Form C. 2118

| Place | Date | Hour | Summary of Events and Information | Remarks and references to Appendices |
|---|---|---|---|---|
| R/S | 16 | | No movement. Enemy shelling still heavy on Bihucourt line. | |
| | 17 | | Early morning of 17th patrols of 2 Dis Middlesex from Bihucourt line reported Bihucourt much dry occupied, it was ordered to push forward to Bihucourt. Moved forward into Bihucourt passing through the village enemy to snipers machine guns — | |
| Bihucourt | | | Batt'n concentrated by mid-day in G.28.C. moved forward to enemy Bihucourt line, 1 gun - p/s on South side of it — to Bihucourt line, 1 gun p/s on South side of it — | |
| | 18 | | Battalion moved in advance (road to Behagnies – left, Ervillers rd. right) 2 coy's of cavalry + a section of Field guns & occupied without resistance Behagnies to BAPAUME ARRAS road from Sapignies to Behagnies. After Cavalry scouts sent into the enemy on the hill (between Sapignies & St Leger — | |
| Sapignies | 19 | | Battalion moved forward with 2 squadrons of cavalry + a company of cyclists & occupied St Leger. This was only accomplished finally after 4 o'clock, 2nd Battalion came into Battalion on the St Leger-Mory front and was established. 2nd Division on the left — Batt'n in touch with 7th Division + 3 cavalry patrols — at Judas Farm north of 6th 7th Division — Battalion held an outpost line on both sides of the valley running from | |
| St Leger | | | St Leger to Croisilles, on the Northern edge of St Leger — | |

| Place | Date | Hour | Summary of Events and Information | Remarks and references to Appendices |
|---|---|---|---|---|
| ST LEGER | 20 | | Battalion made a reconnaissance in force assisted by cavalry on our flanks — the Lucknow Brigade being in our centre as well as the troops early. at 7.30 a.m. Four companies in line to R.D.C from right & left. A Coy was unable to emerge from the wood at the N.E. corner of ST LEGER owing to heavy artillery machine gun fire & suffered considerable casualties. B Coy worked up the valley & stopped in advance for the enemy had considerable preparation shell & heavy shelling. C.D Coys advanced on the type N.W of the valley but after going 800 or 500 yards came under heavy machine gun fire & met with considerable shelling. At about 10.30 a.m. it was seen that casualties so too steady. Refused to make any further advance — Consequently the wire is still & it the (her that) we were supported by one battery R.F.A. one valley R.H.A. — practically. Orders were given for companies to withdraw to their original start positions. This was done chiefly (9 about 12.30 & about 4.30 p.m. | |

# WAR DIARY or INTELLIGENCE SUMMARY

Army Form C. 2118

| Place | Date | Hour | Summary of Events and Information | Remarks and references to Appendices |
|---|---|---|---|---|
| ST LEGER | 21 | | D Company, who were in a field of [turnips?] with [?] were to advance from in daylight. They decided to wait till dark however about 4 p.m. a party of Germans came out from crossroads & very nearly succeeded to outflank them. They [?] fire came [?] a shell [?] intact country — many however returned & amongst them [?] who were received by the 8th Devon Regiment who relieved the Battalion last evening. Battalion proceeded to billets in ACHIET LE GRAND. Battalion moved to WARWICK HUTS nr. IRCHLAND back from MIRAUMONT. | |
| WARLOY | 22 | | Battalion moves to WARLOY, reaching 1st Corps Commander at SINUS | |
| VILLERS BOCAGE | 23 | | Battalion moves to VILLERS BOCAGE | |
| | 24 | | Battalion moves by 'bus from VILLERS BOCAGE to DURY | |
| DURY | 25 | | Church Parade & conference inspection by C.O. | |
| | 26 | | Battalion left DURY at 8.30 p.m. to entrain at BACOUEL (two hours march) | |
| | 27 | | Battalion entrained about 5 a.m. trains moving from BACOUEL station at 7.15 a.m. | |
| | 28 | | Battalion detrained at BREQUETTE station at about 7 a.m. | |

# WAR DIARY
## or
## INTELLIGENCE SUMMARY

Army Form C. 2118

| Place | Date | Hour | Summary of Events and Information | Remarks and references to Appendices |
|---|---|---|---|---|
| THIENNES | March 28 | | Marched to huts at THIENNES | |
| | 29 | | Training for all Companies in trenching, bayonet fighting &c. Spent morning under assistant adjutant | |
| | 30 | | Training as above. Message of thanks taken from 5th Army Commander to 18th Division on leaving his army | |
| | 31 | | Training as above | |

R. Turner Lt Colonel
6th Bn Northamptonshire Regt

Army Form C. 2118

# WAR DIARY
## or
## INTELLIGENCE SUMMARY
(Erase heading not required.)

APRIL 1917

6 & 8 Bn Northamptonshire Regt

Vol 2

| Place | Date | Hour | Summary of Events and Information | Remarks and references to Appendices |
|---|---|---|---|---|
| THIEPVAL | 1/4/17 | 11am | Church parade in afternoon all ranks paraded. Inspection of kit. The blankets of 2 Coys and transport men were aired during the day | |
| " | 2/4/17 | 9am | Company training. Thorough kit inspection. One corporal inspected by the C.O. Small Bore printers total. | |
| | 3/4/17 | 10am | Battalion route march. Specialty talks by Capt W Roberts to officers and NCO's | |
| | 4/4/17 | | Company training. Lecture to 6 Coy & Major Johnson on map reading | |
| | 5/4/17 | | Coy training. Coy and reft. ranges during the day | |
| | 6/4/17 | | Coy training. CO inspection of organization shall Coys during the day Training of 2 Coys with Bradshaw with our Bombing Officer | |
| | 7/4/17 | | Coy training. Medical officer's inspection of feet | |
| | 8/4/17 | | Church parade. Presentation of medal ribbons decorations etc. gained in connection with recent operations on the Somme | |

# WAR DIARY
## or
## INTELLIGENCE SUMMARY

Army Form C. 2118

| Place | Date | Hour | Summary of Events and Information | Remarks and references to Appendices |
|---|---|---|---|---|
| THIENNES | 8.4.17 (cont) | | by the Corps Commander. Military Cross to 2nd Lt J.N. Beachey DSO, MC to Cpl R.S.M.C at 2 P.M. Military Medals. 9 Other Ranks. Bar to Military Medal to Other Ranks | |
| | 9.4.17 | | Coy training. Coys used range during the day. | |
| | 10/4/17 | | Battalion training (Outpost Scheme) | |
| | 11/4/17 | | Musty Parades all Coys. Coys used range during the day. | |
| | 12/4/17 | | Coy training. | |
| | 13/4/17 | | Battalion Route March (Gonehn) | |
| | 14/4/17 | | Company training. Coys instructed in Bayonet fighting etc by C.S.M Burns. Army Gymnastic Staff during the day. Rifle made return of 2 Coys review of instructors made. Bombing officers. Jackson yesterday was not awarded to 5 other ranks. Bar to Military Medal to 1 Other Rank. Coys and Personal Comdrs sent congratulations to the respects | |
| | 15/4/17 | | Baths at AIRE allotted to the Battalion all day. All Ranks bathed. Church Parade for 2 Coys | |
| | 16/4/17 | | Company training | |

# WAR DIARY or INTELLIGENCE SUMMARY

Army Form C. 2118

| Place | Date | Hour | Summary of Events and Information | Remarks and references to Appendices |
|---|---|---|---|---|
| THIENNES | 17/4/17 | | Brigade Outpost Scheme cancelled owing to wet weather. Instruction under Platoon Commds in billets. | |
| | 18/4/17 | | Bath.Spot cancelled owing to wet weather. Preparations made for Bath Spot. Instruction (Lectures etc) by Platoon Comds in billets. | |
| | 19/4/17 | | Bath. Spot. weather dull. Spot very satisfactory. Firing Kimpel inspected by Col Greer & D.S. Broan (new billets). Coy training. Battalion moved to MANGUEVILLE | |
| | 20/4/17 21/4/17 | | | |
| | 22/4/17 | | Church parade. Voluntary Service during morning and evening | |
| | 23/4/17 | | Battalion took part in Brigade Tactical Exercise (Outpost scheme) | |
| | 24/4/17 | | Company training. Muster parades for all Coy during the day. (Checking of equipment) | |
| | 25/4/17 | | Company training. Baths at THIENNES allotted to Bn all day, all Bn bathed | |
| MANGUEVILLE | 26/4/17 | | Brigade Tactical exercise cancelled owing to motor lorries not used to be prepared to move out and tent after 1 pm. Bath moved to near Gileb at BOURS. | |

Army Form C. 2118

# WAR DIARY
or
## INTELLIGENCE SUMMARY
(Erase heading not required.)

| Place | Date | Hour | Summary of Events and Information | Remarks and references to Appendices |
|---|---|---|---|---|
| BOURS | 27.4.17 | | The Batt. less transport went to entrain at PERNES for ARRAS at 10.30am but on arriving at PERNES at 9.20am information was received that owing to an accident on the railway in PERNES the batt. was to march to BRYAS and entrain there. left PERNES and arrived at BRYAS at 2.40pm and entrained for ARRAS. Arrived at ARRAS at 10.45pm, the train detrained at railway near the station for about 12 hours, marched to bivouacs at NEUVILLE V. TASSE arriving there at about 1.45am 28.4.17 | |
| NEUVILLE VITASSE | 28.4.17 | | Made arrangements to relieve the 2nd WWFS and 18 King's Liverpools (30th Division) in the trenches (These two batt'ns were not in my Bde.) It was explained that we should take up the line (O.31.c.3.) to 31.6.5.7 by Marshes [illegible]. Relief started at 6.15pm and was complete at 1 [illegible] 29.4.17. There were no casualties. Weather fine. | |
| In the trenches | 29.4.17 | | A & D Coys in front line with C & B Coys in support. B Coy holds shoppard A Cliff abutting to the enemy on Bronko [illegible] during the day. Lt F.D.S. Walker and 4 OR wounded (remaining at duty.) Weather fine. | |
| In the trenches | 30.4.17 | | Intermittent shelling all day. B Coy worked on dump line on road from B Coy dugout to right of front line | |

1875 Wt. W593/826 1,000,000 4/15 J.B.C. & A. A.D.S.S./Forms/C. 2118.

# WAR DIARY
## or
## INTELLIGENCE SUMMARY

*(Erase heading not required.)*

Army Form C. 2118

| Place | Date | Hour | Summary of Events and Information | Remarks and references to Appendices |
|---|---|---|---|---|
| Little Kursh | 3rd… | | C Coy worked on improving a long sap from front line from which good observation could be obtained. Front line had to be extended to the left for 150 yards. 1 platoon of C Coy occupied this distance. | |

Instructions regarding War Diaries and Intelligence Summaries are contained in F. S. Regs., Part II. and the Staff Manual respectively. Title Pages will be prepared in manuscript.

# WAR DIARY
## or
## INTELLIGENCE SUMMARY.
(Erase heading not required.)

Army Form C. 2118.

| Place | Date | Hour | Summary of Events and Information | Remarks and references to Appendices |
|---|---|---|---|---|
| In the trenches W. of CHERISY. | 1.5.17 | | Weather fine. Quiet all day. Very little shelling. 2 Officers patrols went out at 9.30 p.m. and returned at 11.30 p.m. Right patrol reported that the enemy were not strong in their front line, but judging from enemy very lights the trench further North was strongly held. On returning were fired at. No casualties. The Left patrol went along CABLE TRENCH where they were held up by an enemy patrol. Shots were exchanged. No casualties. Later they went further - nothing to report. The Battalion was relieved by the 12th MIDDLESEX Regiment and the 7th Bedfords and marched back to bivouacs at NEUVILLE VITASSE arriving there 2 p.m. 2.5.17. | |
| NEUVILLE VITASSE. | 2.5.17 | 2 p.m. | Orders received that the Division would attack on a two Brigade front - the 54th on the right and 55th Brigade on the left. The 21st Division would attack on the right and 14th Division on the left simultaneously. Objectives blue and red lines - Map attached. The Battalion were held in Brigade Reserve. Preparations for battle made during the day. Only 20 Officers to go into action, the remainder to be with Transport. Conference of Officers held at Battalion Headquarters. Details explained. | |
| | 3.5.17 | 12.30 a.m. | Battalion left NEUVILLE VITASSE by Companies. 1st Company at 12.30 a.m. remaining Companies 5 minutes interval, and marched to trenches at N.29.C. (Map 51 S.W.) arriving at 1.45 a.m. | |
| | | 3.45 | Zero hour 3.45 a.m. The Battalion was not engaged in the first part of the operations. | |

Army Form C. 2118

# WAR DIARY
## or
## INTELLIGENCE SUMMARY.
(Erase heading not required.)

| Place | Date | Hour | Summary of Events and Information | Remarks and references to Appendices |
|---|---|---|---|---|
| | 3.5.17 cont. | | After retirement from positions W of CHERISY and FONTAINE-CROISILLE the Battalion was ordered to counter attack and occupy FONTAINE TRENCH from O.32.a.5.3. to O.26.c.2.0. and the circular trench in rear of it. Orders had been received that the bombardment would start at 5-30 p.m. for half an hour, then a pause for a quarter of an hour and the rolling barrage would open at 6-15 p.m. 200 yards in front of our trench, but this was later postponed for one hour. Battalion was in position at 5-30 p.m. (all in front line trench) with the LEICESTER-SHIRE REGIMENT (110 Infantry Brigade) on the right and 7th QUEENS (55th Brigade) on the left. These Battalions were to attack simultaneously after a preliminary bombardment as stated. The rolling barrage opened and the Battalion attacked with 2 Companies, 2 platoons in the front line and 2 platoons 2nd line A and D Companies were in support. Of the attacking Companies, B Company under Captain Mobbs were on the right and C Company under Captain Shepherd on the left. A company were on the right, D Company on the left as supporting Companies. D Company furnished a bombing party (1NCO and 8 men) who advanced down CABLE TRENCH with the leading wave of the assaulting Company. They also furnished carrying parties for bombs and S.A.A for C Company, down CABLE TRENCH running towards CHERISY from O.31.b.4.9. B and C Companies advanced as close to the barrage as possible having several cas-ualties from the barrage. The hostile Machine Gun fire which swept the area they had to cross was as bad as in the attack of the morning. B Company (right | |

Army Form C. 2118.

# WAR DIARY
## or
## INTELLIGENCE SUMMARY.
(Erase heading not required.)

| Date | Hour | Summary of Events and Information | Remarks and references to Appendices |
|---|---|---|---|
| 3.5.17 contd | | assaulting company) having 50% casualties by the time they reached within 50 yards of the enemy wire - having covered nearly 900 yards. They found the wire intact, the bombardment not having touched it, and the Machine Gun fire from the right flank as well as from the front rendered further advance impossible. C company (left assaulting Company) were able to get down CABLE TRENCH owing to the Stokes Gun having totally cleared the trench of enemy. They started over the top but found Machine Gun fire rendered further advance in that way impossible. They pushed their way by bombs and rifle grenades down CABLE TRENCH to the junction of FONTAINE TRENCH, and worked their way along that trench for about 70 yards after a severe bombing and grenade fight, where several enemy were killed. This Company finding its flanks in danger was compelled to get back to the original front line. No blame can be attached to the Company Commander, on the contrary he personally and the Officers of the whole company put up a very big fight. The right Company were then ordered to withdraw to original front line - One of the objects of this attack was to enable wounded men and others who were lying out since morning to get back. A considerable number of men did so. No: of casualties 120 including 6 Officers - lack of success in this operation was due to intensive Machine Gun fire. | |
| 4.5.17. | | Two patrols were sent out at 12.15 a.m. The right patrol found nothing to report. The left patrol detected a Machine Gun on ridge - point O.31.b.6.5. | |

Army Form C. 2118

# WAR DIARY
## or
## INTELLIGENCE SUMMARY.
*(Erase heading not required.)*

| Place | Date | Hour | Summary of Events and Information | Remarks and references to Appendices |
|---|---|---|---|---|
| | 4.5.17 cont'd | | Considerable shelling was done by the enemy on our front for 3 hours after the attack. Active rifle and Machine Gun fire was maintained throughout the night (3rd to 4th). The ground in front of the line was searched for wounded and though the task was rendered difficult by enemy fire, ten men were brought in and several wounded crawled back. | |
| NEUVILLE-VITASSE | 5.5.17 | | Weather fine throughout the day, and front quiet. All spare Lewis Guns drums, Machine Gun belt boxes, bomb buckets and spare ammunition was salved, dumped, and handed over to the incoming Battalion. At 9 p.m. the enemy were discovered to be working on the wire between our trench and FONTAINE TRENCH. Our Guides met the incoming Battalion (8th SUFFOLKS) at Battalion Headquarters at 10 p.m. and conducted them to their positions. Relief was completed at midnight. The Battalion marched back to their Bivouacs at NEUVILLE-VITASSE arriving at 1.30 a.m. | |
| | 6.5.17 | | Clearing out of dug-outs, erecting bivouacs, cleaning equipment. Re-organisation of Companies. Colonel Turner went to Rest Camp WARLEY with an inflamed knee. | |
| | | 9 am | Strong Points taken over from 8th NORFOLKS at N 22.c. 27.b. 21.d. | |
| | 7.5.17 | | Battalion continued General Training - Working parties were supplied at night for digging in front line. Above strong points given up. | |

Army Form C. 2118.

# WAR DIARY
## or
## INTELLIGENCE SUMMARY.
*(Erase heading not required.)*

| Place | Date | Hour | Summary of Events and Information | Remarks and references to Appendices |
|---|---|---|---|---|
| NEUVILLE-VITASSE cont'd | 8.5.17 | | General Training. | |
| | 9.5.17 | | General Training. Working party supplied at night. Captain Gadsden and 5 O.R. left for Rest Camp at BOULOGNE. | |
| | 10.5.17 11.5.17 12.5.17 | | General Training. | |
| Bivouacs N of HENIN | 13.5.17 | 11 am | Battalion marched to point N 32.a. and bivouaced. Night working party supplied. | |
| | 14.5.17 | | General Training. | |
| | 15.5.17 | | do do Night working party supplied. | |
| | 16.5.17 | | do do Colonel Turner returned. Battalion attack practice. | |
| | 17.5.17 | | do do Night working party supplied. | |
| | 18.5.17 | | do do | |
| | 19.5.17 | | Battalion attack practice. Night working party supplied. | |
| | 20.5.17 | | General Training. | |
| | 21.5.17 | 11 am | Battalion attack by Royal FUSILIERS, our Battalion defending and carrying for attacking Battalion. | |
| | 22.5.17 | | General Training. Night working party. | |
| | 23.5.17 | | Very wet day. Proposed attack practice postponed. | |
| | 24.5.17 | | General Training. Positions of frontage when next in the line reconnoitred. Night working party supplied. | |
| | 25.5.17 | | General Training. The Commanding Officer and company commanders reconnoitred strong points. | |

Army Form C. 2118.

# WAR DIARY
## or
## INTELLIGENCE SUMMARY.

(Erase heading not required.)

| Place | Date | Hour | Summary of Events and Information | Remarks and references to Appendices |
|---|---|---|---|---|
| Bivouacs N of HENIN. cont.d | 25.5.17 cont.d | | Working Parties supplied. also small fatigues. | |
| | 26.5.17 | | Weather fine. Little shelling all day. Grenade and bomb training. Trench practice, grenadiers firing over bombers. 4 platoons night working party. | |
| | 27.5.17 | | Heavy shelling during night (26th/27th.) 3 wounded casualties sustained by working party. Day fine. British barrage at 2 pm – 3 pm. 4 platoons night working party. Considerable aerial activity during early evening. German plane versus British – over Camp. No definite result perceived. | |
| | 28.5.17. | | Weather fine. Quiet day. Little shelling. General Training. | |
| | 29.5.17. | | Early shower, followed by fair but cloudy day. All quiet. General Training. | |
| | 30.5.17 | | Fine morning, heavy showers in afternoon. A thunderstorm – 2 runners and 1 guard struck. One man went to hospital. Brigade attack practice. Northamptonshire Regiment – dug-out clearing parties and support to assaulting Battalions. | |
| | 31.5.17 | | Heavy shelling by us and enemy 2 am to 4 am. Fine. Quiet Day. General training. | |

R Turner Lieut. Colonel.

Commdg: 6th (S) Bn Northamptonshire Regiment.

Report on attack by 6th (S) Bn. Northamptonshire Regt.
on FONTAINE TRENCH
by Lieut-Colonel R. Turner D.S.O

On the night of May 3rd after a preliminary bombardment — a pause — and a rolling barrage re-opening 200 yds in front of our front line — the Northamptonshire Regiment attacked on a 2 Company front in three waves. They must have followed the barrage very closely, having of course a certain per-centage of casualties from our own barrage. Immediately they came into view over the crest they were under a very heavy Machine Gun fire and they covered the ground at the double.

The left Company seeing that the way was clear and that there was cover in the CABLE TRENCH O.32.a.3.8. got into this trench, and bombed straight down FONTAINE-TRENCH and were in this trench 10 minutes after barrage opened having a bombing post at O.32.a.5.7. to protect NORTH flank as the Company advanced down FONTAINE-TRENCH they killed a few of the enemy and discovered a few dead from previous artillery fire and could observe from their position the right Company advancing to the attack. The right Company as they neared the trench did so in small rushes from shell-hole to shell hole, when within 30 or 40 yards of enemy wire they were completely held up in shell holes by very heavy Machine Gun fire.

A vigorous resistance was made but the left Company Commander then seeing that the right Company could not possibly gain their objective and as the left attacking Battalion was not in touch with him although he was actually in their area — he retired along CABLE TRENCH back to their original front line.

Some of the right Company started a gradual retirement from shell-hole to shell-hole.

(Cont.)

The Stokes Gun was of considerable assistance in clearing CABLE TRENCH before the infantry advance enabling the CABLE TRENCH to be quite clear for the attack and for forward carrying parties with bombs, grenades and S.A.A.

The Gun was placed at O.31.b.5.9. and fired down the CABLE TRENCH (CABLE and semicircular trenches) NORTH of CABLE TRENCH with great success keeping suspected Machine Gun in semicircular trench at O.26.c.5.2. quiet.

### Barrage:

The barrage was a good one and the attacking companies speak very well of it. The bombardment and barrage also caused a certain amount of dust and smoke which rendered aim fire by the enemy only possible in places.

During and after the attack many men lying out of the previous attacking Battalions who were in shell holes were enabled to get back — in one case about 50 strong of the Bedfordshire Regiment who had dug themselves in SOUTH of our area.

### Position of Affairs

Being in direct touch with right and left Battalions these Battalions were informed of every eventuality and they informed me likewise. When the attacking Companies got back to the front line trench they were immediately re-organised and assisted in taking up the front line system of defence.

### Estimated Casualties;

6. Officers and
105 Other Ranks.

(sgd.) R. Turner
Lieut-Colonel.
commdg: 6th(S) Bn. Northamptonshire Regt.

# WAR DIARY
## or
## INTELLIGENCE SUMMARY

Army Form C. 2118.

| Place | Date | Hour | Summary of Events and Information | Remarks and references to Appendices |
|---|---|---|---|---|
| BIVOUACS N of HENIN | 1.6.17 | | Fine Very Quiet. General Training. Lewis Gunners & Snipers on range. Preparations for handling over Bivouacs to the 10th Essex Regt. | |
| | 2.6.17 | 8 a.5 | 2.6.17 Battalion Marched to trenches via HENINEL & SUSSEX AVENUE. | Map Reference W. of CHERISY 51b SW. |
| | 2.6.17 | 10 p.m. | At 10 p.m. the Battalion relieved the 7th West Kents. Relief carried out with the exception of the HORSE-SHOE TR at the East end of WREN LANE Point O.31.b.7.4. The enemy had taken possession of this trench and a post 70 yards WEST of the HORSE-SHOE in WREN LANE and were holding it strongly. The West Kents organised a bombing party composed of their own men and ours, 2nd Lieut. G.H. Warner 6th NN headed this party. They bombed up WREN LANE and drove the enemy completely out of that trench and established a double bombing block at the junction of WREN LANE and the HORSE SHOE. Here 2nd Lieut Warner was killed. Simultaneously with this operation a platoon of the Royal West Kents, supported by a platoon of the 6th NN under 2nd Lieut A.J. Frost attacked HORSE-SHOE TR from the end of LARK LANE. They were very strongly resisted with pineapples, rifle grenades and machine gun fire and were unable to get a footing in the trench. | |
| | 3.6.17 | | The entire defence of the front system was entirely taken over by the 6th NN Regiment at 4 a.m. on the morning of the 3rd with the enemy still strongly holding the HORSE-SHOE. Consolidation of the trenches and making of fire steps was proceeded with. Copy of Commanding Officers scheme to obtain possession of the HORSE-SHOE submitted to the 54th I.B. The G.O.C. approved of the alternative scheme. | See copy attached. CO's scheme. |

Army Form C. 2118.

# WAR DIARY
## or
## INTELLIGENCE SUMMARY
*(Erase heading not required.)*

| Place | Date | Hour | Summary of Events and Information | Remarks and references to Appendices |
|---|---|---|---|---|
| In the Trenches W. of CHERISY. Bn.H.Qrs. N.30.d. | ~~2.6.17~~ 3.6.17. | 11 p.m. | Zero hour 11 P.m. The Operation carried out as per Operation Order with 3 platoons, one platoon attacking from the end of LARK LANE under 2/Lt. Sucklick supported by a wiring and consolidating party; another platoon attacking from the North under 2 Lieut H. Beckingham. The success of the operation was largely due to Stokes Mortars and the volume of rifle grenades fired. The trench was taken, 11 of the enemy dead were accounted for and about 40 rifles of the 191G. Pattern captured. Consolidation was carried out under extreme difficulty the HORSE SHOE TR being heavily shelled - the shelling continuing during the following day. | See Operation Order Attached. |
| | 4.6.17. | | During the night of the 4th/5th further wiring and consolidating work was done to the front line trenches. | |
| | 5.6.17. | | Intermittent shelling was carried on by the enemy during the day, at 4 p.m. C.E. Company relieved "D" Coy in the front line and at 10 p.m B Company relieved "A". Further consolidation of strong points was carried out and during the night. Front line trenches were shelled occasionally throughout the day. | Map Reference 51b S.W. |
| | 6.6.17 | | At night a party of the Sussex Pioneers connected the extension of SWALLOW LANE with HORSE-SHOE O.31.C.9.6 to O.31.B.6.4. A Company providing a protective screen. During the same night the whole of the HORSE SHOE was filled in and strongly consolidated. The entire portion of the SHOE being filled with tangled wire and a strong protective entanglement being put out in front and on the right + left flank. 280 coils of wire being used for this purpose. Meanwhile a T head was constructed at the junction of WREN LANE and | |

Army Form C. 2118.

# WAR DIARY
## or
## INTELLIGENCE SUMMARY
(Erase heading not required.)

Remarks and references to Appendices

Map Reference. Sheet 51.b. S.W.

| Place | Date | Hour | Summary of Events and Information | |
|---|---|---|---|---|
| In the trenches N. of CHERISY | 6.6.17 | | and the HORSE SHOE. To form a Lewis Gun emplacement. Further work during the night comprised fire stepping deepening and improving the posts and digging a Lewis Gun Sap at Point O 31.b.6.4. | |
| | 7.6.17 | | Little enemy shelling on our front. Machine Guns and Snipers were active. Patrols. An enemy Patrol were observed in front of FONTAINE TRENCH at O.29.d.3.7. Consolidation, firestepping and wiring of our front trenches was done during the night. Two new emplacements were made in WREN LANE. | 1 |
| | 8.6.17 | | Occasional shelling of our front trench. Snipers active. During the day enemy were seen to be working in front of the HORSE SHOE at about O.32.C.2.3. on what was eventually a trench mortar emplacement. It was then arranged for an artillery and trench mortar bombardment to take place at night to demolish this strong point. The first bombardment commenced at 10 p.m. consisting of 18 pds and 4.5". together with Trench Mortar bombardment and lasted one minute. This was again repeated at 2 a.m. Though no patrolling of this point was made, from the observation which was obtained next day, this operation was entirely successful and the enemy position was broken up. The artillery fire was very accurate and the number of the enemy must have been killed. At 11-45 p.m. the enemy opened a bombardment on our front line composed of artillery and a considerable number of MINENWERFERS. A number of rifle | |

Army Form C. 2118.

# WAR DIARY
## or
## INTELLIGENCE SUMMARY

(Erase heading not required.)

Remarks and references to Appendices

Map Reference Sheet 51b. S.W.

| Place | Date | Hour | Summary of Events and Information |
|---|---|---|---|
| In the trenches W. of CHERISY | 8.6.17 | | Grenades were fired from in front of FONTAINE TRENCH and from CABLE TRENCH. The barrage then lifted onto CURTAIN TRENCH and the second in command who was in CURTAIN TRENCH at the time phoned down to Hd.Qrs for the S.O.S. Our own bombardment and that of the enemy had ceased at 12.20 a.m. More wiring was carried out. The wiring done during these five nights was done without screw posts; being made of concertina barbed wire which had been coiled by the Support Companies the preceding day. |
| | 9.6.17 | | During the morning short periods of systematic shelling was done on CURTAIN and STORK TRENCHES. |
| Support Trenches S. of HENINEL | | 9.40 p.m. | The Battalion was relieved by the 7th BEDFORDSHIRE REGIMENT and moved into the Support area. Dispositions were as follows B and C Companies in BOOTHAM TRENCH N.30.C. 'A' Company in CONCRETE TRENCH N.35.C. D Company in SHAFT TRENCH T.6.a. Battalion H.Q. in SHAFT TR. at N.35.C. Relief completed by midnight. |
| | 10.6.17 | | Quiet. Fine. Salvage work done in the day time, and working parties (12½ platoons) were provided by us for digging in front line and carrying. |
| | 11.6.17 | | Quiet. Heavy rain early, followed by fine day. Officers of EAST YORKSHIRE REGIMENT shown round the trenches and situation explained to them. Salvage work and cleaning of trenches a |

Army Form C. 2118.

# WAR DIARY
## or
## INTELLIGENCE SUMMARY
*(Erase heading not required.)*

Instructions regarding War Diaries and Intelligence Summaries are contained in F. S. Regs., Part II. and the Staff Manual respectively. Title Pages will be prepared in manuscript.

| Place | Date | Hour | Summary of Events and Information | Remarks and references to Appendices |
|---|---|---|---|---|
| Bn H.Q. | 12.6.17 | | Night working party of (11½ platoons) | |
| | 13.6.17 | | Salvage work. Night working party (6 platoons.) Fine day. Quiet Salvage work. Night working party (4 platoons) Fine day. Quiet | |
| Bn H.Qrs SHAFT TR. N.35.C. | 14.6.17 | | Fine. From 4 to 6 p.m. considerable shelling was done WEST of D Company's H.Qr. Night working parties (9 Platoons) were detailed for digging & carrying. A special working party detailed to clear damage done by shelling in SHAFT TR. | |
| | 15.6.17 | | A Company moved from CONCRETE TR. to BROWN TR. to hold posts vacated by 12th Middlesex. D Company (1 Platoon) moved into CONCRETE TR. | |
| Bn H.Qrs. in CONCRETE TR. | 16.6.17 | 10 am | Fine. Occasional shelling in the early morning. Bn H.Qrs moved to Headquarters in CONCRETE TR. The Bn was relieved by the EAST YORKSHIRE Regt. All Trench stores were handed over by us. Relief commenced at 6.30 p.m. All Companies reported correct by 7-55 p.m. Bn H.Qr left CONCRETE TR. at 8 p.m. Bn then marched to Camp in S.17. All Bn had reached camp by 9.45 p.m. | |
| Camp S.17 | 17.6.17 | | Fine day. Men bathed during afternoon. | |
| ANDINFER-WOOD | 18.6.17 | | Heavy shower at 2.30 am. Bn marched off at 3.45 am and reached ANDINFER WOOD at 6-10 a.m. billeted there for the day. A clearing party of 25 were left at camp at S.17. and were brought on to PAS by Motor lorry. | |

# WAR DIARY or INTELLIGENCE SUMMARY

| Place | Date | Hour | Summary of Events and Information | Remarks and references to Appendices |
|---|---|---|---|---|
| WARLINCOURT | 19.6.17 | | Bn marched off at 2.45 am and reached WARLINCOURT at 7.45 am when they went into village. Heavy thunderstorm before entering P.A.S. | |
| | 20.6.17 | | Fine early - showery in afternoon. Bathing and General training. Draft of 207 O.R.s joined Battalion. Companies then reorganised into 4 Platoons. | |
| | 21.6.17 | 4.30pm | Ribbons were presented by Corps Commander to three recipients General training as per programme rendered to Brigade | |
| | 22.6.17 | | Heavy showers. Physical Training. Ball firing on range SOUTH of BAYEN- -COURT and WEST of SAILLY-au-BOIS. | |
| | 23.6.17 | | Showery morning. Tunics and trousers fumigated in Foden lorry. Firing on range SOUTH of R in MONDICOURT. | |
| | 24.6.17 | | Overcoats put through Foden lorry. Church parade 11.30. | |
| | 25.6.17 | | Fine. The Battalion fired on range SOUTH of MONDICOURT. General training. Commanding Officer went to Divisional Head- quarters to arrange for sports. Pioneers and a working party provided to erect hurdles at Divisional Sports ground, COUIN. | |
| | 26.6.17 | | Fine. A & B Companies fired on range from 6am to 1pm. C & D Companies Gen- eral Training. Commanding Officers conference with Company Commanders at 2 pm. re promotion of N.C.Os & men. Further arrangements re Battalion, Brigade & Divisional Sports. | |

Army Form C. 2118.

# WAR DIARY
or
## INTELLIGENCE SUMMARY.
(Erase heading not required.)

Instructions regarding War Diaries and Intelligence Summaries are contained in F. S. Regs., Part II. and the Staff Manual respectively. Title pages will be prepared in manuscript.

| Place | Date | Hour | Summary of Events and Information | Remarks and references to Appendices |
|---|---|---|---|---|
| WARLINCOURT | 27.6.17 | | Fine. 150 men bathed at GAUDIEMPRE. C & D Companies fired on range. A Company's rifles inspected by Armourer Sergeant. | |
| | 28.6.17 | | Fine. Battalion Sports. B & C Companies rifles inspected by Armourer Sergt. | |
| | 29.6.17 | | Showery. General Training. Box Respirators tested by Brigade Gas N.C.O. D Company's rifles inspected by Armourer Sergeant. | |
| | 30.6.17 | | General Training from 9am to 11 am. Divisional Sports 2 p.m. very wet. | |

R. Turner
Lieut - Colonel.
Commdg: 6th (S) Bn. Northamptonshire Regiment.

To 54th I.B.                                    Copy.

**Proposed scheme for recapturing the HORSE SHOE TRENCH about M.31.b.80.25.**

There is every evidence that this trench is strongly held. I believe that the enemy occupied shell holes close to and SOUTH of the HORSE SHOE, in addition to the HORSE-SHOE TRENCH.

I consider it necessary to bombard this trench with 4.5s. The artillery officers of 281st Brigade who are now in the line have had a previous operation of bombarding this particular trench; so there will be no difficulty about it, it will only mean withdrawing our bombing post from the bomb block in the communication trench. I consider that a strong bombardment some time during the afternoon might cause them to evacuate without an attack. Patrols would thus find out if the trench was held or not, and if evacuated could quietly take possession.

### Alternative Plan.

Bombardment during the afternoon by 4.5s on junction of CABLE TRENCH and FONTAINE TRENCH (suspected T.M. position) and on HORSE SHOE TR about M.31.b.80.25. also 3 Stokes Mortars two in STORK TRENCH, one in WREN LANE or any other position more favourable to register in the afternoon. At night to attack at 11 o'clock after a second artillery bombardment of 5 minutes, and a Stokes Mortar bombardment 3 minutes on trench and

-2-

Then lift with the artillery to 100 yards in front, and then to 200 yards, the lifting of the barrage to be a signal for the attack by the Infantry of 2 platoons. One platoon attacking on right flank of the HORSE-SHOE TRENCH. The other platoon attacking the left flank of the HORSE-SHOE TRENCH over the top of communication trench. A small party of bombers to push up communication trench, rifle grenadiers to cover advance of both attacking flanks with rifle grenades.

Note.

There are sufficient rifle grenades and bombs in bomb store, PELICAN LANE for this operation.
Stokes Mortars will have to arrange for further supplies of ammunition.

Operation Orders.    3.6.17.
Reference Map Sheet 51$^b$ S.W.
Edition 4.A. 1/20,000.

1. The 6$^{th}$ Northamptonshire Regiment will attack and recapture HORSE SHOE TRENCH. O.31.b.8.0 at 11 p.m. tonight.

2. Method of Attack

At ZERO hour 2 platoons from positions as arranged will rush the objective the moment the shrapnel barrage lifts off at 11.2 p.m.

A third platoon with tools and wiring material will advance from about O.31.b.6.4. and move forward to consolidate the objective.

-3-

3. Artillery Arrangements.

(a) From 6 p.m to 11 p.m 1 - 4·5 Howitzer Battery 281st Brigade R.F.A. will carry out a slow bombardment on the objective at the rate of 1 round per minute.

(b) From 10·58 p.m to 11 p.m 3 Stokes Mortars will bombard the objective. At 11 p.m the Stokes Mortars will lift a 100 yards every minute for 3 minutes.

(c) From 11 p.m. onwards the Howitzer Battery referred to in (a) will lift off the objective on to FONTAINE TRENCH between O.32.a.4.7 and O.32.c.45.50

(d) From 11 p.m to 11·2 p.m four 18 pounder Batteries will open a shrapnel barrage on the objective.

(e) From 11·2 p.m onwards the shrapnel barrage referred to in (d) will lift on to a semi-circular line 250 yards EAST of the objective (From O.32.c. 55.

N.B. The opening of the shrapnel barrage will be the signal for the assaulting platoons to advance and get close up to the objective ready to rush in the moment the barrage lifts.

4. Machine Gun Arrangements.

The 6 Vickers Machine Guns from a position in FRITZ LANE T.6.d will fire on to the ground between objective and FONTAINE TRENCH to cut off enemys retreat and to prevent him from reinforcing the objective.

5. Precautionary Arrangements.

From 6 p.m to 11 p.m the garrison of post at O.31.b.85.30 will be withdrawn to O.31.b.6.4 it will reoccupy its post at 11.2 p.m.

6. Consolidation

The objective must be consolidated and wired immediately it has been occupied, as a counter attack from the enemy is exceedingly probable. The enemy as soon as he discovers that he has lost HORSE SHOE TRENCH will bombard it heavily with rifle grenades and pineapples. The actual trench should therefore be avoided as much as possible during consolidation and small posts with Lewis Guns should be established in shell-holes immediately EAST of the objective to form a screen whilst the consolidation is in progress.

7. Working Parties.

O/C "C" Company will detail 1 platoon to carry up coiled wire and place same in position. "B" Company will carry for the Right as arranged.

8. "A" Company will push forward their withdrawn post at midnight as arranged and take immediate steps for wiring same.

6th Northants Regt

**WAR DIARY** or **INTELLIGENCE SUMMARY**
Army Form C. 2118.

WO 25

| Place | Date | Hour | Summary of Events and Information | Remarks and references to Appendices |
|---|---|---|---|---|
| WARLINCOURT | 1.7.17 | | Church Parade at 11.30. The Battalion bathed at GAUDIEMPRE baths. | |
| | 2.7.17 | | Rifle grenade practice & firing on range. A lecture by Brigade R.E. Instructor. | |
| | 3.7.17 4.7.17 | | The Battalion, less B Coy, marched from WARLINCOURT at 12.30 p.m. to DOULLENS, arriving there at 4.35 p.m. Then entrained at 5.30 & left DOULLENS at 6.19 p.m. arriving at GODEWAERSVELDE at 1·5 am the 4th. | Commanding Officer leave 3rd to 17th |
| | 4.7.17 | | Marched to ABEELE & arrived at billets 3·30 am. Foot Inspection and Company inspection of A, C & D Companies. B Company arrived in billets at 6.45 p.m. | |
| Billets & Bivouacs N.W. of ABEELE | 5.7.17 | | Battalion parade and inspection by Commanding Officer. Conference of all Officers of Brigade held by Corps Commander. | |
| | 6.7.17 | | At 7·45 am 'D' Company and 50 ORs 'C' Company left ABEELE to report to officer in charge 2nd Canadian Tunnelling Co. R.E. at ZEVECOTEN to relieve parties of 30th Division. 2 Officers & 50 ORs 'C' Company reported to officer in charge 171st Tunnelling Co. R.E. at 5·30 p.m. Remainder of Battalion left ABEELE to march to CANAL RESERVE CAMP (H.27.b & 26) Map 28 N.W. and arrived at Camp N.W. of DICKEBUSCH at 9.30 p.m. D Company were billeted in OUERDOM with 2nd Canadian Tunnelling Co. | Map Reference Sheet 28 N.W. H.27.b. |
| Camp N.W. DICKEBUSCH (Canal Reserve Camp) | 7.7.17 | | Box respirator practice. In addition to Permanent Working Parties – 1 Company, night working party, provided by B Company. | Casualties: 2 wounded. |
| | 8.7.17 | | Physical Training 7 am to 7·30 am. Church Parade 11.30. Additional Working Party of 2 Companies reported to 2nd Canadian Tunnelling Co. | |
| | 9.7.17 | | Physical Training. Musketry & Bayonet fighting. Inspection of B Company organisation. Routes reconnoitred by Officers & NCOs | 1 |
| | 10.7.17 | | Physical Training. Musketry. Close & Extended order drill. Moving in Artillery formations. Additional Working Party of 250 men for carrying Stokes Mortars & Gas Shells from ZILLEBEKE to TOP TOR tunnels. | 2 wounded |

Army Form C. 2118.

# WAR DIARY
## or
## INTELLIGENCE SUMMARY.
*(Erase heading not required.)*

Instructions regarding War Diaries and Intelligence Summaries are contained in F. S. Regs., Part II. and the Staff Manual respectively. Title pages will be prepared in manuscript.

| Place | Date | Hour | Summary of Events and Information | Remarks and references to Appendices |
|---|---|---|---|---|
| Camp N.W. DICKEBUSCH. (Canal reserve Camp) | 11.7.17 | | Physical training & Close Order drill | Casualties. Map Reference Sheet 28 N.W. H.27.D. |
| | 12.7.17 | | Physical training. Musketry & Close order drill by worst shots. Firing on range near Brigade Headquarters | |
| | 13.7.17 | | Men bathed at RHENINGHELST. Afterwards 1 hours arm drill. Carrying Parties supplied - 200 ORs. Trench Mortar Ammunition carried from ZILLEBEKE to support line. 1 man killed, 1 wounded. | 1 Killed, 1 wounded. |
| | 14.7.17 | | Physical training. Firing on range at Brigade Headquarters. Arm drill. Night working party - 2 officers & 150 ORs - Carrying from ZILLEBEKE. | 2 killed, 7 wounded. |
| | 15.7.17 | | Firing on range. Church Parade at 5.30 p.m. Carrying party 100 men to unload lorries at Divisional bomb store. | |
| | 16.7.17 | | Close & Extended order drill. Rifle grenade instruction. * | |
| | 17.7.17 | | Night carrying party of 100 men to unload lorries to form divisional dump. Firing on range by less expert shots. {* afterwards cancelled.} Musketry. Close & Extended order drill. Bombing practice. | 3 wounded. |
| | 18.7.17 | | Physical training. Bombing & Rifle Grenade Instruction. Box Respirator drill. Musketry & Close Order drill. Colonel Turner returned from leave. | |
| | 19.7.17 | | 2 Platoons, A Company, on Working Party from 4 am to 7-15 am constructing track W of CHATEAU SEGARD. | |
| | 20.7.17 | | B Company bathed at Cornwall Camp. Musketry, Bayonet fighting, & Bomb-throwing. | |
| | 21.7.17 | | Physical training. Musketry. Bomb throwing. Bayonet Fighting. Party of 1 officer & 7 men to Rest Camp. 150 Carrying ammunition. Additional night working parties. 80 on Divisional Track. Instructions by Company Commanders regarding coming operations. | 5 killed 5 wounded. |

Army Form C. 2118.

# WAR DIARY
## or
## INTELLIGENCE SUMMARY.

*(Erase heading not required.)*

Instructions regarding War Diaries and Intelligence Summaries are contained in F. S. Regs., Part II. and the Staff Manual respectively. Title pages will be prepared in manuscript.

| Place | Date | Hour | Summary of Events and Information | Remarks and references to Appendices |
|---|---|---|---|---|
| Camp N.W. DICKEBUSCH (Canal Reserve Camp) | 22.7.17 | | Battalion relieved by 19th Kings Liverpool Regiment in Canal Reserve Camp. At 8-45 am The Battalion marched to DALLINGTON CAMP, WHIPPENHOEK E & arrived at 11-50 am. Working parties attached to 2nd Canadian Tunnelling Company, returned to their Companies (C and D) Physical Training, Grenade Instruction, and Organisation preparatory to operations | Map Reference Sheet 28 N.W. H.27.b. |
| Dallington Camp WHIPPENHOEK E. | 23.7.17 | | | |
| | 24.7.17 | | The Battalion left DALLINGTON CAMP at 7 am and reached STEENVOORDE at 11 am. | |
| Bivouacs N.W of STEENVOORDE | 25.7.17 | | Physical training. Organisation of Companies, and forming up practice. Inspector of physical training lectured to Officers & Men at 2.30 p.m. | |
| | 26.7.17 | | Physical training. Further organisation and explanation of operations — Tape diagram set out on ground illustrating Objectives and features of Corps area. | |
| | 27.7.17 | | Physical training. Organisation & Explanation of Operations. Practice of assault. Bathing at STEENVOORDE. | |
| | 28.7.17 | | Physical training. Explanation of Operations. 1 hour Musketry & Bayonet fighting. Bathing at Baths STEENVOORDE. | |
| | 29.7.17 | | Left Bivouacs (N.W. of STEENVOORDE) at 5.40 am. Arrived at Dallington Camp, WHIPPENHOEK E at 9.15 am — Left Dallington Camp at 9.20 p.m. and arrived at MICMAC Camp at 11-30 p.m. All Box Respirators examined | H.31.b. central. |
| MICMAC Camp, West of Dickebusch | 30.7.17 | | | |
| | 31.7.17 | 1.30 am | Left MICMAC CAMP and arrived Canal Reserve Camp at 2.30 am | |

Army Form C. 2118.

# WAR DIARY
## or
## INTELLIGENCE SUMMARY

*(Erase heading not required.)*

| Place | Date | Hour | Summary of Events and Information | Remarks and references to Appendices |
|---|---|---|---|---|
| CANAL RESERVE CAMP, N.W of DICKEBUSCH. | 31.7.17 | | Battalion marched from camp, proceeded as far as the point where the Divisional Track crosses the road at H.29.b. where orders were received to return to Canal Reserve Camp. | |

R. Turner
Lieut - Colonel.
Commdg: 6t.(S) Bn. Northamptonshire Regiment.

Army Form C. 2118.

# WAR DIARY
## or
## INTELLIGENCE SUMMARY

(Erase heading not required.)

| Place | Date | Hour | Summary of Events and Information | Remarks and references to Appendices |
|---|---|---|---|---|
| CANAL RESERVE Camp. N.W. of DICK-EBUSCH. | 1.8.17. | | Very wet all day. No training possible | Map Ref. 28 N.W. H.27.b. |
| | 2.8.17. | 10am. 2.0 pm. | Physical training & rifle inspection. Battalion Commanders Conference at Brigade Headquarters. | |
| In the Line, Bn H.Q. S.E. of IGNORANCE CRESCENT | 3.8.17. | 4.30 pm. 9.30 pm. | LEFT CANAL RESERVE CAMP to march for support area at 4.30 pm. Headquarters arrived at Battalion Headquarters at 9.30 pm. S. EAST of IGNORANCE CRESCENT. Companies were distributed as follows. B & C Coys SANCTUARY WOOD I.18.d. A Coy OLD BRITISH FRONT LINE I.24.b. D Coy WELLINGTON CRESCENT I.23.b. The 12th Middlesex were holding the front line with 55th Bde on their right and Loyal North Lancs Regt. (25th Div.) on their left. there were no dugouts in this area owing to the water-logged state of the ground and headquarters occupied one of the Machine Gun emplacements, with 3 ft walls and 3 ft 6" roof, the latter having double iron girders — the concrete being reinforced by 3/4" round iron. These emplacements effectually resisted direct hits by the enemy's 5.9s. Weather fine. | J.B.C.5.8. |
| | 4.8.17. | | B & C Coys having no shelter and having been heavily shelled moved forward 75 yards into SANCTUARY WOOD. C Coy moved to WELLINGTON CRESCENT I.23.b. Weather fine. | |

# WAR DIARY or INTELLIGENCE SUMMARY

Army Form C. 2118.

Map Ref: ZILLEBEKE 28. N.W. x N.E.

| Place | Date | Hour | Summary of Events and Information | Remarks and references to Appendices |
|---|---|---|---|---|
| In the Line. B"HQ.S. S.EAST of IGNORANCE CRESCENT | 5.8.17 |  | Heavy shelling around H.Q.s and WELLINGTON CRESCENT throughout the day and at 9.30 pm a fierce bombardment commenced lasting till 10.45 p.m. Enemy aircraft were active during afternoon. 3 planes flew over our front line. Companies salved a number of Grenades and bombs, cleared up the trenches and buried the dead in their areas. Weather fine. | J.B.c.5.8. |
|  | 6.8.17 |  | Tools were salved along the MENIN Rd (J.13.a.) and dumped J.13.a.9.3. Burial Party sent to bury dead lying along MENIN Rd. west of H.Q.dparters at the tunnel. Enemy artillery active during the morning. Weather fine. Received Brigade Orders relative to attack to be made on INVERNESS COPSE GLENCOURSE WOOD, & South end of WESTHOEK RIDGE — 18th Division on right. 25th Division on left. 18th Division to attack with 55th Brigade on right & 54th Brigade on left. Line of attack for 54th Brigade approx:– J.14.d.5.8 — J.14.b.5.1. – J.8.c.6.3.  54th Brigade to attack with 11th Royal Fusiliers on right – 7th Bedfords on left. The rôle of this Battalion, 6th (S) Bn. Northamptonshire Regt., was as follows:– A & D Coys – Moppers up to assaulting Battalions. A Coy with Royal Fusiliers D Coy with Bedfords. C Coy to garrison & consolidate the strong points. B Coy Carrying Party – to carry from Dump in MENIN Rd. to forward area. |  |
|  | 7.8.17 |  | Shell holes on A.T.N. Track filled in. Tape which had been broken by shell fire relayed. Considerable shelling with 5.9s round Jd Q.r.s Dir: Track x WELLINGTON CRESCENT |  |

Army Form C. 2118.

# WAR DIARY
## or
## INTELLIGENCE SUMMARY.
(Erase heading not required.)

(3)

| Place | Date | Hour | Summary of Events and Information | Remarks and references to Appendices |
|---|---|---|---|---|
| In the Line Bn.H.Q. EAST of IGNORANCE CRESCENT | 7.8.17. continued | 9-30 p.m. | At 9.30 p.m. a big bombardment developed on both sides were severe round IGNORANCE TRENCH and lasted till 11 p.m. About 6 p.m. several enemy planes flew over our lines at a high altitude. | Major ZILLEBEKE J.8.C.5.8.2nd M.C. |
| | 8.8.17 | | Enemy artillery active all day. Our aircraft were in the air all day preventing the enemy planes flying so near our trenches. Attack arranged to take place on the night of 8th/9th, but owing to heavy rain, was postponed. | |
| | 9.8.17. | | Quiet during the day, about 7 p.m. artillery on both sides became more active. Received orders for the attack to take place on the night 9th/10th. | |
| | 10.8.17 | 4.35 a.m. | Zero hour fixed for 4.35 a.m. Weather Fine. All units were formed up at Zero hour with only a small number of casualties. Our barrage which opened at Zero was a wonderful one, and the advance had very little check. On the extreme left as the barrage rolled over the enemy came out 2 manned a Machine Gun in a Strong Point. (map reference J.8.C.2.4.) in JARGON TRENCH N.W GLENCOURSE WOOD. 2 Lewis Gunners of the Moppers up seeing the assaulting party were temporarily held very clever rushed the gun and killed the enemy gunners. The advance then continued on the left without check. The right assaulting Battalion appeared to loose direction somewhat and their advance continued N.E. instead of E. Possibly this change of direction was due to enemy Machine Gun fire. The assaulting Battalion on the right pushed forward to JARGON SUPPORT and occupied that trench from J.14.b.3.1 to J.14.b.3.7. | J.8.C.2.4. |

Army Form C. 2118.

# WAR DIARY
## or
## INTELLIGENCE SUMMARY.
(Erase heading not required.)

| Place | Date | Hour | Summary of Events and Information | Remarks and references to Appendices |
|---|---|---|---|---|
| In the Line | 9.8.17. | | The left of the right assaulting Battalion was held up by 3 Machine Guns behind a barricade at J.14.b.7.5. Some of the Moppers up directly behind the Royal Fusiliers at this point pushed up into JARGON SUPPORT and southern end of GLENCOURSE WOOD. One Lewis Gunner Lance-Corporal Norris did very good work in the southern end of GLENCOURSE WOOD. He succeeded in knocking out two of the enemy's Machine Guns. The right of the assaulting Battalion was seriously held up by the enemy bombing up trenches from FITZCLARENCE FARM and the N.E. and the E. of INVERNESS COPSE. More than half the Moppers up had then joined up and reinforced the front line in JARGON SUPPORT. The enemy then counter attacked very determinedly and drove us back to JARGON DRIVE at Point J.14.a.3.2. on the right to JARGON TRENCH J.8.C.4.2. on the left. The casualties of the mopping up on the right :— 1 Officer killed 3 missing O.R's 5 killed 40 wounded 20 missing The left assaulting Battalion were for a time more successful and pushed thro' GLENCOURSE WOOD, the enemy eventually counter-attacked and drove them back into JARGON TRENCH. The casualties of this Company were :— 2 Officers wounded O.R's 4 killed 26 wounded 3 missing The Moppers up took about 50 prisoners and killed a considerable number of the enemy. Total Casualties. Officers killed 1 O.R's killed 27. wounded 6 wounded 123. missing 3 missing 26. | J.14.b.7.5. J.14.a.3.2 and J.8.C.4.2 Map Ref. ZILLEBEKE 28 N.W. |

Army Form C. 2118.

# WAR DIARY
## or
## INTELLIGENCE SUMMARY.
(Erase heading not required.)

| Place | Date | Hour | Summary of Events and Information | Remarks and references to Appendices |
|---|---|---|---|---|
| CHATEAU WOOD In the Line | 10.8.17. | 1-40am | Headquarters left CHATEAU WOOD 1-40 a.m. for WELLINGTON CRESCENT 1.23.B and left WELLINGTON CRESCENT at 7 a.m. for RITZ STREET | 2.11.B.N.W. 1.23.B.N.W. 1.23.a |
| | | 7 am | Artillery on both sides was fairly active during the day and aerial activity very marked - one of our airmen riddling an enemy plane with tracer bullets and brought it down in flames. | |
| | | 8.30 pm | Headquarters left RITZ at 8.30 p.m and arrived CHATEAU SEGARD at 11 p.m. | Belgium Sheet H.33a N.W. H.30.a. |
| | | | 53rd Brigade relieved 57th Brigade in the line. | |
| CHATEAU SEGARD H.30.a. | 11.8.17. | 5. am | The battalion reached CHATEAU SEGARD 5 a.m. H.30.a. Weather Fair. | |
| | | | The battalion left CHATEAU SEGARD at 2.45 p.m and went to New DICKEBUSCHE CAMP. H.33.a. | H.33.a. |
| New Dicke- busche Camp H.33.a. | 12.8.17 | 8.45 am. | Left New DICKEBUSCHE Camp at 8.45 a.m and marched to HOOGRAAF where the battalion enbussed for STEEN- VOORDE. Billets N.E. of STEEN- VOORDE. | Belgium + Part of France No 27. K22.b.2.8. |
| N.E. of STEENVOORDE K22.b.2.8 | 13.8.17. | | Physical Training ½ hour, remainder of day devoted to cleaning up & haircutting | for H.Q.S. |
| | 4.8.17. | | Physical Training ½ hour. Company drill 1 hour. Reorganisation of Companies | |
| | 15.8.17 | 5 am. | Left billets N.E. of STEENVOORDE (5am) arrived at ABEELE 6.15 a.m. entrained and arrived ARNEKE at 12.15 p.m. Marched to billets at HOOG HUYS arrived 2-10 p.m. | |
| Billets at Wt. HOOG HUYS | | 2-10pm | Hd Qrs G.30.b.30.45. A Co G.30.a.8.8. B Co G.30.c.1.6. C Co H.32.a.8.9. D Co H.25.c.8.7. | |

Army Form C. 2118.

# WAR DIARY
## or
## INTELLIGENCE SUMMARY

(Erase heading not required.)

(6)

| Place | Date | Hour | Summary of Events and Information | Remarks and references to Appendices |
|---|---|---|---|---|
| Billets at W. HOOG HUYS | 16.8.17. | | Physical training. Rifle & Gas Helmet inspection, Musketry & Bayonet Fighting. Instruction in Guard mounting duties for all Sergeants by R.S.M. Weather fine. | |
| | 17.8.17 | | Bathing & change of clothes. Organisation and cleaning of rifles, equipment &c. Sgt Bumstead Physical Training Instructor reported & was at the disposal of the Battalion for 4 days. Took all Sgts, Lance-Corporals and 3 Corporal's per Coy. Guard mounting duties for Junior Officers & all Corporals. Draft arrived (7 O.R) | |
| | 18.8.17 | | Inspection by the Commanding Officer. Physical Training, Coy and Close order drill, Musketry and Bayonet Fighting. Junior Officers, Sgts & Cpls under Sgt Bumstead. Guard mounting duties for Lance Corporals under R.S.M. Companies fired on Range at EPERLECQUES | |
| | 19.8.17 | | Working Party. 60 men on range at BOIS DE HAM. (N.W. of H in HEEBERG) | Maps ref HAZEBROOK 5a |
| | 20.8.17 | | Physical training. A and C Companies Wiring Instruction. B and D Coys - Guard duties Company and Close Order drill, Bayonet Fighting. Bombing under bombing officer. Communication drill for all Sergeants. | |
| | 21.8.17 | | Physical training. A Company - Guard mounting. Saluting, Musketry & Bayonet Fighting. B and D Coys. Wiring Instruction. Guard duties & Bayonet fighting. C Company - Judging distance. Fire Orders Bayonet Fighting. | |

# WAR DIARY or INTELLIGENCE SUMMARY

Army Form C. 2118.

| Place | Date | Hour | Summary of Events and Information | Remarks and references to Appendices |
|---|---|---|---|---|
| Billets at Wg HOOG-HUYS. | 22.8.17 | | Physical training. Box Respirators tested by Div. Gas N.C.O. | |
| | 23.8.17 | | A & B Companies inspected by Brigade Armourer Sergeant. A Coy fired on Brigade Rifle Range at BOIS de HAM during the morning. C & D Coys rifles examined by Armourer Sergeant. C Coy Bombers under bombing officer. Remainder of C Coy - Guard mounting duties, Musketry, Bayonet fighting. B & D Coys Physical training, Judging distance, Fire Orders, Bayonet Fighting. | |
| | 24.8.17 | | Physical training. Company and Close Order drill. Musketry & Bayonet Fighting. Battalion Inspection by Corps Commander. | |
| | 25.8.17 | | Church Parade - 9.45 am. | |
| | 26.8.17 | | | |
| | 27.8.17 | | Firing on Range at BOIS D'HAM by B Company and 2 Sections and best shots of other Companies. C Company Bombers under 2nd Lt Dunstan - Remainder of Company Physical training, Musketry & Bayonet Fighting. A & D Companies - Physical training, Wiring, Musketry & Bayonet Fighting & Judging distance. | |
| | 28.8.17 | | Draft 72 arrived. Bathing. Organisation. Physical training. Draft 18 OR arrived. Firing by sections and men entered for Brigade Competition. | |
| | 29.8.17 | | Physical training. Wiring Practice. Musketry, Visual training. Close and Extended Order drill. Bayonet fighting. Draft 9 OR arrived. | |

Army Form C. 2118.

# WAR DIARY
## or
## INTELLIGENCE SUMMARY

(Erase heading not required.)

(8)

| Place | Date | Hour | Summary of Events and Information | Remarks and references to Appendices |
|---|---|---|---|---|
| Billets at HOOG. HUYS | 30.8.19. | | Firing by best shots and picked Sections on Range at BOIS D'HAM. Physical training. Extended Order drill by signals. Musketry and Bayonet Fighting | |
| | 31.8.19. | | Physical training. Attack practice according to new formation. Musketry. Firing on Range at BOIS D'HAM. by picked shots. | |

R. Turner
Lieut - Colonel.
Comndg: 6t (S) Bn. Northamptonshire Regt.

# OPERATION ORDERS
## BY
### Lieut-Colonel R. Turner D.S.O.,
### Commanding 6th.(S)Bn.Northamptonshire Regiment.

Copy No. 1

7-8-17.

The 11 Corps will capture, at an early date, INVERNESS COPSE, GLENCORSE WOOD and the southern end of the WESTHOEK RIDGE.

"Z" Day and Zero Hour will be notified later.

The attack will be carried out by the 18th Division on the right, and the 25th Division on the left.

The 18th Division will attack with the 55th Brigade on the right and the 54th Brigade on the left. The 7th Brigade will attack on the left of the 54th Brigade.

The 54th Brigade will attack on a two Battalion, and the 55th Brigade on a one Battalion, front. Boundaries between Brigades and Battalions are shewn on attached map, Appendix "A".

The objective is the YELLOW LINE on Appendix "A". For the 54th Brigade it runs approximately J.14.d.5.8. - J.14.b.5.1. - J.14.b.4.5. - J.14.b.2.9. - J.8.c.6.3.

The 54th Brigade will attack with the 11th Royal Fusiliers on the right and the 7th Bedfordshire Regiment on the left. The 6th Northamptonshire Regiment will attach one Company to each of the two assaulting Battalions for "Mopping-up", one Company for carrying and one for garrisoning and consolidating Strong Points. Boundaries between Battalions are marked in black on Appendix "A".

"A" and "D" Companies ("Moppers-up") will be attached to the 11th Royal Fusiliers and 7th Bedfordshire Regiment respectively.

"C" Company will garrison the Strong Points.

"B" Company will furnish the carrying parties.

The two Companies of the 6th Northamptonshire Regiment to be used for "Mopping-up", will be attached, one Company to each assaulting Battalion some hours before Zero Hour so that these Companies come under the direct command of the Assaulting Battalions before forming up commences. Officers Commanding Assaulting Battalions will issue orders direct to the "Mopping-up" Companies both as regards forming up and objectives.

The "Mopping-up" parties will on no account proceed East of the unamed trench running parallel to and just E. of JARGON TRENCH. There are strong dugouts on the line of advance; these must all be cleared and sentries left over them.

"C" Company will be used for garrisoning and consolidating Strong Points 3, 4, 5, 6, 7, shewn on map Appendix "A". Nos. 3 and 4 will each be garrisoned by two sections, Nos. 5, 6 and 7 each by a platoon.

This Company will be assembled at Zero ∓ 1 hour 30 minutes in the trenches round J.13.a.9.4. They will move forward by bounds at Zero Hour complete with their attached Machine Guns, the first bound being to line CLAPHAM JUNCTION - SURBITON VILLAS - JARGON SWITCH. They will then feel their way forward and commence consolidation of their Strong Points immediately the ground on which they are situated has been captured.

"B" Company will be employed in moving the dump at present situated at J.13.a.9.3. to the forward position J.14.a.8.4. At Zero Hour it will be assembled in JACKDAW AVENUE. The O.C.Carrying party will be at the Headquarters of the two Assaulting Battalions. As soon as the situation is favourable he will move his Company forward to J.13.a.9.3., the Headquarters of the assaulting Battalions, and begin to move forward the dump.

The O.C., 54th Machine Gun Company, will detail one gun for each of the Strong Points 3 and 6 and these guns will move forward with the Strong Point garrisons. Strong Points 4, 5 and 7 will, after the attack, be filled by the Vickers Guns sent forward with the assaulting Battalions; Strong Points 4 and 5 by the 7th Bedfordshire Regt., and Strong Point 7 by one of the guns with the 11th Royal Fusiliers.

On X/Y Night Companies will be in the trenches they at present occupy.

The Signal for the advance will be the opening of the Shrapnel Barrage, when bayonets will be fixed.

EQUIPMENT, S.A.A., GRENADES & TOOLS.

Each man of the "Mopping-up" Companies will carry 5 Bombs - 50% No.5. and 50% No.23.   Two sandbags per man.

"B" Company will not require bombs, they will carry 120 rounds S.A.A.

"C" Company will be equipped as follows:-

Riflemen............170 rounds S.A.A.
Bombers.............120 rounds S.A.A. 5 Mills No.5.
Rifle Grenadiers....120 rounds S.A.A. 5 Mills No.23.
Lewis Gunners....... 50 rounds S.A.A.
Sandbags............  3 per man.

Runners etc., will carry their usual complement.

Men must carry rations for one day plus one iron ration.

Steel Helmets must be covered or mudded, so as to ensure that they do not shine in the moonlight.


(sd)  B.C.Gillott, 2nd.Lieut: and Actg:Adjt.,
        6th.(S)Bn.Northamptonshire Regiment.

Issued at.......... .m.

Copies to:-
    No.1. Commanding Officer
    No.2. O.C. "A" Company
    No.3. O.C. "B" Company
    No.4. O.C. "C" Company
    No.5. O.C. "D" Company
    No.6. Office Copy.

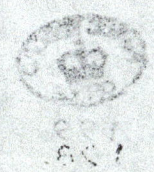

**Army Form C. 2118.**

# WAR DIARY
## or
## INTELLIGENCE SUMMARY

*(Erase heading not required.)*

6th Northants.

WO 27

| Place | Date | Hour | Summary of Events and Information | Remarks and references to Appendices |
|---|---|---|---|---|
| | | | Map Ref: Headquarters: I.2.a.2.2. Belgium and France Sheet 27. | |
| Billets at HOOG-HUYS Hd Qrs. (G30.b.30.45.) | 1.9.17. | | Seaside Outing. | |
| | 2.9.17. | 10 a.m. | Church Parade. Brigade Boxing Comptn in afternoon. | |
| | 3.9.17. | 12-45 p.m. | Battalion left billets at HOOG HUYS at 12-45 p.m. arrived at billets N.E. of ARNEKE at 4. p.m. | |
| Billets N.E. of ARNEKE. | 4.9.17. | | Practice of attack formation. Musketry. Bayonet fighting under Staff-Sergeant. Divisional Gymkhana in afternoon. | |
| | 5.9.17. | | Divisional Boxing Tournament | |
| | 6.9.17. | 10 a.m. | Brigade Rifle Competition at EPERLECQUES. Our section teams 1st first, 1 second Draft of "C" & "D" Coys paraded at Battalion Headquarters at 10 a.m under R.S.M. | |
| | 7.9.17. | | Intensive digging was carried out by A & B Companies. Remainder of C & D Companies - Musketry Instruction &. Physical Training. Draft of A & B Companies paraded at Battalion Headquarters under the R.S.M. During the morning C & D Companies - Intensive digging. Remainder of Companies - Musketry, Saluting drill &. | |
| | 8.9.17. | | Firing on range at EPERLECQUES by Companies. | |
| | 9.9.17. | 10.30 a.m. | Church Parade 10.30 a.m. Attack Practice. | |
| | 10.9.17. | | | |
| | 11.9.17. | | 100 men per Company firing on range at EPERLECQUES Remainder :- General training. | |

Army Form C. 2118.

# WAR DIARY
## or
## INTELLIGENCE SUMMARY

2.

*(Erase heading not required.)*

Instructions regarding War Diaries and Intelligence Summaries are contained in F.S. Regs., Part II. and the Staff Manual respectively. Title Pages will be prepared in manuscript.

| Place | Date | Hour | Summary of Events and Information | Remarks and references to Appendices |
|---|---|---|---|---|
| Billets N.E. of ARNEKE | 12.9.17. | | A & B Companies Mopping up parties for attack practice by 7th Bedfords. C & D " bathing. | Map. Ref: Headquarters. I.2.a.2.2. |
| | 13.9.17. | | P.H. Helmets inspected by Divisional Gas N.C.O. Scouts commenced training. | |
| | 14.9.17 | | Practice of attack and consolidation of a position. 2 Companies of 12th Middlesex as 'Moppers up'. Route March. | |
| | 15.9.17 | | Church Parade 10-45 a.m. | |
| | 16.9.17. | | Physical Training. Judging distance. Siting of ground for line of defence. Bayonet Fighting. | |
| | 17.9.17. | | Physical Training. Close Order drill. Practice in taking up irregular line. B & C Companies acting as marked enemy for attack practice by Royal Fusiliers. | |
| | 18.9.17. | | A & D Companies Bayonet Fighting under Staff-Sergeant Bumstead and Musketry. | |
| | 19.9.17 | 3 p.m | Wiring demonstration by Officer of 80th Field Coy. R.E. Brigade attack at dawn. B & C Companies attached to 12th Middlesex as moppers-up. A & D Companies represented the enemy and delivered a counter attack. The attack commenced at 6 a.m. The practice completed by 7-30 a.m. Companies bathed at ARNEKE. | |
| | 20.9.17 | | Route March. Kit & foot inspection. | |
| | 21.9.17 | | Left billets - entrained at ARNEKE at 9 a.m. arrived HOPOUTRE 12.30 p.m. | F.27.a.4.0 (sheet 27) |
| | 22.9.17 | | Marched to camp (St JAN der BIEZEN area) Tunnelling Camp | |

Army Form C. 2118.

# WAR DIARY
## or
## INTELLIGENCE SUMMARY.
*(Erase heading not required.)*

**Remarks and references to Appendices:** Map Ref. F.27.a & C (Sheet 27)

| Place | Date | Hour | Summary of Events and Information |
|---|---|---|---|
| Tunnelling Camp. F.27.a &C Sheet 27 | 23.9.17 | | Church Parade 10.30 a.m. |
| | 24.9.17 | | Physical training. Inspection of B & C Companies, by platoons, by Commanding Officer. Squad drill, Musketry & Bayonet Fighting. 4 Days Course for Coy Commanders and Senior Officers at XVIII Corps School commenced. |
| | 25.9.17 | | Physical Training. A Company - Practice in capture of strong points under Bombing Officer in conjunction with riflemen. B & C Companies - Wiring practice, Squad drill & Musketry. D Company - Consolidation of a position. Intensive digging. (This was previous to Brigade order prohibiting digging in the area) Musketry Lecture by the Commanding Officer at 2.15 p.m. |
| | 26.9.17 | | Physical training. B Company - Bombing under Bombing Officer. A & D Companies - Wiring, Squad Drill and Musketry. C Company - Instruction in entrenching, taping out and consolidation of trenches. |
| | 27.9.17 | | Physical Training. C Company - Bombing Instruction. A Company - Entrenching and Consolidation. B & D Companies - Wiring instruction, Squad Drill and Musketry. A & D Companies - Bathing in the afternoon. |

Army Form C. 2118.

# WAR DIARY
## or
## INTELLIGENCE SUMMARY.
(Erase heading not required.)

| Place | Date | Hour | Summary of Events and Information | Remarks and references to Appendices |
|---|---|---|---|---|
| Tunnelling Camp F.27.a & c Sheet 27 | 28.9.17 | | Physical Training – Bombing Instruction<br>D Company – Entrenching and Consolidation.<br>B Company – Entrenching and Consolidation.<br>A & C Companies – Wiring instruction, Musketry and Squad Drill.<br>B & C Companies – Bathing in the afternoon. | Map Ref:- F.27. a & c (Sheet 27) |
| | 29.9.17 | | Physical Training<br>Battalion parade and Drill.<br>General Training | |
| | 30.9.17 | | Church Parade<br>Kit inspection. | |

R. Turner
Lieut-Colonel,
OFFICER COMMANDING
5th Bn. NORTHAMPTONSHIRE REGT.

# WAR DIARY or INTELLIGENCE SUMMARY

Army Form C. 2118.

54/18 6 North'n / 2 / 3

Vol 28

F 27. a 80. Sheet 27. BELGIUM.

| Place | Date | Hour | Summary of Events and Information | Remarks and references to Appendices |
|---|---|---|---|---|
| TUNNELLING CAMP | 1.10.17 | | Attack Practice | |
| | 2.10.17 | | Physical Training. Intensive Digging. Musketry. Bayonet Fighting. | |
| | 3.10.17 | | Attack Practice. Erecting Bayonet Fighting Course. | |
| | 4.10.17 | | A. B. & D Companies. Bathing. | |
| | 5.10.17 | | C Company. Bayonet Fighting Course. | |
| | 6.10.17 | | A & D Companies. Range. | |
| | 7.10.17 | | B Company. Outpost Duty. | |
| | 8.10.17 | | Attack Practice. Lectures and Explanation of Attack. | |
| | 9.10.17 | | Very Wet. Completion of Bayonet Fighting Course. | |
| | 10.10.17 | | Church Parade. 2 Companies. Lecture to men. | |
| | 11.10.17 | | Route March. A Company 160 Strong left to carry XVIII Corps. Sir Henry Arbit- | |
| | 12.10.17 | | Physical Training. Route March. Attack Practice. curtailed owing to rain. | |
| | 13.10.17 | | B. C. D. Companies. Attack Practice. | |
| | 14.10.17 | | B & D Companies :- Bathing. | |
| | 15.10.17 | | A & C Companies :- Musketry Bayonet Fighting | |
| | 16.10.17 | | Lectures. Very Wet. Lectures and Instructions Bayonet Fighting | |
| | | | Physical Training. | |
| CANAL BANK | | | Vacated Camp. Battalion embussed at 10-40 am arrived CANAL BANK 1-30 p.m. | |

# WAR DIARY
## or
## INTELLIGENCE SUMMARY

*(Erase heading not required.)*

Army Form C. 2118.

| Place | Date | Hour | Summary of Events and Information | Remarks and references to Appendices |
|---|---|---|---|---|
| | 17.10.17 | | Reconnoitring of Route by Commanding Officer and Company Commanders. Physical Training. | St. JULIEN 28. N.W. C 25.a. |
| POELCAPELLE | 18.10.17 | | **Operations in Poelcapelle** | |
| | | 3-0 pm | The Battalion relieved the 12th Bn Middlesex Regt in the front line at POELCAPELLE | |
| | | 7.30 pm | 2nd Lt. CANAL BANK. Bn Hdqrs reached their Headquarters at V.19. a. 6.2. Disposition of Companies:– | |
| | | | 'B' & 'C' Coys first line. 'B' on right. 'C' on left. 'D' Coy in support. 'A' Coy in reserve. | |
| | | | Map Refs:– 'B' Coys strong posts extending from V.19. b.6.2 to V.19. b.5.4. (Dispositions) | |
| | | 5.50 pm | Posts were pushed forward at 5.50 pm and extended from the Church on the right to point V.19. b.7.8. on the left. At 5 am following morning posts were withdrawn West of the line running N & S through the Church. During the day, 'C' Coys line extended from V.19. b.25.50 to V.19. 10.90. At night from V.19. b.7.9 to V.13. d. 95.45. | |
| | | | D Company:– 3 Platoons in concrete emplacements on road, near point V.19. b.32 and 1 Platoon V.19. d.2.4. | |
| | | | A Company:– at PHEASANT FARM. U.30. b.1.6 | |

Army Form C. 2118.

# WAR DIARY
## or
## INTELLIGENCE SUMMARY
(Erase heading not required.)

3

St JULIEN 28. N.W

| Place | Date | Hour | Summary of Events and Information | Remarks and references to Appendices |
|---|---|---|---|---|
| POELCAPELLE | 18-10-17 | | The 7th Bedfords were on the right of the Battalion, and the 22nd Northumberland Fusiliers on the left. Time – Wind Slight – Southerly. Intermittent Shelling commenced over the front at 8pm and continued throughout the night. Calibre :- 4.2's and 5.9's from WESTROOSBEKE | |
| | 19-10-17 | 5 a.m. | Our Artillery opened in fair strength and continued till 6 a.m. Enemy replied shelling strongly round B. Hdqrs :- along Front Line and back to PHEASANT FARM. Machine Gun and Rifle Fire :- Nil Work: Consolidation of trenches and shell holes. Between 9-20 a.m. and 9-50 a.m. 10 to 12 rounds of our Whizz Bangs fell short at about V.13.d. 7.2 and V.19.b. Cent. 9 Shots (18 Pounders) burst 75 yds W. of Bn Hdqrs. | |
| | | 12-30p. | Our Artillery shelled MUNIER HOUSE and NOBLES FARM between 2pm and 3pm. The morning bombardment at 5-20 a.m. did not take place on our sector. Intermittent Shelling, with 4.2's and 5.9's by Enemy from 2pm to 3pm. | |

Army Form C. 2118.

# WAR DIARY
## or
## INTELLIGENCE SUMMARY
(Erase heading not required.)

St JULIEN 28 N.W

| Place | Date | Hour | Summary of Events and Information | Remarks and references to Appendices |
|---|---|---|---|---|
| POELCAPELLE | 29.10.17 | 9 pm<br>11 pm | Unusually quiet during remainder of day.<br>Shelling of the Batteries in rear commenced.<br>Intense shelling commenced and continued throughout the night reaching its maximum intensity at 4 am. Calibre:- Whizz Bangs 4·2's and 5·9's from direction of TIENDENBERG and WESTROOSEBEKE.<br>Enemy Aircraft & Bock Planes flew over our line at 6·20 am.<br>A few rounds of M.G. fire were directed against B" Hdqrs from about V.14 C.2.4. about 9 p.m.<br>3 Platoons of 'A' Company took over line from 22nd Northumberland Fusiliers from V14 e.00.00 to V.14.a.10.05.<br>Gas was discharged by us by T.M.s from 10 pm to 10·15 pm. on to the area east of and around the BREWERY.<br>Enemy put a few gas shells over about 4 am.<br>Patrol of 1 N.C.O. and 3 men went out at 7·30pm from V.19 t.8.c. proceeded 100 yards east, when M.G's and Very Lights were fired from emplacement at V.20.a.80.86.<br>Three men were seen to emerge on Working Party which sounded to be working, were heard from V.20.a.38. |  |

**Army Form C. 2118.**

# WAR DIARY
## or
## INTELLIGENCE SUMMARY

*(Erase heading not required.)*

Remarks and references to Appendices: St JULIEN 28 N.W.

| Place | Date | Hour | Summary of Events and Information |
|---|---|---|---|
| POELCAPELLE | 19.10.17 | | A Patrol of 1 Sergt and 6 men went out from point V.19.b.9.6 at 6-30 pm. Concrete Emplacement at V.19.b.95.65 found to be occupied. |
| | 20.10.17 | | Fair generally. - A few showers - Wind S.W. Intermittent shelling by Enemy during the morning. Increasing during the afternoon. A Wiring Being entered V.9 a.y.o at about 5 pm. Wind S.W. |
| | | 6 pm | Battalion relieved by Queens Regt. Relief completed by 7 pm. Marched to IRISH FARM. Entrained: - Arrived W. of POPERINGHE 11 am. Marched to TUNNELLING CAMP. |
| TUNNELLING CAMP | 21.10.17 | | Men Bathed: - Cleaning of rifles and equipment. |
| | 22.10.17 | 4 pm | Received orders to move to forward area as Counter-Attack Battalion. |
| | 23.10.17 | | Battalion entrained 9-15 am, reached CANAL BANK 11 am. Marched to CANE TRENCH. C.9.a. (St JULIEN MAP) At a conference between the Brigadier and the Commanding Officer it was decided that owing to limited accommodation further forward the Battalion should remain in CANE TRENCH. |
| DIRTY BUCKET CAMP | 24.10.17 | 2 pm | The Battalion left CANE TRENCH. Entrained CANAL BANK 5 pm. arrived DIRTY BUCKET CAMP A.24.d (Sheet 28 N.W.) 6-30 pm. |
| | 25.10.17 | | Re-organisation and Cleaning |

Army Form C. 2118.

# WAR DIARY
## or
## INTELLIGENCE SUMMARY

(Erase heading not required.)

Instructions regarding War Diaries and Intelligence Summaries are contained in F. S. Regs., Part II. and the Staff Manual respectively. Title Pages will be prepared in manuscript.

6

MAP REF.
Sheet 27 Belgium & France

| Place | Date | Hour | Summary of Events and Information | Remarks and references to Appendices |
|---|---|---|---|---|
| Billets N.E. of PROVEN | 26-10-17 | | Physical Training. Wet Day. | |
| | 27-10-17 | | Physical Training. Route March. Bathing | |
| | 28-10-17 | | Church Parade. | |
| | 29-10-17 | 10-20am | Left DIRTY BUCKET CAMP reached PADDINGTON CAMP N.E. of PROVEN | F.36 (Sheet 27, Belg. & France) |
| | 30-10-17 | | Physical Training. Cleaning up and re-arrangement of camp. | |
| | 31-10-17 | | Physical Training. Musketry. Firing on Range. | |

R. Turner
Lieut-Colonel
Commanding 6th (S) Bn Northamptonshire Regt

Army Form C. 2118.

WAR DIARY
or
INTELLIGENCE SUMMARY.

6/Northants

(Erase heading not required.)

| Place | Date 1917 | Hour | Summary of Events and Information | Remarks and references to Appendices |
|---|---|---|---|---|
| | | | | Map ref. Sheet 27 Belgium & France 28 N.W. |
| PADDINGTON CAMP N.E. of PROVEN F.3.b | Nov 1 | | Physical Training - Musketry - Route March | |
| | 2 | | Cleaning up and re-arrangement of Camp. | |
| | 3 | | P.T. Musketry - General Training. | |
| | 4 | | do | |
| | 5 | | Church Parade. | |
| | | | Battn. evacuated Camp. Marched to Proven Stn: entrained - detrained ONDANK - marched to a.d.a | |
| DYKES CAMP A.4.b. | | 12.15 p.m. | Battn. arrived Dykes Camp. 12.15 p.m. | |
| | 6 | | P.T. Improvement of Camp - Bathing. | |
| | 7 | | P.T. Musketry. Genl. Training - Lecture | |
| | 8 | | P.T. General Training | |
| | 9 | 6.45 | 9 Offrs and 369 O.Rs to Sutton Camp east of PROVEN | |
| | | | Battn left Camp - entrained ONDANK - arrd POPERINGHE 10.45 am | |
| | 10 | | Battn took over line from 8th Norfolks. | |

Army Form C. 2118.

# WAR DIARY
## or
## INTELLIGENCE SUMMARY.
*(Erase heading not required.)*

Instructions regarding War Diaries and Intelligence Summaries are contained in F. S. Regs., Part II. and the Staff Manual respectively. Title pages will be prepared in manuscript.

| Place | Date | Hour | Summary of Events and Information | Remarks and references to Appendices |
|---|---|---|---|---|
| In the LINE. EGYPT HOUSE U.6.d.a.o. | Nov 10 1917 | 3.30 p.m. | Left BOESINGHE – Bn Hqrs reached Egypt House 6 p.m. Our line extended from TURENNE CROSSING (V.l.d.2.3.) inclusive on the right to COROMBO HOUSE V.l.b.4.3 exclusive on the left. Front line held by a series of strong posts. Distribution of Coy:– A on right (Hqrs V.l.d.a.3) D on the left (Hqrs V.l.d. LES CHEMINS crossroads. V.a.oo.50.) B in close support. Hqrs with A Coy. C Coy in reserve – 3 platoons at VEE BEND. V.ll.d.2.7. Coy Hqrs and 1 platoon PASCAL FARM. V.17.e.6.2. 11th Royal Fusiliers were on my left. 17th Manchesters on right of Brigade. French on left. Night quiet. Work on posts. Very wet mid day to mid night. Front posts. Consisting of shell holes flooded. Little artillery activity. Considerable intermittent M.G. fire. Enemy aeroplanes active during the day. Night spent in consolidating shell holes. Missing post at V.6.a.75.90. | Map ref 20.S.W.4. |

| | | | Remarks and references to Appendices |
|---|---|---|---|
| Place | Date 1917 | Hour | |
| In the line Egypt House V.C.4.4.0 | Nov 11 | 6.30 pm | Map ref 30.S.W.4 |

Patrol 1 O/R 10 O.R's started from V.6.6.3 - to V.6.6.3.6. to V.6 cent. Figures seen moving to the north. Wire to V.6.6.6.6. Very lights were put up, and M.G. observed fire at V.6.6.6.6. Faint wind. Slight NW.

12 — Morning quiet. Artillery active from 3.30 pm to 4 pm. Front line and Bn Hqrs shelled. Enemy aeroplanes flew over our lines at 6 am - at 10-11 am and 5 pm.

At night. Consolidation of ground at CAIRO HOUSE. Improvement of posts. Guide lines fixed on left sector.

6.30 pm — Patrol went out from V.6.6.7.1. moved north. Wire found south side of road. In good condition. Proceeded to V.6.6.9.4. Sounds of working party estimated 20 strong near V.6.11.5. Held up 50 yds further not up by M.G. fire. Gun near V.6.11.a.3.5. No signs of huts of were seen. Fine. Wind slight N.W.

# WAR DIARY
## INTELLIGENCE SUMMARY

Army Form C. 2118.

| Place | Date 1917 | Hour | Summary of Events and Information | Remarks and references to Appendices |
|---|---|---|---|---|
| In the line. | Nov 13 | | Enemy Artillery active from 11 a.m to 1 p.m. and 2.30-5 p.m. Front line-Battn Hqrs- CHEMINS shelled. | St JULIEN M.40 28 N.W |
| EGYPT HOUSE V.C.4.a.o. | | | Enemy aircraft active during the day. Battn relieved by 13th MIDDLESEX- relief completed by 10.30 p.m | |
| | | 10.30 pm | Marched via HUNTERS St. to CANAL CAMP BRASINGHE. (Map ref B.5.d.) Total casualties sustained. Killed 1, Sgt. Wounded 3 O/R  { Looking Between Killed 8 O/Rs and Casua. 9.10 O.R Killed 8 O/Rs } Missing O.R. 9 | |
| CANAL CAMP B.5.d | 14 | | Fine. Cleaning of men and Camp- 150 O/R's brought from SUTTON CAMP a similar number being returned- Men at 3 pm 1 Coy were moved forward to TWISDEN DRIFT in case of need as a counter attack Coy. Were not required and returned at 9 pm- Working Parties found- 60 men to carrying from R.E dumps. | |
| | 15 | | Clearing. Working Parties 60 men 30 carrying |  |

Army Form C. 2118.

# WAR DIARY
## or
## INTELLIGENCE SUMMARY.
(Erase heading not required.)

Remarks and references to Appendices: Map ref: 28.N.W. / Map ref 20. S.W. 4

| Place | Date 1917 | Hour | Summary of Events and Information |
|---|---|---|---|
| DYKES CAMP. A.H.G. | Nov 17 | | Bn. Vacated Camp. Entrained at POPERINGHE 11.30am arrived DYKES CAMP. 12 noon. Details arrived at 3.0pm. 1 Platoon of ea. Coy detailed for loading at ONDANK. |
| | 18 | | Cleaning and improvement of Camp. 1 Coy in Bayonet Fighting Course. |
| | 19 | | P.T. General Training. Improvement of Camp. Construction of Bayonet fighting Course. P.T. |
| | 20 | | do do |
| | 21 | | do do |
| | 22 | | Bn. left DYKES CAMP at 12-15pm. Entrained at ONDANK arrived at BOESINGHE at 1-30pm. |
| | | 3-45pm | left BOESINGHE. Went up line via RAILWAY STREET. Bn H.Q reached EGYPT HOUSE at 7pm. Relieved 8th NORFOLKS in sector of line extending from TURENNE CROSSING (V.I.d.2.3) |

**Army Form C. 2118.**

# WAR DIARY
## or
## INTELLIGENCE SUMMARY.
*(Erase heading not required.)*

Instructions regarding War Diaries and Intelligence Summaries are contained in F.S. Regs., Part II. and the Staff Manual respectively. Title pages will be prepared in manuscript.

Map Ref. SCHAAP-BALIE. EDITION. 2.

| Place | Date 1917 | Hour | Summary of Events and Information | Remarks and references to Appendices |
|---|---|---|---|---|
| In the line EGYPT HOUSE U.6.d.4.0. | Nov. 22 | | inclusive on the night to COLOMBO HOUSE (V.6.c.1.3) inclusive on the left. Front line held by a series of posts. Distribution of Coys:- C Coy on the right (H.Qrs V.6.d.9.3.) B Coy on the left. H.Qrs LES CHEMINS CROSS ROADS (N.a.00.50.) A Coy in close support (U.6.c.8.3. & U.6.c.4.4.) H.Qr with C Coy D Coy in reserve at PASCAL FARM. V.12.c.5.2. 11th Royal Fusiliers were on our left. The LINCOLNS (51st BDE) were on our Right. Night was quiet. Making they standing in posts. Reserve Coy reconnoitred RAILWAY STREET and tunnel some dead. | |
| | | 11.30pm | Patrol 1 N.C.O. 3 men started from V.I.C.7.5, went along S. side of ditch running E to V.I.C. 95.50. Then along E side of track going N. as far as V.I.C. 9.7. They found road Boche posts about V.I.C. 9.2.90. Coughing was heard, and about 10 Boxxxx heads were seen. A Very light was fired from V.I.C.8.9. Patrol 3. O.R. went from V.I.C.0.7. for 30 yards along road running N.E. Patrol was fired on by a M.Gun from a point about V.I.C. 25.90. Weather generally fine. Fairly low Intermittent shelling all day in vicinity of EGYPT HOUSE En: aeroplanes not active during day | |

23

Army Form C. 2118.

# WAR DIARY
## or
## INTELLIGENCE SUMMARY.
(Erase heading not required.)

Map Ref. SCHAAP-BALIE. ED: 2.

| Place | Date 1917 | Hour | Summary of Events and Information | Remarks and references to Appendices |
|---|---|---|---|---|
| For the time EGYPT HOUSE | Nov 23 | | and fired with their M. Guns into the hoots of our left Coy. During night 23/24 duckboards were taken up and put in hoots. The hoots were covered with tarred paper on low louses pickets. Reserve Coy salvaged R.E. material between VEE BEND and EGYPT also improved accommodation at PASCAL FARM. Owing to moonlight, no patrols went out early part of night. Listening patrols were sent out 1½ hrs before dawn, owing to rumours of the Boche contemplating making an attack on the PASCHENDAELE area. | |
| | 24 | | Morning dull, afternoon fine. Visibility very high. Wind S.W. fresh. Enemy activity shelled EGPT HOUSE during day. Owing to strong wind, no aerial activity took place. | |
| | | 12.M.N. | D Coy relieved B Coy in the left sector without incident. Owing to close proximity of A Coy to C Coy, no Coy relief was considered necessary in the right sector. Listening patrols were sent out. It dw. before dawn. | |
| | 25 | | Weather dull and stormy. Wind. W.S.W strong + blustery. Our artillery were active all day. Enemy artillery shelled EGYPT HOUSE and area around. A hit was made on our left front Coy H.Q. (at N.D. 20. 50.) causing slight damage. H.Q. at Sulphur Coy were transferred to V.6.d.4.4.) | |

Army Form C. 2118.

# WAR DIARY or INTELLIGENCE SUMMARY

(Erase heading not required.)

4th Northants

Map Ref. BELGIUM. SHEET 28. N.W.

| Place | Date 1917 | Hour | Summary of Events and Information | Remarks and references to Appendices |
|---|---|---|---|---|
| In the line | Nov 25 | | B⁰ relieved by 12th MIDDLESEX Regt. Night was fine and moon was up. Relief completed by 2 a.m. B⁰ went out via HUNTER ST. to BABOON CAMP (B.G.C.) Total casualties sustained Killed 2 O.R. Wounded 1 officer 6 O.R. Missing 4 O.R. | |
| EGYPT HOUSE | | | | |
| BABOON CAMP B.G.C. | 26 | | Cleaning of men and camp. Carrying party of 1 officer & 40 O.R. to EGYPT HOUSE. | |
| | 27 | | Improvement of Camp. Carrying parties to EGYPT HOUSE at 4-30 & 6-30 consisting of 1 officer 30 O.R. & 1 officer 40 O.R. to carry R.E. material. At 9 p.m. 1 officer 30 O.R. carried elements of Elephant Shelters to EGYPT HOUSE. | |
| DYKES CAMP | 28 | 12-30 p.m | B⁰ evacuated Camp. Entrained at BOESINGHE to ONDAM arrived at DYKES CAMP at 2-45 p.m. | |
| | 29 | 2 pm | 3 Officers 130 O.R. arrived from "H" Camp under MAJOR ROBERTS. Cleaning of clothing, equipment etc. Foot inspection. Working party of 1 officer 50 O.R. under 92nd R.E. Coy at ONDANK CABARET. | |
| | 30 | | Physical training. Company drill. Musketry. Box respirator drill. Same working party as for 29th. | |

G.F. Mummery Major
Commanding 6th (S) Bn. Northamptonshire Regt.

Army Form C. 2118.

# WAR DIARY
## INTELLIGENCE SUMMARY
(Erase heading not required.)

6th (S) Battalion Northampton[on]shire Regt.

Vol 30

MAP REF:
BELGIUM. SHEET 28. N.W.   SCHAAP-BALIE
                          ED II

| Place | Date 1917 | Hour | Summary of Events and Information |
|---|---|---|---|
| DYKES CAMP | Sept 1 | | The Battn. were allotted the baths at ELVERDINGHE from 10 a.m. to 2 p.m. A working party off 1 off. & 50 men employed at ONDANK STATION under the 92nd Field Coy R.E. |
| | 2 | | B & D Coys were allotted the baths at ELVERDINGHE. Two working parties of 1 off. 36 O.R. & 1 off. & 39 O.R. were employed at ONDANK under 9th F. Coy R.E. |
| | 3 | | "B" Coy were all employed at ONDANK under 92nd F Coy R.E. 1 off. & 52 O.R. worked on "bullet & bayonet" course at DYKES CAMP. Remainder of Battn. were employed in making bomb proof emplacements round the huts. |
| | 4 | | Battn. evacuated DYKES CAMP. Entrained at ONDANK STATION 2 p.m. & detrained at BOESINGHE 2.45 p.m. Proceeded up line via RAILWAY STREET at 8.45 p.m. Battn. relieved the 8th NORFOLK REGT in front line. Battn. Right boundary being the BROEMBEEK (inclusive) at V7 d 4 4. Left boundary at U 6 d 2.7. Battn. H.Q. at EGYPT HOUSE. U.6.d.2.00. "D" Coy occupied R. sector of Bn. front with Coy H.Q. at U.6.d.90.35. "A" Coy occupied L sector of Bn. front with Coy H.Q. at U.6.d.25.45. |
| EGYPT HOUSE | | | |

Army Form C. 2118.

# WAR DIARY or INTELLIGENCE SUMMARY.
(Erase heading not required.)

6th (S) Battalion Northampton shire Regt

**MAP REF. SCHAAP BALIE.**

| Place | Date | Hour | Summary of Events and Information | Remarks and references to Appendices |
|---|---|---|---|---|
| In the line | 4/12/17 | | C Coy were in support with Coy H.Q. at U.12.d. 65-95. D Coy were in reserve at PASCAL FARM (U.12.c.5-2). Relief was complete at 2. a.m. Front line was held by a series of posts with 3 platoons of each front Coy in front line & one platoon in support. Support Coy had 2 platoons in & around Pill box at U.6.d. 2545. 1 platoon at V.1.c.3.3. in consolidated shell holes & one platoon on railway at V.7.a.2.5. Reserve Coy had 2 platoons at PASCAL FARM. 1 platoon at V.18.a.55-65 & 1 platoon at U.12.d. 30.00. The 12th R. FUSILIERS were on the "left", the 6th DORSETS 50th BDE. 17th DIV. on the Right. Enemy artillery intermittently shelled EGYPT HOUSE & vicinity. | |
| EGYPT HOUSE | 5/12/17 | 1.35% | One of our aeroplanes brought down by A.A. fire near WATERVILLEBEEK. Weather fine & frosty. Visibility high. Wind fresh S.W. | |
| | | 6 am | Patrols. Object. To locate suspected Boche post at V.1.C.15-80. 2 N.C.Os & 2 men proceeded about 150+ along W side of ANGLE Rd when they heard talking. The post was located at V.1.C.30.90. Patrol returned at 7hrs. | |
| | | 11.00 | Patrol Object. to find out if there were any at V.1.C.99 were held 15+ 3 men proceeded to within 20+ of corner but did not see any of the enemy. 4 dead STAFFORD soldiers were seen in a shell hole near corner. Ground was very badly broken up. Patrol returned 11-40+. | |

Army Form C. 2118.

# WAR DIARY
## or
## INTELLIGENCE SUMMARY.
(Erase heading not required.)

1st (S) Battalion Northumberland Fus.

**MAP REF. SCHAAP-BALIE.**

| Place | Date | Hour | Summary of Events and Information | Remarks and references to Appendices |
|---|---|---|---|---|
| In the line | 5/12/17 | 11pm to 12·15 am | **Patrol.** Object:- to patrol road 200+ to a front V.I. d. 60.45. & observe. 1 N.C.O. & 5 men advanced parallel with road keeping about 30 to the right. They were fired on by a M. Gun firing from about V.I. d. 85. 30. After leading 15 men patrol returned the same route. 6th DORSET REGT on our right were relieved by 14th GLOUCESTER Regt 105 BDE. 35th DIV. The 2 front boys worked on their boats, putting in new duckboards & setting in front of posts. Wired in front of main line of defence. Supply, boy wired in front of posts. Reserve boy carried of wiring materials & other R.E. stores. Artillery generally quiet. Intermittent shelling around EGYPT HOUSE and vicinity of LES 5 CHEMINS. Ground was quite hard due to frost. Wind slight S.W. Weather - fine. Visibility high. |  |
|  |  | 11pm | Wind was contained as for previous night. |  |
| EGYPT HOUSE | 6 | 10pm to 10·40 pm | **Patrol.** Object:- to reach front at V.I.c. 9.5. & observe of enemy had a post between V.I.c. 1.7 & V.I.c. 9.5. 1 Sgt & 2 men proceeded from post V.I.c. 1.7 in a N.E. direction to within 20+ of road leading to COLBERT. CROSS. R[ro]d then turned in easterly direction parallel with road. Patrol was fired on by M.G. from about V.I.C. 3.9. & V.I.C. 40.85. After continuing for about 100+ the ground was too broken up to make further progress. |  |

Army Form C. 2118.

# WAR DIARY
## or
## INTELLIGENCE SUMMARY.
(Erase heading not required.)

**MAP REF.** BELGIUM. SHEET. 28.N.W.
SCHAAP-BALIE.

6th (S) Battalion Northamptonshire Regt.

| Place | Date | Hour | Summary of Events and Information | Remarks and references to Appendices |
|---|---|---|---|---|
| In the line ECYPT HOUSE | 6/12/17 | 10pm | Patrol. Object:- To find out if a Boche post existed at V.I.c.85.95. 1 N.C.O. & 3 men proceeded from post at V.I.c.8.6. on northerly direction. Owing to darkness, observation was difficult, but some of the enemy were seen in the post, but number was not ascertained. Patrol returned by same route at 10-45 p.m. | |
| | 7 | 2-0am | Patrol. Object:- To locate Boche post on N. side of railway. 1 N.C.O. & 3 men proceeded from V.I.d.00.30 in N.E. direction. Railway was badly cut up by shell fire which made progress slow. Boche post was found to be on N. side of railway about V.I.d.45-6.5. Patrol returned by same route at 4-0am. Enemy artillery generally quiet. Intermittent shelling of ECYPT HOUSE & vicinity, also vicinity of LES 5 CHEMINS. Before dawn, guides were sent back to BOESINGHE to meet & arrange about the conducting of the relieving Regt. up the line. Weather: dull. State of ground: soft owing to thaw. Visibility: low. Wind: Great S.W. | |
| | 8 | 3-0am | Battⁿ were relieved in the line by 12th MIDDLESEX Regt, 54th BDE. 18. DIV. Battⁿ marched out the line by platoon. The rendezvous being BOESINGHE RAILHEAD. Entrained at 8-15 am. detrained at ONDANK STATION 8-50 am and proceeded to DYKES CAMP vacated by SUFFOLKS, 5-3rd BDE. 18th DIV. Battⁿ rested remaining part of the day. | |
| DYKES CAMP | | | | |

Army Form C. 2118.

# WAR DIARY
## or
## INTELLIGENCE SUMMARY.

(Erase heading not required.)

6th (S) Battalion (or Bedfordshire Regt)

MAP REF.  BELGUIM. SHEET 28. N.W.

| Place | Date | Hour | Summary of Events and Information | Remarks and references to Appendices |
|---|---|---|---|---|
| DYKES CAMP | 8/12/17 | | Total casualties in the line from night of 6th/7th to night of 7th/8th:- Officers Nil. O.R. Killed 3. Wounded 4. Missing 1. | |
| | 9 | 8am to 5pm | Baths at BOX CAMP allotted to A, B + C Companies. Remainder of day devoted to cleaning of arms, accoutrements and clothing. | |
| | 10 | 8am to 10.30am | "D" Coy + details at transport lines allotted baths at BOX CAMP. Companies carried out organisation + interior economy. | |
| | | 4.30pm | 1 Officer 35 O.R's worked on new transport lines of 9th BEDFORDSHIRE Regt at ONDANK. from 8.45 am to 3.30 pm. A printed paper "GAZETTE DES ARDENNES" dated 8/12/17 was dropped from an aeroplane + fell in a field about A.5.d. It was immediately handed over to 54th BDE HQ. | |
| | 11 | 9am | All N.C.O's paraded under R.S. Major. | |
| | | 9-9.30 | All Coys. P.T. under platoon officers. | |
| | | 12-30 pm | During day all available men making emplacements round huts. "D" Coy supplied 1 Officer 5 O.R's for work on new transport lines. All aviation officers received special physical instruction | |

Army Form C. 2118.

6th (S) Battalion Northumberland Regt

# WAR DIARY
## or
## INTELLIGENCE SUMMARY.
(Erase heading not required.)

| Place | Date | Hour | Summary of Events and Information | Remarks and references to Appendices |
|---|---|---|---|---|
| | | | | MAP. REF. BELGUIM. SHEET 28.N.W.   BELGUIM. SHEET 19.S.E. |
| DYKES CAMP | 12/12/17 | 9-9.30 | Physical training under platoon officers. Examination of N.C.Os. Companies at disposal of Coy Commanders | |
| | 13. | 9-9.30 11- | Physical training. A & D Coy inspected by Commanding Officer. " instruction for available officers | |
| | 14. | 9-9.30 6- 11- | " " B & C Coys inspected by C.O. B'n H.Q. " " All N.C.Os taken in communication drill | |
| | 15. | 9-9.30 | Physical training. Saluting drill. Musketry Kit inspection | |
| | 16. | 11- | Batt" evacuated DYKES CAMP and proceeded by march route to HARINGHE area. Batt" were billeted in huts at BAPAUME CAMP | |
| BAPAUME CAMP | 17 | 9-9.30 am 9.45-11am | All boys physical training under by N.C.Os. Squad drill, close order drill. Musketry & Bayonet fighting. Improvement of camp accommodation | |
| | 18 | 9-1-0. | Physical Training. Section drill under Section Comm'ts. Platoon drill. Musketry & Bayonet fighting. The Commanding Officer expected A & B Coys that they return. | |
| | 19 | 9-1- | Physical Training. Squad drill. Musketry, Squad training in full marching order. | |
| | 20. | 9-1- | Adjustment of equipt, leading marching order. Close order drill. Bath. Route March. | |
| | 21 | 9-1- -4.30 | Physical training. Baths. Route march. Lecture in "Discipline of Warfare + Elephant Commanders" by CAPT. LONG. Officer i/c Haurteu Fourth Army. | |

# WAR DIARY or INTELLIGENCE SUMMARY

Army Form C. 2118.

6th (S) Battalion Northamptonshire Regt.

MAP REF.
BELGUIM and FRANCE.
19. S.E.

| Place | Date | Hour | Summary of Events and Information | Remarks and references to Appendices |
|---|---|---|---|---|
| BAPAUME CAMP | 22/2/17 | 9-1 | Physical Training. Musketry. Sectional drill under section commrs. | |
| | | | Battn (short) Route March. | |
| | 23. | 10-15 | Church Parade. Box Respirators tested during morning. | |
| | 24. | | General Holiday. A & C Coys had their single climax in HARINGHE. B & D Coys had their climax | |
| | 25. | | Church Parade. | |
| | 26. | | Dinner in HARINGHE. General Holiday. | |
| | 27. | 9-1 | Physical Training. "D" Coy on rifle range, A & C Coys communication of shell holes, "D" Coy. Close order drill, extending by section under covering fire, passing fire orders & alteration of sights. Lecture by the Brigadier on "Communications". | |
| | 28. | 2 p | B Coy on rifle range. D Coy close order drill. | |
| | | 9-1 | Physical Training. B Coy on rifle rifles. A Coy adjutants parade. Short route march. D Coy same as for "A" | |
| | 29. | 9-1 | Physical Training. D Coy on rifle range. B & C Coys tested the part of enemy on a Brigade tactical scheme. A Coy covering under supervision of R.E. Officer. HARINGHE. | |
| | 30. | 9.8 Sat. | H.Q., A, B & C Coys were allotted the "Baths" at ROUSBRUGGE. | |
| | | 10 a | Church Parade in school room HARINGHE. | |
| | 31. | 8 a | Batt" inspected by Brigade Commander on Batt" parade ground. | |
| | | 9.30a | Mass formation afternoon inspected in a tactical scheme which took place on large ground. | |

W. Turner Lt Col

1st M[...] 6th Batt. Northamptonshire

6th (S) Battn. NORTHAMPTONSHIRE. REGT

Army Form 2118.
(1)

## WAR DIARY
## or
## INTELLIGENCE SUMMARY.
(Erase heading not required.)

Instructions regarding War Diaries and Intelligence Summaries are contained in F. S. Regs., Part II. and the Staff Manual respectively. Title pages will be prepared in manuscript.

WM 31

| Place | Date 1918 | Hour | Summary of Events and Information | Remarks and references to Appendices |
|---|---|---|---|---|
| BAUPAUME CAMP | Jan 1 | | New Years Day. | HAZEBROUCK |
| HARINGHE | 2 | | A.L. Coy Bren Drill - Bayonet fighting | S.A. 1/10000 |
| H.I.S.O. | | | At A Coy Firing | |
| | 3 | | A & B Coys moved to Beacon Camp B.6.b. with sand | Ref 28 1917 |
| | | | to 7th Royal West Kent Regt. | |
| | | | B Coy Coy Firing on Range. C Coy Bren Musketry | |
| | | | D Coy Battn left BAPAUME CAMP arrived DYKE CAMP Drefelm | |
| | 4 Jan | 9am | Battn | |
| DYKE CAMP | 5 | | A Coy Coy Bren Drill Musketry Bayonet fighting | Ref 28 1917 |
| | 6 | 11am | Church Parade | |
| A.H.A. | 7 | | B Coy Rifting | |
| | | | C Coy Visual and Rector drill Musketry Bayonet | |
| | 8 | | C Coy Firing Lewis march | |
| | | | B Coy Musketry Route march | |
| | 9 | | A & B Coy Musketry authelics - lecture organization | |
| | 10/11 Jan | | Rifts DYKE CAMP - entrained onibark old men | |
| | | 12.30am | Alfred BOULOGNE 12.30 Atrem | |

# WAR DIARY or INTELLIGENCE SUMMARY

Army Form C. 2118.

| Place | Date 1918 | Hour | Summary of Events and Information | Remarks and references to Appendices |
|---|---|---|---|---|
| In the Line | Jan 10 | 3 p.m. | Battalion marched via WINDMILL and RAILWAY ST. to front | Map: 70/8: DIXSCHOOTE 30 S.W.¼ SCHAP-BALIE 20 S.E.¼ |
| BREAK FARM | | 5.30 p.m. | line. Bttn reached BREAK FARM at 5.30 p.m. | |
| FARM U.12.c.5.2. | | | Distribution of O.C's:- David B Co in front line "D" on the right from V.9.a.9.5. to V.18.b.8.9. U.12.a.65.95. | |
| | | | A. from V.18.c.50.45. to V.6.d.90.25. | |
| | | | B. Coy in support right U.6.d.40.35. | |
| | | | C. Coy in support. | |
| | | | Coy "Reserve" by BREAK FARM | |
| | | | Battn "Blayes" - 8th EAST SURREY REGT | |
| | | | Battn on right - 11th LANCS FUSILIERS | |
| | | | Battn on left - 11th ROYAL FUSILIERS | |
| | | | Battn O.P. - 11th ROYAL FUSILIERS. | |
| | | | Intermittent shelling around ADEN Rd and EGYPT Ho. | |
| | | | 6.30 - 9 a.m. 11th Jan. night seemed front | |
| | | | to be very wet. Informed 9 posts | |
| | 11 | | Intermittent shelling during the morning and from 3 to 4 p.m. around EGYPT HO. ADEN HD. and ANGLE POINT. APACCAR. | |
| | | | FARM with T.M. fire on our front posts. | |

# WAR DIARY
## INTELLIGENCE SUMMARY

Army Form C. 2118.

| Place | Date 1918 | Hour | Summary of Events and Information | Remarks and references to Appendices |
|---|---|---|---|---|
| In the LINE PECHAR FARM | Jan 12 | 3 am | One enemy aeroplane flew over our front both ways. Improvement of posts - Revetted woods at V.7.a.9.6. All posts connected by wire or tape. Fair | |
| | | 4-5 pm | Fwd Hq. ADEN Ho: ANGLE POINT killed at 4.2.5.5 and 77 mm and Stokes posts on 4th 4.2 and T.M's between S.O and 60 Aun PECHAZ FARM shelled during afternoon with bursts of 77 mm further enforcement of posts and wiring up our wire. | BIXSCHOOTE and GHELUVELT BAILIE MAPS |
| | | 8.20 am | Inter company Relief completed by 8.20 am. C Coy Relieving D Coy and B Relieving A Coy | |
| | 13 | Sam 4.20 am 4.30 am | Shelling with 77mm around ADEN HOUSE Salvoes of 100 to 150 77 mm around PECHAZ FARM and N RAILWAY CT. T M's active on front at 5 hm A strong hostile T.M will attempt to support our attack to try to force ADEN to to RAILWAY turning then to endeavour to turn ADEN to | |

# WAR DIARY or INTELLIGENCE SUMMARY

Army Form C. 2118.
(4)

| Place | Date | Hour | Summary of Events and Information | Remarks and references to Appendices |
|---|---|---|---|---|
| In the Line PICHE WOOD | | | to BRAYBECK. Camp WITH | |
| FROM | | 7am | So unloads & instruct for ELEPHANT Shelter arrive) from Kit-Kit Camp to Brayvet to advance her to right Coy. | |
| | | | Shells at CAIRO HOUSE continued. | MAP |
| | | | Next two units at V.17.a.65.55. and reaching Front line | POTIJZE BAUE |
| | | | Artillery fairly quiet during the day. Between hours of shell fire in the hours of EAST HOUSE fair Battalion relieved by 1/8 MIDDLESEX Regt. 6 to 4 | |
| | | 10 am | Battalion marches to MOOL | |
| | | 6.25 | Completed by 6.25 am. Battalion marches to MOOL WOOD camp reaching there 8.30am. | BIXSCHOOTE |
| ABRI WOOD J.25.d. | | | Pct - All fell hopeneuch. Wiring Parties - Officers and Men detailed Wiring Parties. Officers and charge of Wiring squads attend to taking out of the from & line to be wired. | MAP 20 S.W |

Army Form C. 2118.

# WAR DIARY
## or
## INTELLIGENCE SUMMARY.
(Erase heading not required.)

(5)

| Place | Date 1918 | Hour | Summary of Events and Information | Remarks and references to Appendices |
|---|---|---|---|---|
| ABRI WOOD CAMP U.25.d. | | 8pm | N.I. and Tool Treatment. Firing Practice. Ten experts (10 strong) under 3 Officers left more camp and marched to the line. On entering trench 49 O.B's to wait in front of right sector posts. Two R.E. Officers in charge. The remaining Officers repairing the O.B.K. Wiring done:- A double apron fence of 65ft with 10ft gaps between sections from U.6.c.6.9. to V.1.c.6.7. and V.1.c.7.5.7. to V.1.c.8.0.15. Commenced 9pm. Completed 4.30am. | MAP 25/1/18 Bosch Scouts? 20 Jan 4 |
| | 18 | | Baths located ABRI CAMP. Entrained ONDANK 3.30pm Reached DYKES CAMP. 4.30pm. | MAP 25N.W |
| DYKES CAMP | 19 | | Cleaning of men arms equipment. Foot Treatment. | |
| | 20 | | Church Parade. Kit Inspection. Cleaning of Camp. | |
| A.H.Q. | 21 | | A.M. & B. Baths. B.Co.s & D.Co Inspection & clo. Close Order Drill. Musketry — Fire. | |

Army Form C. 2118.

# WAR DIARY
## or
## INTELLIGENCE SUMMARY.
(Erase heading not required.)

Instructions regarding War Diaries and Intelligence Summaries are contained in F. S. Regs., Part II. and the Staff Manual respectively. Title pages will be prepared in manuscript.

| Place | Date 1916 | Hour | Summary of Events and Information | Remarks and references to Appendices |
|---|---|---|---|---|
| DYKES CAMP Jan 21 | | | P.T. Close order drill, Musketry, Bayonet fighting | |
| | 22 | | Short Rout march. | |
| | | | XI Brigadier inspected B.n. Capbenator instructor | |
| | 23rd | | Bathing in vats. Camp to take over from 8th EAST SURREY REGT. Carrying parts of 60 O.R's to HOUSKOW CAMP | |
| | 24 | | BARASTON CAMP. Detail to HOUSKOW CAMP Bat'n entrained ONDANK- Left Bat'n CROCHE 2.40 p.m. | |
| In the Line PASCAL FARM VIERST | | | Night reached PASCAL FARM 6.15 p.m. B of Coy Coupled B.Q.O.hm Map. out of line and difficulties of Co. are also Staff (there was takenover on a 2 Coy front and re-distribution) Artillery quiet, occasional shelling. passed PASCALFARM Carrying parties (340 O.R strong) formed from B.n. Details carried forward shelters and dumps | |
| | 25 | | Arts arrived and consolidated. Fine. Generally clear. Patrol went out to no mans land, but owing to bright light nothing of importance took place | |

# WAR DIARY / INTELLIGENCE SUMMARY

Army Form C. 2118.

| Place | Date | Hour | Summary of Events and Information | Remarks and references to Appendices |
|---|---|---|---|---|
| In the Line PASSCH- ENDAEL. | Jan 25 1918 | | Artillery fairly quiet. M.G. fire active from TURENNE crossing. Aerial activity considerable. All Coy posts wired. Cooker's funnels &c - posts crenelated & from the to parapet &c to which staped. Work commenced on two new L.G. posts at V.1.c.35.20 and V.6.a.96 as ordered by the Brigadier. | |
| | | 9.55 | Inter-Coy relief completed by 9.55am. 'B' Coy left front, 'C' Coy right front. 'A' Coy supp'd, 'D' Coy Reserve Line. | M.G. 1xScheme 1M.G. 20 S.A.A. |
| | | | Very quiet all day. At 6.30pm our artillery bombarded Wet Wall Strts to a minute. TM supplement- W area. | 132 |
| | | | TURENNE CROSSING - Do. At 6 A.C.A. Retaliated by bombarding 6 Eine CYMS CHEMINS - FOREST HOUSE - RAILWAY STATION - all over. | |
| | | 6.35 | Ceased by 6.35pm | |
| | | | Two new L.G. posts were established at V.1.c.40.25 and V.6.a.90.65. | |
| | | | Battn was relieved in the Line by the 13th Middlesex Regt. | |

**Army Form C. 2118.**

# WAR DIARY
## or
## INTELLIGENCE SUMMARY.
*(Erase heading not required.)*

Instructions regarding War Diaries and Intelligence Summaries are contained in F.S. Regs., Part II. and the Staff Manual respectively. Title pages will be prepared in manuscript.

| Place | Date | Hour | Summary of Events and Information | Remarks and references to Appendices |
|---|---|---|---|---|
| 18R.I. CAMP | 26 | | Relief completed by 9.0 p.m. Battalion marched to 18R.I. Camp, reaching there by 10.30 p.m. A carrying party from BETHUNE carried forms with ? for EXTRA SHELTERS. | |
| | 27 | | All tents received. Cleaning up & putting up tents & equipment. | |
| | 28 | | Details at HOUNSLOW CAMP Bathed. Batt. left 18R.I. Camp and arrived EMILIE CAMP 12 noon. Details arrived 12.30 p.m. Batt. bathed afternoon. | Half Rest Rest 2.30 p.m. |
| | 29 | | Cleaning of kits and equipment. | |
| | 30 | | Batt. left EMILIE CAMP 9 a.m. marched to CROMBEKE via New Rest Camp East of CROMBEKE × 13 B.4. | Camp Rest 19.00 |
| CAMP E. of CROMBEKE | 31 | | Physical drill Close Order Drill Musketry. Cleaning and improvement of the camp | |

R. Turner Lt. Col.
Commanding 6th (S)
Battn. Northamptonshire Regt.

# WAR DIARY
## or
## INTELLIGENCE SUMMARY.
(Erase heading not required.)

Army Form C. 2118.

6 Northamptonshire 1/2/18

| Place | Date | Hour | Summary of Events and Information | Remarks and references to Appendices |
|---|---|---|---|---|
| CAMP. W. of CROMER | 1 | | A.M. Ordinary Drill. A.P.C. Inspection. Makeover | |
| X.13.d.3.8. | | | P.M. Inspection by the C.O. Co. Musketeer Instructor. | |
| | 2 | | A.M. A & C Platoons (1st) and Co Co Programme resumed | |
| | | 2.30pm | Church parade | |
| | 4 | | A.M. Packing of kits. Cleaning of equipment etc | |
| | | | P.M. Route March, relatives still | |
| | 5 | | A.M. Special training for 7 hr. musketry classes | |
| | | | P.M. Inspection & noting of next draft of 64 O.R.s | |
| | | | Grand Field Day. | |
| | | | Divisional Tactics | |
| | 6 | | A.M. R.E. Co. co. tactics – Brigadier Inspection | |
| | | | Canals under field batteries Red. | |
| | 7 | 9-0 to 12.45 | P.T. Close Order Drill. Musketry. Box Respirator drill. | |
| | | 2-2.45 | Special musketry squads under the B.M. Instructors. | |
| | | | General Sharpening & specialist training | |

Army Form C. 2118.

# WAR DIARY or INTELLIGENCE SUMMARY.
(Erase heading not required.)

Instructions regarding War Diaries and Intelligence Summaries are contained in F. S. Regs., Part II. and the Staff Manual respectively. Title pages will be prepared in manuscript.

| Place | Date | Hour | Summary of Events and Information | Remarks and references to Appendices |
|---|---|---|---|---|
| CAMP W. of CRUMBEK | 1918 Feb 8 | 9-00 6-4.30 2-4-2.45 | P.T. Organization & general training. Mobility squads on fr.S. Lecture to all mobility squads by Commanding Officer. Squad training for junior officers and N.C.Os. Mounting & communicating drill. | |
| X 13 d 3.8 | 9 | 4-15p | Bn. entrained at PROVEN station & proceeded by train to NOYON. | |
| MORLINCOURT | 10 | 10-00 | Bn. arrived at NOYON, & marched on to MORLINCOURT. | |
| J 28 c & D (Sheet 70 E.) | 11 | 9-00 12-1.00 | P.T. Inspection by bn. comm. Mobility, Bayonet fighting &c. Special Mobility squads for N.C.Os. | |
| | | 2-0-2.45 | Go mounting & communicating drill | |
| | 12 | 1/- | Bn. with Transport proceeded by march route to BETHANCOURT. | |
| CAMP 700° N.N.W. of JUSSY MAP REF: ST QUENTIN | 13 | 11-00 | " " " " " " " " " JUSSY | |
| | 14 | 9-11 | A & B Coys. P.T. Improvement of camp, making trenches for protection against air raids. C & D Coys digging cable trench for 14th DIVL SIGNAL COY at CLASTRES | |
| | 15 | " | A, B, C & D Coys employed as at 14th. Special stores held during day. | |
| | 16 | " | Same as 15th. C & D Coy & Transport had baths at FLAVY-LE-MARTEL |  |

# WAR DIARY
## or
## INTELLIGENCE SUMMARY.
*(Erase heading not required.)*

Army Form C. 2118.

| Place | Date 1918 | Hour | Summary of Events and Information | Remarks and references to Appendices |
|---|---|---|---|---|
| CAMP 400x N.N.W. of TUSSY | Feb 17 | 8-15 to 2-20 | A.B.C. & D Coys employed in digging cable trench for III Corps Signal Coy. Special classes for N.C.Os. in Musketry, Lewis Gunners, Signallers. | |
| MAP. REF. SI QUENTON. | | | "B" Coy & part of "B" H.Q. had baths at FLAVY-LE-MARTEL. | |
| | 18 | 7-45 | All Coys digging, as on 17th. Specialist classes held during day. | |
| | 19 | | Same as for 18th. | |
| | 20 | " | Same as for 18th. | |
| | 21 | " | Same as for 18th. Coys inspection by Coy Commanders. | |
| | | 4-pm | Inspection of Regulation & Reserve L Gunners by Major McCLASHAM. | |
| | | | (G.H.Q. School) & lecture to all officers. | |
| | 22 | 7-45 | Same as for 18th. Lecture for officers at REMIGNY by Major McCLASHAM. | |
| | | 5-0p | Coys parade. | |
| | 23 | | Same as 16th inst. | |
| | 24 | 1pm | 6 Officers and 300 O.R's moved to PONT D'EVEQUE and attached to 109 Fd. Co. R.E. to work on Guanineton Intrenm. | |
| | | | Same as 16th inst. Much fog. Classes continued | |

Army Form C. 2118.

# WAR DIARY
## or
## INTELLIGENCE SUMMARY.
(Erase heading not required.)

Instructions regarding War Diaries and Intelligence Summaries are contained in F.S. Regs., Part II. and the Staff Manual respectively. Title pages will be prepared in manuscript.

| Place | Date 1914 | Hour | Summary of Events and Information | Remarks and references to Appendices |
|---|---|---|---|---|
| CAMP N.W. JUSSY | 26 | | B Coy O.C. completed cook trench. Clearing up & later equipment and camp. | |
| Billet at | 26 | | B Coy Rets reached Camp, marched to Billets at CHAUNY | ST QUENT IN MAP |
| CHAUNY | 27 | 4.30am | Aroused by H.M. 2nd. Army firing on Range | |
| | | | L.S. Much Em firing or Range | |
| | 28 | 10.30 | Orders received 70 Battalion to hold itself in readiness to M.O.L. at 15 minutes notice. No action incurred to 7 hour | |

S. Stewart
Major Commanding
6th (S) Bn Northamptonshire Regt

54th Inf.Bde.
18th Div.

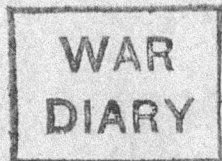

6th BATTN. THE NORTHAMPTONSHIRE REGIMENT.

M A R C H

1 9 1 8

# WAR DIARY or INTELLIGENCE SUMMARY

Army Form C. 2118.

6th Northants

(Erase heading not required.)

Instructions regarding War Diaries and Intelligence Summaries are contained in F.S. Regs., Part II. and the Staff Manual respectively. Title pages will be prepared in manuscript.

| Place | Date | Hour | Summary of Events and Information | Remarks and references to Appendices |
|---|---|---|---|---|
| Billets CAULOYEN (Map E.24) | 1/1/18 | | Battns. Lewis Gun School to all Platoons | |
| | | | Recruits Rifle Practice & Drill | |
| | | | Band in Rehearsal. Runners Lecture Reconnaissance | |
| | 2 | | Practice of attack. Reorganisation of Anti-Gas Section | |
| | | | Bombing in Lewis Gun Instruction | |
| | 3 | | Three O.R.s to G.H.Q. Batt. Routine. Ranges the Coy at | |
| | | | North on school of B.S. Coyd non-com explained A.P.M. | |
| | 4 | | Morning ranges of first Platoons by A.P.L. and | |
| | | | C.O. Rifles to by 2 Pltns, and runs | |
| | | | Rifle Inspection | |
| | 5 | | Stretcher drill Batt. Intelligence. worked at way | |
| | | | Musketry. Battn. Att. of Rifle Rock Platoon | |
| | | | Rifle Inspection | |
| | | | Attack practice D Coy L/Rt Hammersfield 11/R.F. | MAP 1/40,000 |
| | | | 10th and NCO's, and young Battn billeted BETHANCOURT | MAP 1/70 B 1/40,000 |
| | 6 | | Field Training D Coy Young class B Coy Co Commanders | |
| | | | and cleaning up A Coy | |

# WAR DIARY or INTELLIGENCE SUMMARY

Army Form C. 2118.

| Place | Date 1918 | Hour | Summary of Events and Information | Remarks and references to Appendices |
|---|---|---|---|---|
| Billets CAILLOUEL | Feb 19 | | Firing on Range. Field Firing. Continuation of programme. | |
| | | | Bombing range. A & B Coy Baths | |
| | 5 | | Parades as for 7th | |
| | | 9.16am | B & C Cos moved to JUSSY to work on CIZERCOURT – LIZEROLLES – CAMAS First number E.S.S. III Coys. | |
| | | 2pm | A Coy (2 Offs 131 ORs) moved to FAILLOUEL for advance number 365 Forest Central Coy. | |
| | | 6am | Scheme. Attack with Rose Trenches N of CAILLOUEL | |
| | 9-11 | | Battn left CAILLOUEL (Sunday) and worked to billets at | |
| Battn Hd Qrs | 10 | 10 Am | JUSSY. M & C. arrived here 5 pm. | |
| JUSSY M.I.S.C. | 11 | | Cleaning Camp and instructing our brokes billets. | |
| | | | D.Coy continued work on B.Coy construction of Camp for | |
| | | | work on 115th Ind. | |
| | 12 | | Remainder of A Coy rejoined Hd Cos from C Coy | |
| | | | and RE unters turned A 552. | |
| | 13 | | Working parties as 115 Ind. Firing on range by B Coy | |

# WAR DIARY or INTELLIGENCE SUMMARY.

Army Form C. 2118.

| Place | Date 1918 | Hour | Summary of Events and Information | Remarks and references to Appendices |
|---|---|---|---|---|
| CAMP HUSSEY | Mar 14 | | Working parties as usual. Firing practice and musketry during afternoon. Officers & N.C.O.s went to instructional school | |
| | 15 | | As for yesterday | |
| | 16 | | Working parties as returned to R.E. Platoon joined "A" Field Coy R.E. at M.I.&d.2.6. | |
| | 17 | | Working parties as usual. Church parade 9 am. | |
| | 18 | | do. Working parties of "B" & "C" Coys | |
| | | | Relieved by 9th Imperial Cavalry Regiment. Battn. returned to CARNOY. | |
| | | | CARNOY. Arrived there 9 pm. | |
| | 19 | | General training. Battn. recommenced of reserve centre | |
| | 20 | | do. | |
| | 21 | 16.30 | Battn. left CARNOY. 16.30 Coys embussed BUCHANCOURT 6 km roads | |
| | | | at WOOD of NESSY-FAILLOUEL Rd. Moved forward at 4 pm to take over British line in front of LY FONTAINE | |
| In line LY FONTAINE | | 9 am | From the right and GRICOURT on the left. Relieved to hold front of QUENTIN CANAL at LA MONTAGNE Ridge and took up | |
| | | 10.30 pm | | |

# WAR DIARY or INTELLIGENCE SUMMARY

Army Form C. 2118.

| Place | Date 1918 | Hour | Summary of Events and Information | Remarks and references to Appendices |
|---|---|---|---|---|
| In the Line SE of JUSSY | Mar 22 | 5:30 am | A.M. A Bitter on Railway embankment about M.22 d in Bellenne Ridge at LA MONTAGNE and the BEDFORDS now on the high ground of the R. FUSILIERS on the C.of L had to blow up, but this was only partially successful. The Bn had to hold itself in readiness to counter attack in case the enemy crossed the Canal. Enemy aircraft was very active during the afternoon and a heavy bombardment was made against the position and the enemy twice made an unsuccessful attempt to cross the Canal but were repulsed. The line was continued on west continuing from the Bridge on the Canal at M.23.a.8.9. to Dvo 70s SE of MONTAGNE BRIDGE. | |
| | 23 | 7:30 am | The enemy attacked against the 3rd BEDFORDS and Fusiliers northly against the Royal Fusiliers working back both flanks. We held on to our position and the 2 Bridges when were the 2 most intricate points in the line were kept and continued | |
| | | 11:30 | to carry on until relieved by the Brigadier to withdraw attacking down | |

Army Form C. 2118.

# WAR DIARY
## or
## INTELLIGENCE SUMMARY.
*(Erase heading not required.)*

Instructions regarding War Diaries and Intelligence Summaries are contained in F. S. Regs., Part II. and the Staff Manual respectively. Title pages will be prepared in manuscript.

| Place | Date | Hour | Summary of Events and Information | Remarks and references to Appendices |
|---|---|---|---|---|
| In the line | 1918 Nov 23rd | am | Reinforcements of STRATHCONA'S HORSE arrived & billeted immediately in Huvers | |
| SUSSY | | 12 noon | The Batt. hitherto in BOIS DE FOURÈS where the enemy voluntarily pulled out, move from RÉNIGNY and reconnoitre towards whilening as far from WEST of FAIRIER | |
| | | 3 pm | The Batt. hitherto thru VILLEROUGE AUMONT and moved into billets at CAILLOUIL | |
| CAILLOUEL | 24.10.30 | am | The Brigade took up defensive positions on high ground N. of CAILLOUEL 6th NORTH'N Regt on the right and 7th BEDFORDS on the left. The R.F. riflemen were at CREPIGNY in Reserve. the EAST FORTRESS were on the right. The early movers were on the left of a Brigade | |
| | | 7pm | The enemy attacked on the left of the BEDFORDS and the other Pioneers and French Cuirassiers were forced back. | |
| CHAUNY | 25 Jany | | Brigade withdrew to N.W. of CREPIGNY and at 10.30 am | |
| ATTINOLES | | 3pm | to GRAND RU — 3pm to BE+ FRECOURT, thence V.E. to about | |

# WAR DIARY
## or
## INTELLIGENCE SUMMARY.

Army Form C. 2118.

| Place | Date 1914 | Hour | Summary of Events and Information | Remarks and references to Appendices |
|---|---|---|---|---|
| BABOUEF | Nov 25 | Am 4:30 | 1000 yards W of BABOUEF. Here the Brigade drew up with a small body of French Troops into Artillery formation to attack BABOUEF. The 11th Regt further on the right. The 7th Rochfort on the left and Scots & North Regt in support. The advance commenced about 5 am. The village was reached with a few casualties caused by rifle and machine gunfire. The advance continued and 2 Cos of the 6th North Regt were sent to reinforce the 7th Scottish. The line eventually taken and entrenched was East of the Village. This ran [?] from the railway K21.a.5.2. along line running NW to junction of roads at H.15.c.2.5. | |
| | 26.2.14 | | At 6.15 am the Brigade was evacuated and the Brigade retired along the main road to NOYON, then via DER the CANAL through PONTOISE to CAISNES. Marching to ADSINCOURT billeted in the Conv. | |
| Andigncourt | 27.4.45 | 4 pm | Marched from ANDIGNICOURT to ST AUBIN into billets | |

# WAR DIARY
## or
## INTELLIGENCE SUMMARY.
*(Erase heading not required.)*

Army Form C. 2118.

| Place | Date 1918 | Hour | Summary of Events and Information | Remarks and references to Appendices |
|---|---|---|---|---|
| ST AUBIN | Mar 29 | | Cleaning up and Reorganisation | |
| | 30 | 6am | do | |
| | | 9.R. | Marched via ANDIANCOURT to NAMPCEL - Embussed and | |
| | | 9.am | Enbussed via COMPIEGNE to RIBES Arrived 9 Am. | |
| CENTELLES | 31 | 6.30am | Marched to CENTELLES. | |
| | | 2.30 | Recd. orders to attack HANGARD, DOMART and HOURGES. Found | |
| IN THE | | | Huns already (upper) lines and trenches at hill 2nd/Australians | |
| LINE | | | and CANADIENS (in sight) S.D.L. on the left. | |
| N. of | | 9am | Recd. orders to relieve Royal BERKS N W. of HANGARD | |
| HANGARD | | | Line extended from U 29.A.3.7. in front of CESSE 29.90 | |
| | | | Rd. to CAYUT/BOIS DE HANGARD to about U 21.9.4.4.7. | |
| | | | 10th F. & Ry together with French Tranch on Right. | |

S. le Flemming Stephens. Major.
Commanding 6th Northamptonshire R.

54th Inf.Bde.
18th Div.

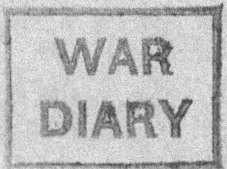

6th BATTN. THE NORTHAMPTONSHIRE REGIMENT.

A P R I L

1 9 1 8

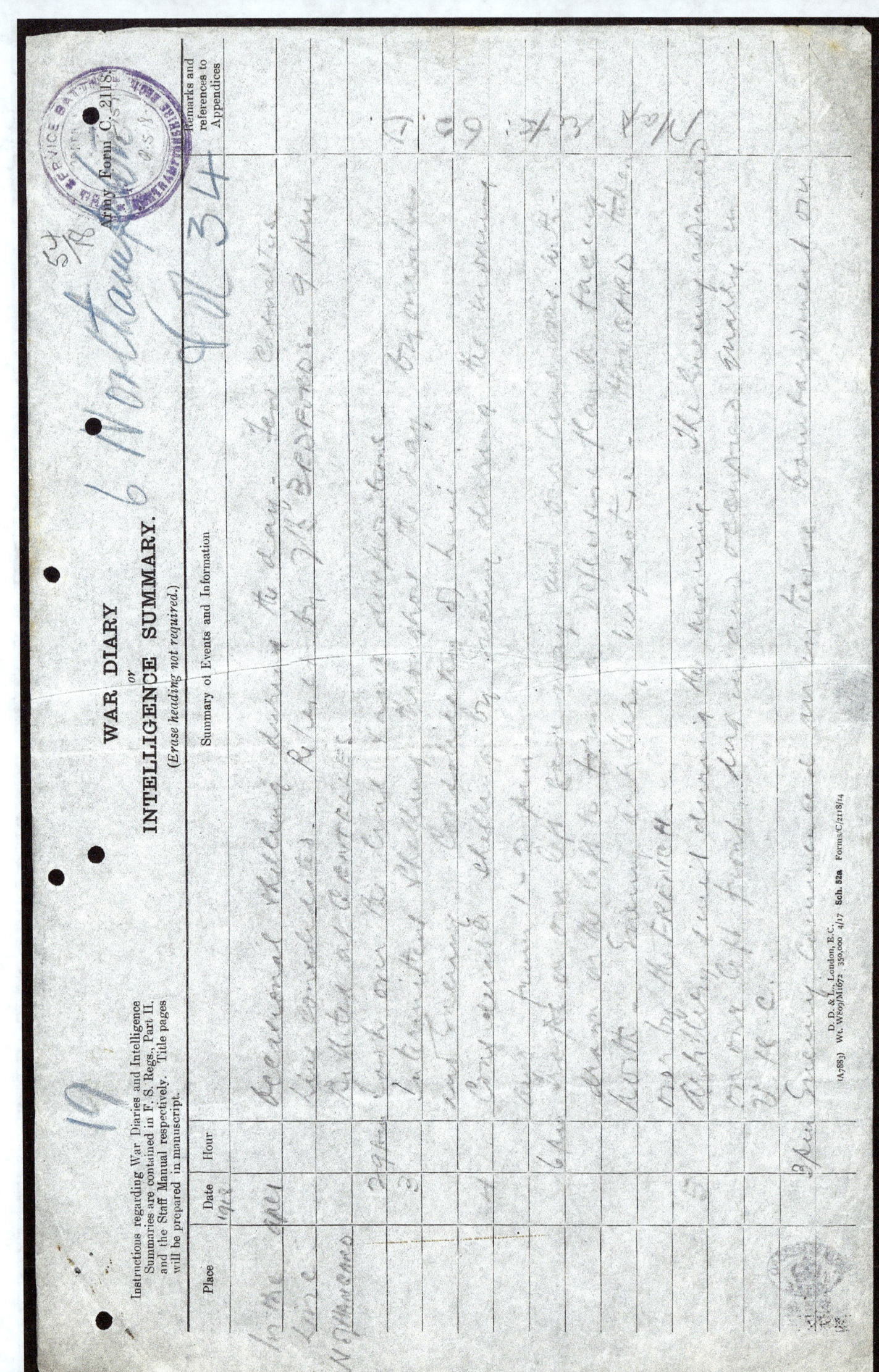

# "War Diary"

| PLACE | DATE | SUMMARY OF EVENTS AND INFORMATION | REMARKS AND REFERENCES TO APPENDICES |
|---|---|---|---|
| In the Line | 1918 Aug 5 | The whole of our Bn'ns and HANGARD and HANGARD WOOD the forward posts and advanced on their CARD and our Line North. The Battn N° 51 and 1 Coy of 76 Bedfords lined the Ridge V 21 d and V 22 e. At 6.45 p.m. a message was received from the Commanders of the our Coys/2 Coys in a Cunnets attack. By Capture of the left flank and "Brand" the trunk lines in V 23. d. 7.27pm 1 Coy of Mc Bedfords coming up in support advanced under a Creeping Barrage. The enemy aircraft interfered by searching ordnance up by very heavy machine gun fire to 8.30 pm. The Barrage moved there A. which was found a m. gun nest at the C.T. of our front. Infantry to rush and dug in and ??? in | 9 9 2/3 3 3 |
| No Advanced | | | |

# "WAR DIARY"

| PLACE | DATE | SUMMARY OF EVENTS AND INFORMATION | REMARKS AND REFERENCES TO APPENDICES |
|---|---|---|---|
| In the Line Mylterngem | Apl 1918 Thurs 5 | At 10 p.m. on 4th inst. relieved by the 27th Australian Brigade. The Battalion sustained several casualties on the trek back, 5 staff including [?] O.C. who was wounded in the throat and Mr. [?] Capt Garrard who was killed. The Bn then marched back to CENTURES to be clothed and fed. | |
| | 6 | Bn marched to Will o Spin. | |
| | 7 | Billeted in CROSS ROADS. Cleaning up and reorganisation. Returns rendered and Lewis Guns to be issued to replace all that had been lost in action. Given orders to stand to at an hour's notice Ready to check the enemy's advance and to defend the [?] town at [?] costs. | |
| | 8 | Cleaning up. 2.30 p.m. the Battn marched to BOUTILLERIE — SE of AMIENS. | |
| BOUTILLERIE | 10 | Cleaning up and reorganisation | |
| | 11 | General Training. Inspection and reorganisation | |
| | 12 | do Col. Packe took on command of Battn. | |
| | 13 | do Bath. Box Respirator Inspection | |

Army Form C. 2118.

# WAR DIARY
## or
## INTELLIGENCE SUMMARY.
(Erase heading not required.)

| Place | Date 1918 | Hour | Summary of Events and Information | Remarks and references to Appendices |
|---|---|---|---|---|
| BRILLION-SUR-LYS | 15 | | Church Parade. | |
| | | | Bus Respirator Inspection. Baths Inspection. | |
| | 16 | | General training. | |
| | 17 | | do | |
| | 18 | | do | |
| CACHY | 19 | | | |
| | 20 | | Moved to Cachy. Entered Training. | |
| In line | | | Firing rifles at targets. B Coy. | |
| I/F of CACHY | | | B & D Coy took over Inner line in front of CACHY and | |
| | | | In front of CACHY. Working parties for returning and | |
| | | | constructing the defensive line. | |
| | 21 | | B & D Coys relieved by A & C Coys. Further activity | |
| | | | to this. | |
| | 22 | | Considerable hostile artillery activity. B & D Coys | |
| | | | continued training at CACHY. | |
| | 23 | | B & D Coys General training. | |
| | | | A & C Coys in the C CACHY and Rue Marie at CENTELLES | |

# WAR DIARY or INTELLIGENCE SUMMARY

Army Form C. 2118.

| Place | Date | Hour | Summary of Events and Information | Remarks and references to Appendices |
|---|---|---|---|---|
| In the Chetty Sector | 6/6 | | After intermittent shelling throughout the day, the enemy shelled | |
| | 24 | | Enemy attacked after a short bombardment lasted from 11am to 5am. Bn Co sent forward from enemy and took up a position in rear of enemy. | |
| | | 9am | The enemy attacked and informed no progress but not much in front to be in front of the Bn. = an enemy in sight. (R.W.R.) We withdrew our line. | |
| | | | to the front trench. Fairly quiet throughout the day. Intermittent shelling. | |
| | 25 | 6.30 | A considerable bombardment on the Chetty Sector. The Bn has orders and are withdrawn. All ranks died down by 7.15pm and no clash took place. Relieved by a Batt of Moroccan Troops - Rily | |

Army Form C. 2118.

# WAR DIARY
## or
## INTELLIGENCE SUMMARY.
*(Erase heading not required.)*

| Place | Date | Hour | Summary of Events and Information | Remarks and references to Appendices |
|---|---|---|---|---|
| GENTELLES | 1918 | | Complete by 5 a.m. Bn. marched to Gentelles and N.W. of GENTELLES | |
| | | 2 Noon | Left GENTELLES and entrained at AMIENS arrived at HERCUVET Valle 6 a.m. Next in to R.16.b. (General and reorganisation. Church Parade 3 p.m. Bath parade and General training | |
| HEU COURT | | 9 | | |
| | | 30 | | |

S. Hemming Shipton Major
Commander i/c
6 (S) Batt Northampton Bat

Army Form C. 2118.

# WAR DIARY
## or
## INTELLIGENCE SUMMARY.
(Erase heading not required.)

6th Northants.
Vol 35

| Place | Date | Hour | Summary of Events and Information | Remarks and references to Appendices |
|---|---|---|---|---|
| Haucourt | May 1st | | Ordinary Battalion Parade. General Training. | |
| " | 2 | | General Training. | |
| " | 3 | | " Brigade Parade at Bailly. Relieved by Corps Reserve | |
| " | 4 | | Inspection March Out. Bn H.Q. Buses left to return towards WP | |
| " | | 10.30 | Recon. came to transport lines at 12.30 to Battalion | |
| | | | Continued | |
| Oh An thur | 5 | 5.30 | Bn moved from Haucourt Hansker to Banks and in orders | |
| " | | 4.9.m | Situated at Vadencourt — marched to trenches | |
| Oulay | 6 | 7.am | Battle moved off to take over trenches about 11 | |
| | | | Reinforcement of B.H.Q. Support & Reserve Posts | |
| | | | Cot. in Bw Hq. in Cory in reserve | |
| | 7 | | Very quiet — our trenches 9 a very quiet nature very quiet | |
| du du shiri | 8 | | Ordinary routine in trenches | |
| Laurien | 9 | 1.30 | Patrol of 8 men went out under Lieut Pruck bost relief to Bisacourt & Biencourt | |
| | 10 | | Zinas Shells was about which caused much damage N°10 of Ravin | |
| | | | A Coy relieved Bw Coy in the line | |

Army Form C. 2118.

# WAR DIARY
## or
## INTELLIGENCE SUMMARY.
*(Erase heading not required.)*

Instructions regarding War Diaries and Intelligence Summaries are contained in F. S. Regs., Part II. and the Staff Manual respectively. Title pages will be prepared in manuscript.

| Place | Date | Hour | Summary of Events and Information | Remarks and references to Appendices |
|---|---|---|---|---|
| NR CUI DE LAVENTIE | 18 | | Our line extended from E.19.b.4.0 to E.12.a.8.0 (about 620 MLE) | |
| | | | Bn Hqrs at E.24.a.2.7 near B Coy in front line A & C Coys in Support and D Coy in reserve. Quiet day | |
| " | 19 | 2 am | C Coy in conjunction with Australians on R right attempted a raid on Death Trench just in front of our line. Owing to wire and (concrete?) (machine?) gun emplacements uncut they were unable to enter though (Death?) Trench was examined for (...)| |
| | | 9 am | D Coy relieved B Coy in the front line | |
| | | | to 24.6.3 a dawn shift to E.24.a.3.7 as the situation of trenches | |
| " | 20 | | Artillery quiet. Aircraft active. | |
| | 21st | 10 pm | Strong patrol was sent out to 24.a.4.9. (...) and L.B.24.b.4.9. | |
| | | | Intermittent shelling. Strong patrols entered and went (...) | |
| | 22nd | | Quiet day. (...) was located at A.16 for (...) our (...) | |
| | 23 | 9 am | Queen (...) of NW of Bn Hqrs by enemy exploded. Sap (...) | |
| | | | Our line was registered upon. (Strong?) patrols sent out. New front line was (...) in the (...) | |
| | | | E.18.d.4.1 to E.13.a.6.0 was (...) this (...) | |

Army Form C. 2118.

# WAR DIARY
## or
## INTELLIGENCE SUMMARY.
(Erase heading not required.)

Instructions regarding War Diaries and Intelligence Summaries are contained in F. S. Regs., Part II. and the Staff Manual respectively. Title pages will be prepared in manuscript.

| Place | Date | Hour | Summary of Events and Information | Remarks and references to Appendices |
|---|---|---|---|---|
| 4th Line 2 Lancville | May 11th | | Enemy shelling just west of our camp was fairly heavy. Shelling from 1-2.5 | |
| | 12 | | Usual trench warfare | |
| | 13 | 10 am | Enemy shelled Lancville with traces on Bn. C.U. [?] had on Bn. H.Q. O.C. was blown in to Col & Capt [?] supplied and the Capt to said [?] wounded and evacuated. | |
| | | 10 pm | Battn. was relieved in the line by East Surreys and marched back to Bivouacs & shelters in valley | |
| | 14th | | Whole Bn. bathed at Prisoners Camp N. of Bazincourt. Difficult did not turn [?] on [?] Bn. Ground & heavy shells. Capt King 7th Bedfords took command of Bn. | |
| | 15th | | Enemy firing of 400 was found to having cable towards ourselves also top of W [?] shells 7 & 8 hrs. for 1st Bn AEG Post on Albert Rd. | |
| | 16th | | Some working parties were found. | |
| | 17 | | C.O. prepared to [?] details was changed owing to Lt Col (Acting) Booth on command of Capt Kirk was relieved 7th Bedfords. | |
| | | 6:45 pm | Bn. in which I'll [?] the 4th on said [?] Royal Berks. Yesterday Nr. 9. Villa-Lu-Vois. | |

# WAR DIARY or INTELLIGENCE SUMMARY

Army Form C. 2118.

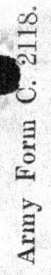

| Place | Date | Hour | Summary of Events and Information | Remarks and references to Appendices |
|---|---|---|---|---|
| 4th Bn Line SE of Neuville | May 24th | | Quiet day. Disposition un altered. B Coy sec support to right of line | |
| | | | Front line 2nd & C Coy Support less platoon to left of line | |
| | 25th | 10 p.m. | Bn was relieved by 2/4th London Regt. Relief proceeded with out active enemy interference but was badly hampered by enemy casualties on support trench and our own casualties on way down during Bn moved to new Billeys & billets in wood north of Bully-Grenay arriving in wood at 2 W 1, 62 D | |
| | 26th | 2 p.m. | Bn wood and 1 was a new aug 2 Coy ha ter C14 W 1 | |
| | 26th | | Church Parade. Bn bathed at the Baths at Vancouver | |
| | 27th | | Bn Parade and Coy drill | |
| | 28th | | " " " " | |
| | 29th | | General Training. Major H Ashton took over command from Lt Col A Michelsk (evacuated sick) | |
| | 30th | | General Training | |
| | 31st | 9.30 a.m. | Bn passed through gas chamber | |
| | | 3.35 p.m. | Bn moved from Camp to billets in Warley | |

Con'g 6(5)Bn Northamptonshire Regt
H Ashton Lieut Col

**WAR DIARY**
or
**INTELLIGENCE SUMMARY.**

(Erase heading not required.)

Army Form C. 2118.

(1) Yorkshire Rgmt.

WN 36

| Place | Date | Hour | Summary of Events and Information | Remarks and references to Appendices |
|---|---|---|---|---|
| Warloy | June 1st | | General Training under Coy arrangements. Reconnaissance parties visited front line | fl Cpt |
| " | 2nd | 11 am | Enemy shelled in vicinity of Bn Hdqrs. was hit. Church parade was arranged | fl Cpt |
| | | | Parties visited tks 4.2s. Church parade was arranged cancelled and Hdqrs and C Coy moved out of billets to billets on the southern outskirts. Battalion bathed. | |
| | 3rd | | Training under Coy arrangements. | fl Cpt |
| | 4th | | Training and preparation for the Line | fl Cpt |
| | | 5.30 pm | Totals (battle supplies) marches off to Divisional Brighton camp at Millencourt au Bois. | |
| | | 8.30 pm | Battn moved off to the line and took up position as Garrison Batt of Royal Warloy Keep, front line B and A Coy in CAPEY TRENCH (B. W26a.) (A. W20d) | |
| In the line West of | | | D Coy Melbourne TR. W.19.d @ Murky TR. Keep was VERA Rest | 517N.J. |
| ALBERT | | | R.C.H. Campbell Batt relieved Zoke ???? Construction & strong Points | W. |
| | | | Construction Continued Btn. moved to Keep relieved by M Melbournes TR. W.19.a.5.0 |

# WAR DIARY
## or
## INTELLIGENCE SUMMARY.
*(Erase heading not required.)*

Army Form C. 2118.

| Place | Date 1916 | Hour | Summary of Events and Information | Remarks and references to Appendices |
|---|---|---|---|---|
| In the field | | | Quiet day. | 3rd Cdn |
| Line | 6th | | A Coy relieved RCR Royal Irish in Desire Trench | |
| W of | | | Torpens [?] Trench - Wired and improving strong points | |
| the Pozieres | | | and Trenches | |
| | 7 | | Held artillery wire nature. I.M. turns on Trenches | MdCy |
| | | | W21 and 6. Bn 7th Brig at L.27.d.9.6. Casualties | 2/L |
| | | | Consumed 4 hours W.9 & 23 to Chalk Trench at W20c.9.6. | M/Cdy |
| | | | T Head of Battn HQ at Columbia [?] of Strong Point | |
| | | | W15 & and W21 a. | |
| | 8 | | Received gas shelling in Chalk Trench and Desboro [?] | M/Cy |
| | | | Trench and both HQs. A Coy moved back to Chalky Trench 3 | |
| | | | Becoming l. Shelling with H2S gas T.M.s on Sunday and | M/Cy |
| | 9 | | Infant Lines. They bombarded T Kern Centre 3 | |
| | 10 | | Gun shelling was received. Casualties and Ammn. | M/Cy |
| | | | Gas shelling engaged in cutting wire in front of 3/Bde | |
| | 11 | | Quiet day. Operations arranged to capture Boche Trench | M/Cy |

# WAR DIARY
## or
## INTELLIGENCE SUMMARY.

Army Form C. 2118.

| Place | Date 1918 | Hour | Summary of Events and Information | Remarks and references to Appendices |
|---|---|---|---|---|
| In the Line | 11th | | W 27 6 and N of train - R&D Cos to be coys to attack Bri: operation instructions. | |
| W of MBECT | 12 | | Dull day. Patrol went out at 11.30pm to obtain information. Enemy were encountered. | J. Roh |
| | 13 | | Spent a fairly quiet interim hrs. | J&Cpl J&Cpl |
| | 14 | 1 am | R Coy, B Coy, 2/Queens Regt. relief completed 1.30 am. Bathe moved to Pithiviers in V.36.a and W. of HENENCOURT | |
| B&vourses W of HENENCOURT WOOD | 14 | | Rest of Battn. billeted WARLOY-BAILLEUX line Battn. working parties found all night 270 RE dugouts Craters (A Davies) V.23.c | J&Cpl |
| | 15 | | Cleaning and organising. Remainder D. Smith Bath. Completion of Cadre formed. | J&Cpl |
| | 16 | 10 am | Church Parade 10 am. | J&Cpl J&Cpl |
| | 17 | 9.15 am | Practice of morning setter of parade. | |
| | 18 | | Firing General Training. Musing practice Lewis Gun. General Training. L.G Inspection J&Cpl | J&Major |

# WAR DIARY
## or
## INTELLIGENCE SUMMARY

Army Form C. 2118.

| Place | Date | Hour | Summary of Events and Information | Remarks and references to Appendices |
|---|---|---|---|---|
| Bivouac ed of G.R | | | | |
| W. of HENENCOURT WOOD | 18 | 6 am | Details of Bn. left WARLOY to march to ALBERT and BOUZINCOURT AREA. | |
| | 19 | | Moving Parties superintending digging of trenches by R. Eng. | 2nd Lieut. |
| | | | All Coys. Practising an attack on a Trench. | Pop. Capt. |
| N.W of ALBERT | 20/21 | night | A & C Coys took over Reserve trenches in counter-attack batts. CARSON TRENCH | 11.20.00 2nd Lt. |
| | | | from 8th E. Surrey Regt. Quiet. | |
| | 21 to 25 | | A & C Coys in Reserve trenches. B & D Coys training daily for operations. | 2nd Lt. |
| | | | B as assault Coys, D in wiring Coy. Practice in rapid wiring. Rehearsals. | 2nd Lt. |
| | 25/26 | night | A & C Coys took over front line trenches, A Coy in HAIRPIN, C Coy (in W.21. a & b) | 2nd Lt. |
| | | | support) in TORRENS and TORRENS Support (SENLIS map 1:20000, W.21 a & b) | SENLIS |
| | 27 | 10 am – 6 pm | Enemy registered on support line with heavy and light T.M. Patrolling by | 2nd Lt. |
| | | | Day by A Coy discovered several gaps in enemy wire, opposite HAIRPIN. | |
| | | | B & D Coys still rehearsing attack just west of MARTOY. | 2nd Capt. |
| | 28 | | Some shelling by enemy of front and support trenches. Our Lewis | |
| | | | [fire?] on enemy front trenches and wire | |
| | 29 | | Quiet day. | 2nd Lt. |
| | 29/30 | night | Relieved by 2nd Bedfordshire Regt. & moved to right sector, relieving 11th R. Fusiliers | 2nd Capt. |

# WAR DIARY
## INTELLIGENCE SUMMARY

Army Form C. 2118.

| Place | Date | Hour | Summary of Events and Information | Remarks and references to Appendices |
|---|---|---|---|---|
| N.W. of ALBERT | 29/30 | night | B + D Coys took over our front line (SWAN TRENCH) C Coy in reserve (MELBOURNE TRENCH) Final preparations for attack in moving front system in W21.B+d | SENLIS 1:20,000 |
| | 30 | 9.35 pm | Zero hour 9.35 pm. Good barrage by our own guns, enemy barrage late in starting. Advance under creeping screen. No news from front line at 12.30 am. Patrols sent out. Found prisoners coming down (July 1st 12.40 am) Signals from front line positions established and consolidated. Very light casualties. | J.M.Coy Capt + M/A Capt 2nd North'n R |

# WAR DIARY or INTELLIGENCE SUMMARY

Army Form C. 2118.

6 Northamptons
Vol 51 37

| Place | Date | Hour | Summary of Events and Information | Remarks and references to Appendices |
|---|---|---|---|---|
| N.W. of Albert | July 1st | 2.0 am | Arno. shelling of captured line by enemy. No infantry action. Fairly quiet day. Consolidation and establishment of communication. | Sentries special at posts 1-8 here |
| " | | 9.25 pm | Heavy shelling | |
| " | 2 | 2.35 am | "S.O.S" from front line. Heavy shelling. | |
| | | 3.15 am | "Crown sur" all well | |
| " | | | Order to relieve 6/7 Queens (Pursuing Regt) Relief proceeded without incident on left of Bn line that night & Bedfords. South attack much ???? by A Coy | |
| " | 3 | 9.35 pm | Enemy attempted counter attack against A Coy who were in ???? much Zero hour fixed 3.10 ???? but bombardment at 3 am ???? (assisted ???? - avances Brit 1st/ Buffs E.Kent R.) ???? him ??? | Regt not engaged |
| " | | 6.35 pm | Relief ???? | |
| " | 4 | 1.45 am | Relief complete and position taken up to bivouacs along Henencourt - Bouzincourt Rd. Cleaning up. R.E. ???? on day night. | |

Army Form C. 2118.

# WAR DIARY
## or
## INTELLIGENCE SUMMARY.
*(Erase heading not required.)*

Instructions regarding War Diaries and Intelligence Summaries are contained in F. S. Regs., Part II. and the Staff Manual respectively. Title pages will be prepared in manuscript.

| Place | Date | Hour | Summary of Events and Information | Remarks and references to Appendices |
|---|---|---|---|---|
| HUMENCOURT-BOUZINCOURT Rd | July 5th | | Cleaning and improving dugouts. No Parades. Precautions to observation | |
| " | 6th | | 1 Off and 3 O/R went to MOLLIENS-au-BOIS. RE fatigue party | |
| " | 7th | | RE fatigue. Reveille at 7am. Breakfast from 8 to 9am. | |
| " | 8th | | Church Parade 9.10.11 to pub Lowis Mass at 7am | |
| " | 12th | | Bath was relieved by 10th Bn of London Bde at 3.15pm and marched (ON TAP) Bus on arrival 9.45pm | |
| SAISSEVAL | 13th | | to Huts at SAISSEVAL. Arrived at 9.45pm | |
| " | 14th | 10 am | Cleaning up. Billets very dirty. Battalion very dirty | |
| " | 15th | 8.15 am | Bn Parade. Inspection by Bn 2nd in CO. | |
| " | 16th | 9.30 | EA to field. As usual. Physical drill, arms drill and march off by coys | |
| " | 17th | | Drew BA on 15th. Afternoon football | |
| " | 18th | 8.45 | Training as on 15th Battalion Concert in Evening. | |
| " | 19th | | " " Place Van Blergs School | |

Army Form C. 2118.

# WAR DIARY
## or
## INTELLIGENCE SUMMARY.
(Erase heading not required.)

Instructions regarding War Diaries and Intelligence Summaries are contained in F. S. Regs., Part II. and the Staff Manual respectively. Title pages will be prepared in manuscript.

| Place | Date | Hour | Summary of Events and Information | Remarks and references to Appendices |
|---|---|---|---|---|
| Naissard | July 20 | | Marched by Coupeaux to Picquigny for billets & Training | |
| " | 21 | 10.30am | Bn Church Parade | |
| " | 22 | 8.45am | Bn Parade. General Training. | |
| " | 23 | | Bn Parade " | |
| " | 24 | | Same as for 23 | |
| " | 25 | 12.30am | Bn paraded and marched to Divisional Race Meeting at Cross Road Crouy-Cauelon and Sous-Picquigny. | |
| " | 26 | 8.30 | Bn attended Presentation of Medal Ribbons by G.O.C. III Corps B4s. March Past. | |
| " | | 3 pm | Bn Rifle Meeting. | |
| " | 27 | | TALAVERA DAY. Bn marched to B2 Sports at Run Divisional Cinema Invited Lathe. | |
| " | 28 | 10.30 | Bn Church Parade. | |
| " | 29 | 10.30 | Bn marched to entraining point at Fienvilliers. 12 am Bn entrained Delvey at Pont Noyelles and marched to Vignacourt on either side of ALBERT-AMIENS Rd. Bivouac La Houssoye & FRANVILLERS | Sheet 62 D. N.E. |

**Army Form C. 2118.**

# WAR DIARY
## or
## INTELLIGENCE SUMMARY.
(Erase heading not required.)

| Place | Date | Hour | Summary of Events and Information | Remarks and references to Appendices |
|---|---|---|---|---|
| SW FRANKVILLERS | July 30 | 5pm | Bn marched off to the line by Platoons. A 3 hours halt at HEILLY where Bn bathed in ANCRE and had tea. Marched off at 9pm and relieved the 53rd Bn Infantry, Australian Imperial Forces, in the line N.E. of SAILLY LAURETTE, west of the front captured by them from the enemy on the 29/30th. Relief complete 1 a.m. 31st. Work the 31st on deepening &  connecting trench known as front line. | |
| In the line | 31 | | | |

Yrs [signed] Crosse[?]
for Lt. Col.
Comdg the 6(S) Bn Northamptonshire Regt.

54th Inf. Bde.

18th Division

6th BATTALION

NORTHAMPTONSHIRE REGIMENT

AUGUST 1918

# WAR DIARY
## or
## INTELLIGENCE SUMMARY.
*(Erase heading not required.)*

Army Form C. 2118.

| Place | Date | Hour | Summary of Events and Information | Remarks and references to Appendices |
|---|---|---|---|---|
| Loane W. of ALBERT | 17th | | Quiet day. Daylight patrols in ALBERT. | |
| | 18th | | Moderate activity during the day. | |
| | | 9.30pm | Battalion was relieved by 1st Queens Regt. and came out to BENENCOURT WOOD. | |
| | 19th | | Day spent in cleaning and reorganising. | |
| | 20th | | Men rested during the day. | |
| | | 8.30pm | The Bn. moved off and relieved 139th Bde American Regt on Railway Cutting S.W. of ALBERT. | |
| S.W. of ALBERT | 21st | | Bn. rested all day in existing Railway Cutting handle for forward Bn. Very heavy M.G. fire. | |
| | | 11 pm | A Coy took up forward position near Rivers ANCRE but between met by heavy M.G. fire. | |
| | 22nd | 4.30am | The whole Bn with the exception of C Coy had crossed River ANCRE | |
| | | 4.45am | Covering Barrage on front of Bn commenced. Line 4.5-5am the Bn attacked. C + B Coys gaining first objective R.T.S Coys gaining through and gaining final objective 3,000 yards E. of River ANCRE. Over 600 Prisoners including 1 Major + 1 Field gun numerous M.Gs + | |
| | | 6.0pm | T.Ms. were captured by the Bn. A Coy attacked and obbay fatirud out from Bouzeaux to known were taken during the attack. | |
| | 23rd | | The Bn. consolidated positions captured on 22nd. | |

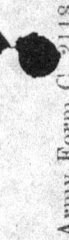

Army Form C. 2118.

# WAR DIARY
## or
## INTELLIGENCE SUMMARY.
*(Erase heading not required.)*

Instructions regarding War Diaries and Intelligence Summaries are contained in F. S. Regs., Part II. and the Staff Manual respectively. Title pages will be prepared in manuscript.

| Place | Date | Hour | Summary of Events and Information | Remarks and references to Appendices |
|---|---|---|---|---|
| | 25th | 4.0am | A & D Coys further advanced their line 1000/1500 yards nearly reaching their objective. | |
| | 26th | 2.30am | C. B Coys went through A & D Coys advancing under a barrage and dug in on a line E. of FRICOURT. 11th Royal Fusiliers plus some units and carried on the advance. Total casualties up to this day of 3 offs. 112 O.R. | |
| FRICOURT | 26th | | The Bn. held in the same position for the day. | |
| | 27th | | Bn. still in the same position. Day was spent in resting & cleaning up. | |
| | 28th | | Bn. in same position. | |
| | | 7.30pm | Bn. moved off and took over position from 7th R.W. Kents B. & C. Coys. on eastern edge of TRONES WOOD. A. & D. Coys in support in BERNAFAY WOOD. | |
| | 29th | 7.30am | News of Enemy Retreat. The Bn. formed up and halted on Ridge S. of LEUZE Wood. The Enemy was seen retiring from COMBLES. | |
| | | 4.30pm | The Bn. advanced. B. & C. Coys in front and took up a position on high ground S.E. of COMBLES. Fairly heavy Enemy shelling. Enemy Machine Gunning from N. of COMBLES. | |
| | 30th | 4.30am | 1 & D. Coys. 11th Royal Fusiliers & 2nd Bedfordshire Regt. attacked through the Bn. & D. Coys. then came into line on left of B.C. Coys. 2nd Beds. Regt. on the left were held up by Hostile M.Gs. The Bn. dug in on their position. Movement on left was impossible owing to M.G. and rifle fire. | |

6th (S) Bn. Northumberland Fusiliers Regt    Aug 18

Army Form C. 2118.

# WAR DIARY
## or
## INTELLIGENCE SUMMARY.
(Erase heading not required.)

Vol 38

| Place | Date | Hour | Summary of Events and Information | Remarks and references to Appendices |
|---|---|---|---|---|
| Bois N. of SAILLY LAURETTE | 1st | | Quiet day. Active patrolling all night. A & B Coys were relieved in the front line by C & D Coys. | |
| " | 2nd | 10.30pm | Enemy artillery active all day. The Bn. was relieved by 2nd Lancashire Regt. and came into billets N of SAILLY-LE-SEC | |
| billets N of SAILLY-LE-SEC | 3rd | | Trenches in very bad condition owing to heavy rain. Whole Bn. employed on burying parties at ETINEHEM. | |
| " | 4th | | The Bn. employed as on the 3rd. | |
| " | 6th | 11.0pm | The Bn. battled on the SOMME. My Coys. moved into support to left sector astride the BRAY-CORBIE Road. | |
| " | 6th | 4.0am | Heavy Enemy barrage on front line. | |
| | | 4.30am | Enemy attacked. B & D Coys. supported by C Coy Artillery formation advanced and re-occupied support line S of BRAY-CORBIE Road who have now consolidated and held. | |
| | 7th | 4.40am | In conjunction with 11th Royal Fusiliers on Right, B and D Coys attacked in two waves and recaptured original front line. During the day the enemy made repeated counter attacks. | |
| | | 4.30pm | Enemy consisted during afternoon from heavy shell. A platoon of B Coy. Road. The whole front being held. A platoon of B Coy. re-established the line. | |

Army Form C. 2118.

# WAR DIARY
or
# INTELLIGENCE SUMMARY.
(Erase heading not required.)

Instructions regarding War Diaries and Intelligence Summaries are contained in F.S. Regs., Part II. and the Staff Manual respectively. Title pages will be prepared in manuscript.

| Place | Date | Hour | Summary of Events and Information | Remarks and references to Appendices |
|---|---|---|---|---|
| | 8th | 1.0AM | Bn was relieved by 9/R.F. 12th Division and A.B. & D. Coys came out to dispositions N of Sailly-Sec. C. Coy to Sailly N. of VAUX. Bn Hqrs with C. Coy. | |
| | | 3.30PM | The Bn moved to Baths N of HENCY | |
| | 9th | 2 AM | The Bn moved up in support of 18th Division and took up position along MERICOURT-VAUX Road. B of MERICOURT. Day spent in cleaning and organizing. | |
| | 10th | 10.30AM | The Bn marched to HENENCOURT WOOD and reached there for the day | |
| | | 9.0PM | Bn moved off and took over line W of ALBERT from the London Irish Regt. "C" D Coys in front line with "A" "B" Coys in support. | |
| Line W. of ALBERT | 11th | 4.0AM | Very heavy enemy shelling of front line to Infantry action Allie holding carried out shorlynt the day in ALBERT. | |
| " | 12th | | Quiet day. Patrolling carried on in ALBERT | |
| " | 13th | | Enemy very quiet during these 3 days. Nothing of interest to report | |
| " | 14th | | Quiet day | |
| " | 15th | 10 PM | Relieved by 2 Coys and Resistance Bn. A coy came out to HENENCOURT WOOD | |
| HENENCOURT WOOD | 16th | | Battalion housed in huts at WARLOY | |
| | | 1.0PM | Returned to same position in line "A" B Coys in front line with C + D in support | |

(A8004) Wt. W777i/M231 750,000 5/17 Sch. 52 Forms/C2118/14
D. D. & L., London, E.C.

1st Northants ... 
6 Northants 1st ...

Army Form C. 2118.

# WAR INTELLIGENCE SUMMARY

(Erase heading not required.)

Instructions regarding War Diaries and Intelligence Summaries are contained in F. S. Regs., Part II. and the Staff Manual respectively. Title pages will be prepared in manuscript.

| Place | Date | Hour | Summary of Events and Information | Remarks and references to Appendices |
|---|---|---|---|---|
| COMBLES | 1st | 1 AM | B & D. Coys took up a line of outposts in rear of their positions. A Coy then taking over D Coys line and withdrawing their outposts. 3 Platoons of C Coy attached to D Coy. | |
| | | 3 AM | A Coy withdrew to CHALK PIT in S.E. outskirts of COMBLES. | |
| | | 5.30 | 55 I.B. attack through 6th I.B. | |
| | | 7 PM | 6 N.B. Coys took up a defensive position on the line running from FREGICOURT to PRIER FARM. D Coy withdrawing to Chalk Pit S.E. of COMBLES. C Coy & Bomb. S. of COMBLES. | CO4 CO4 |
| | 2nd | | The Bn. in same position, resting and refitting. The Bn. in same position under orders to move up. Orders was cancelled at 5.30 am. | CO4 CO4 |
| | 4th | | The Bn. moved to huts & bivouacs round Cross Roads immediately E of GUINNEMONT. | CO4 |
| | | | Bn. spent the day in charge of reorganisation. | CO4 |
| | | | The Bn. bathed at COMBLES. | CCR |
| | 7th | | The Bn. spent the day in Camp & made Coy arrangements E. | CC4 |

(48109) Wt. W1972/M137 725,000 3/17 Sch. 52 Forms/C2118/14. D. D. & L., London, E.C.

# WAR DIARY
## INTELLIGENCE SUMMARY.

Army Form C. 2118.

| Place | Date | Hour | Summary of Events and Information | Remarks and references to Appendices |
|---|---|---|---|---|
| East of GUILLEMONT | 8th | | Church Parade Service. Congratulatory notice by Corps Commander read out to all ranks on parade. | |
| | 9th | | Bn. training non commissioned officers and young NCOs, indent resumed. | |
| | 10th | | Inspection of held Athletics by the Corps Commander. The Ellaney horse show only occurred who won cup, attended by 6 Offrs & 160 OR. The remainder of the Bn were training under company arrangements. Training continued. Bn. having now considerable training in new formations. This held lecture at MONTAUBAN. The men were very good. | |
| | 11th | | Reorganisation of Coys manners and specialist Platoons was taken in hand. Training of young soldiers carried out by the Battalion in conjunction with the remainder of the Bde. and with the explanation with 38 on LONGUEVAL + DELVILLE WOOD). | |
| | 12th | | | |

**Army Form C. 2118.**

# WAR DIARY
## or
## INTELLIGENCE SUMMARY.
(Erase heading not required.)

Instructions regarding War Diaries and Intelligence Summaries are contained in F. S. Regs., Part II. and the Staff Manual respectively. Title pages will be prepared in manuscript.

| Place | Date | Hour | Summary of Events and Information | Remarks and references to Appendices |
|---|---|---|---|---|
| | 16th | | The Bn moved forward at 10.0 a.m. and marched to MORLAINS and bivouaced for the night. The EPINETTE WOOD where they bivouaced for the day was exceptionally hot and was followed by a terrific thunderstorm at night. | |
| | 17th | | The Bn rested during the day so no movement was allowed. | C.H. O.A. |
| | | 1 P.M. | Arrived at the line took up a position in Railway Cutting W. of ST EMILE. | |
| | 19th | | The Bn attacked in conjunction with the remainder of the Bde and 7 R.W.K. on a line running E and W and N and S of RONSOY. The scrub being in full view to keep direction. B & C Coys. carrying much it very difficult to keep direction. B & C Coys. advanced in front line A Coy in support D Coy in reserve. The Bn lost heavily in P[?] but did not in T.P. attacking Coys near no german swim before E. W. barrage lifted. The advance continued until held up NW of SERINE F.15.a.5.6 & F.14. b.7.3. We were held up here by | Casualties orders attached to these |

(A8304) D. D/W.L., London, E.C.— Wt. W17711/M2731 750,000 3/17 Sch. 52 Forms/C2118/14

# WAR DIARY or INTELLIGENCE SUMMARY

Army Form C. 2118.

| Place | Date | Hour | Summary of Events and Information | Remarks and references to Appendices |
|---|---|---|---|---|
| | 18th | | All ranks that we came across up to the Western edge of Bois des Foureaux experienced great difficulty in maintaining direction when the E and W barrage started the barrage having been a good one being on the front line running E & W though F.W. Central, though it was anything but a dense barrage and the M.Gs opening against no visible objects fired from shrapnel proof cover. When we had established our line RIDGE RESERVE SOUTH to SUND COPSE notices were put out, to Royal Fusiliers about the Bedfords and Royal Welsh about shorts and these the main W. barrage opened on a line E of ST EMILE at 5.0 a.m. Battalion H.Q. was at ROWNEY WOOD. | |
| | 18th/19th | | During the night we made several unsuccessful attempts to get MAY COPSE. | |
| | 19th | 5 A.M. | The Bn attacked MAY COPSE from two directions and captured it without resistance. We also took two prisoners. We then advanced our right line MAY COPSE corner ENFER WOOD to Ridge Reserve trench at F.15.d.6.8 still maintaining touch with 1/R Fusiliers on the right and 9/R Fusiliers on left. | |
| | | 11 AM | 53rd Bn passed through us when however we supported to be on East edge of ENFER WOOD but still for on N Edge and we had 3 | |

# WAR DIARY
## or
## INTELLIGENCE SUMMARY
*(Erase heading not required.)*

| Place | Date | Hour | Summary of Events and Information | Remarks and references to Appendices |
|---|---|---|---|---|
| Canalnis | 20th | 4 A.M. | The Bn was withdrawn to pt W. Edge of RONSSOY WOOD. Bn Hqrs remained in same position. During the day the Bn was reorganised in 2 Coys "A" & "B" together under Capt FROST and C & D under Capt WESTWOOD. All officers went forward to reconnoitre the ground with a view to a further attack. | |
| | 21st | | The Bn was in position on the forming up line 2 hours before ZERO. A large tell of phone line was patrolled and the gaps not to had been cut by the 7/Buffs were kept clear. The attack was carried out on a 1 Coy frontage of 225 x Idea, the having offered the Enemy any towards any cloudy and suffered several casualties through this. The leading Coy have dashed to about 50 yards carried on close to the barrage with great success, crossing the DUNCAN — DOLEFUL POST LINE and getting on to Yellow line finishing up around ISLAND TRAVERSE. | |

M.Gs. in F.15.d.5.9. and 6 guns in F.15.b. She fired occasionally round in N. part of the Village and slanted down Main St. in S.E. direction. By the time the tank reached F.15.a.9.5. one of the Coys. had moved its many hy. sectional lengths of trench at F.15.a.8.4. the other 2 Coys. attacked the main st. in F.15.b. and Quid Post. Meanwhile taking up a line RIDGE RESERVE TRENCH through Quid COPSE two Platoons of my Coy. for then occupied this was from the N.W. corner of ROMNEY WOOD to the high ground W. of Quid Post eventually turning up a line up to KNOLL POST when they got in touch with 12 Div.

The geographically there is nowhere in the devotions nor the incidence of elevation enemy. It very disadvan. and a great deal of ground there could not the seen at a greater distance than 30 yds. There was also down very awkward and deep trenches to cross, the delayed the troops considerably going E. trudt for which ROMNEY WOOD where we were forced to climb a Quid turning E. and W. through the Wood. At the position but of the store west of the B— L— came our Coy. of the Royal Scots attached to my also met our cox A Coy. who have been working Round the S. end

Army Form C. 2118.

# WAR DIARY
## or
## INTELLIGENCE SUMMARY.
(Erase heading not required.)

| Place | Date | Hour | Summary of Events and Information | Remarks and references to Appendices |
|---|---|---|---|---|

In this trench were captured 1 Off. & 20 O.R. There were not down under cover. At this point we observed that THE KNOLL and the trench system S.E. was strongly held. On the left we got into touch with the R.W. Kents. During the whole of the advance and on arrival in the fellow trench we were very much troubled with M.G. enfilade fire from the right. From this position it was observed that the 4 hours had been put out of action. The 53rd Bde. on our left were unable to advance against the KNOLL and later on showed that the 53rd I.B. were compelled to withdraw to a line further West. We were then in an extremely difficult position have both flanks in the air and the enemy by making an encircling movement compelled us to withdraw to the HOLLAND [MORTERIE crossed out] POST – DURBAN ROAD line.

(Maps &c. attached for Record). cont

# WAR DIARY or INTELLIGENCE SUMMARY

Army Form C. 2118.

| Place | Date | Hour | Summary of Events and Information | Remarks and references to Appendices |
|---|---|---|---|---|
| | 26b. | | The post was captured at 11.55 pm and consolidation was rapidly proceeded with. The ground to the N.E. and West was patrolled and the enemy was discovered to be holding a line of posts running down the Sunken Road from F.7.b.8.9 to F.17.b.8.9. | |
| | 22nd | | Throughout the day the enemy were observed moving approx 1-3 m and moving forward on foot in 2s and 3s through the various communication trenches and along ground approach to Pelican trench. He was at once communicated to the Bde. Every man in the Batt. feeling that an attack was imminent prepared himself. Large quantities of S.A.A. munition were collected during the night. The L. Guns & M.Gs were so placed that they were in no case from enemy M.Gs. & so placed and the expected enemy might the enemy attack quite ready to deal effectively with the enemy attack | |
| | | 3.45 pm | The SOS went up on our light and we saw the enemy advancing in large numbers. The enemy advanced to within 300 y.b. of the Bat. and was mown down by our Rifle and M.G. fire. One large shell and the enemy shed through our lines causing heavy damage | |

(A804) Wt.W1771/M2 31. 750,000 5/17 Sch. 53 Forms/C2118/14

# WAR DIARY
## or
## INTELLIGENCE SUMMARY.
*(Erase heading not required.)*

Army Form C. 2118.

| Place | Date | Hour | Summary of Events and Information | Remarks and references to Appendices |
|---|---|---|---|---|
| | 23rd | 6 PM | During a further attempt by the enemy we captured 39 prisoners. The Bn was relieved by 7th Queens Regt. and came back to QUARRY NW of ST. EMILE. | |
| | 24th | | Bn marching spent the day in cleaning and reorganisation. | cop |
| | 25th | 3.45am | The Bn moved back and occupied old Dugouts in Nurlu area. The Bn spent the day in cleaning and bathing. | cop |
| | 26th | | Bn some advance by the G.O.C. Division. | cop |
| | 27th | | Bn spent the day in preparations for move. | cop |
| | | 3.45am | Bn moved up and occupied area W of EPEHY. | cop |
| | 28th | | The remainder of the day was spent resting. | cop |
| | | 7 PM | The Bn moved to assembly positions prior to its attack on the HINDENBURG LINE. Assembly positions were the VALLEY near ENFER WOOD E. of RONSSOY WOOD. | |
| | 29th | 4 AM | Boys took up positions on forming up Line between LEMPIRE POST and TORTOYS FARM facing NE | |
| | | 5.30AM | The Bn advanced behind the creams. A & D Coys in Front Line B Coy in Support & C Coys in Reserve owing to severe shelling | |

| Place | Date | Hour | Summary of Events and Information | Remarks and references to Appendices |
|---|---|---|---|---|
| | | | Barrage our Coys got mixed up with the Americans. Objective of the Bn. MACQUINCOURT TRENCH, was to run N.E. from Back of support on the Right. A Coy. fell back and formed a defensive flank. | |
| | | 10 AM | 5 A the 8 officers who went with the Coys. had become casualties including B & D. Coy Commanders, therefore 2 Coys. only were organised. A & B together and C & D together. A number of American stragglers were attached to our Coys. Owing to heavy M.G. fire from high ground the forward Coys "B" Coy. were forced to abandon position and withdraw to TOMBOIS SUPPORT. On account of the dense smoke and mist the troops had not mopped up thoroughly and the still held dents behind our troops on the flanks. | |
| | 30th | | Bn. in the same position. Situation Quiet. | |
| | | 1 PM | Orders received from Bde. to proceed to CANAL BANK. A Coy. sent forward put see heavily fired on by M.Gs. from the Right Bank. B Coy. was detailed on bridge in S.S. 26.b.3 the remainder of the Coy. forming a defensive flank in HINDENBURG TRENCH and VENDHUILE TRENCH. | |

| Place | Date | Hour | Summary of Events and Information | Remarks and references to Appendices |
|---|---|---|---|---|
| | 30th | | C. Coy. relieved JAEGER TRENCH | |
| | | 7.30pm | Bde orders were received that the Bn would be relieved by the 2nd Bedfordshire Regt. | out |

R. Turner Lt Col
Commanding 6 (Ok) Northamptonshire Reg.

Copy. No.

Operation Orders No. 30
by
Lieut. Colonel L. Turner, D. S. O.
Commanding 6th Bn. Northamptonshire Regiment.      17.9.18.

Ref. Map. 1/20,000
already issued.

1. The objectives of the Brigade and the present front line are shown on the 1/20,000 map already issued. On Y/Z night the front line will be occupied by the 53rd Infantry Brigade.
Tanks will assist in these operations.

2. The starting Line will be 200 yards West of the Opening Barrage Line, and the Royal W. Kents will attack the first objectives.

3. Battalions will form up in the following order from front to rear at the following times, and will occupy in Depth the following distances :-

| | | |
|---|---|---|
| 7th Royal West Kent Regt. | Zero minus 2 hours. | 250 yards. |
| 2nd Bedfordshire Regt. | " " 1½ hours. | 250 yards. |
| 11th Royal Fusiliers. | " " 1 hour. | 300 yards. |
| 6th Northamptonshire Regt. | " " 30 minutes. | 300 yards. |

4. At Zero the 7th Royal West Kents will advance and capture the Western Outskirts of RONSSOY. On reaching a North and South Line running through E.21.b.4.5. (eastern edge of Cemetery) the barrage will halt and the 2nd Bedfords will pass through them and advance to the Brigade objective. After the 2nd Bedfords are clear of the Royal West Kents, the 11th Royal Fusiliers will advance and pass through the Royal West Kents, form to the left, their Left flank resting on a point 200 yards South of the Cross Roads in F.15.d.8.8. They will be formed on a line running East and West through this point by ZERO plus 116 minutes when the N. and S. barrage will lift and drop on an East-West Line passing through F.15.d.6.8. (see artillery trace) The front of the 2nd Bedfordshire Regt. will be covered by a barrage of 60 lb. and Smoke Shell. At ZERO plus 120 minutes the East and West Barrage will advance, followed by the 11th Royal Fusiliers to the Brigade objective. The 6th Northamptonshire Regt. will form up on the same line as the 11th Royal Fusiliers and at the same time and will advance on their left to the Brigade objective. The Left Flank of the 6th Northamptonshire Regt. will rest on a N. and S. Line through E.14.d.6.6. The E. and W. barrage will halt for 15 minutes at ZERO plus 133 on the Northern edge of RONSSOY to enable Coys. to reinforce front line if necessary.

5. Liaison Patrols commanded by an Officer will be established with flank divisions as follows:-
2nd Bedfordshire Regt.    /4th Division    F.22.d.0.8.
6th Northamptonshire Regt. 18th Division.  May Copse F.9.c.2.6.
"C" Coy. will detail this Officer.

6. The 7th R.W. Kents will leave platoons at the following points also at the same points Vickers guns are placed and will cease fire when Northamptons advance :-
F.13.d.7.4.
F.14.d.4.4.
These platoons will face North East and engage any enemy movement in the valley with Rifle and L.G. Fire.

Any Anti Tank guns which may open fire will be at once ...ged with Rifle and L.G. Fire.

The importance of secrecy is impressed on all ranks. Troops ...p under cover by day as much as possible. All reference to ...ns on the telephone is forbidden, all telephone circuits are ...lic.

9. In the event of the capture of hostile guns, information will at once be sent to Brigade Headquarters for transmission to the artillery, giving exact location of guns, nature of gun, and whether ammunition is at hand.

10. A contact aeroplane will fly over the Corps Front :-
   Zero plus 2 hours 15 minutes.
   Zero plus 5 hours.
   Zero plus 7 hours, and subsequently as ordered.
   Troops will be warned to be on the lookout and indicate their location by placing their rifles in a row in front of their positions.
   A Contact Aeroplane will be up continuously from daylight onwards in order to detect the approach of enemy counter attacks, notice of which it will give by flying towards the Counter Attacking troops and dropping a white flare as near the Counterattacking troops as possible.

11. S.O.S. signal is "red over red over red".

12. Troops will attack in normal fighting kit. Each man will carry 1 bomb. Large tools will be carried - at least 1 spade to each 2 men and 1 pick to each 8 men.

13. Os. C. will impress on all ranks the necessity of keeping under cover by day. Even if all objectives have been captured and the enemy shelling has ceased. If men expose themselves needlessly unnecessary casualties are caused and enemy observers can guage the nature and extent of our dispositions.

14. After the 11th Royal Fusiliers have reached their final objective at Zero plus 168 the creeping barrage will lift. The 11th R.F. will then attack and capture LAMPIRE, YAK, and ZEBRA posts, which will have been bombarded during the proceeding operations. The posts will be captured by fire action and without a creeping barrage.

15. The 6th Northamptonshire Regt. will attack on left of R.F. direction of attack due North, under Barrage. Dividing Line between the two battalions will be a N. and S. Line through the Cross Roads F.15.d.8.8. The left boundaries of the Northamptons will be a N. and South Line F.14.d.5.5.

16. The attack will be carried out as follows:- "B" and "C" Coys. in the Front Line. Attacking Troops "B" Coy. on the right and "C" on the left. "B" Coy. on a frontage of 500 yards and "C" Coy. the remaining frontage. They will attack in two waves, 70 yards in rear of attacking Coys. "A" Coy. will follow if possible, in worm formation, and will assist in clearing the ground and will reinforce the front line if required. All reinforcements by Units, Sections, Platoons, etc. "D" Coy. will be reserve Company, and will follow about 300 to 400 yards in rear of Support Coy.
   When the East and West barrages working North and South lift, "B" Coy. will as rapidly as possible take up a front ENFER WOOD inclusive, thence North or North West until they are in touch with the 12th Division. "B" Coys. area will be F.9.c. and will include a little of F.15.a. "C" Coy's area will be F.8.d. and part of F.14.b. When this Company is in touch with the 12th Division they will form a line of posts parallel to and facing the front line.
   "A" Coy. will take as their area part of F.15.a. and b. This Coy. also having ascertained clearly the situation of the front line, will form a defensive line also parallel to the front line.
   "D" Coy. will take as their area RONSSOY WOOD. This Coy. as the attack proceeds will detach 2 platoons to mop up the areas in rear of F.13.b. and the whole of F.14 a. and b. They will collect all prisoners at the North End of RONSSOY WOOD where they will be sent down to Brigade. Having mopped up this area these two platoons will join their Coy. in RONSSOY WOOD.

   Battalion H.Qrs. will follow in rear of Battalion and take up position at the Northern End of RONSSOY WOOD about F.15.c.2.8.

   sgd. Chas. C. Hill. Lieut. & Adjt.
   6th

18

The attack of the 6th Northamptonshire Regt. in this part of the 5th Infantry Brigade attack was as follows.

Barrage opened to time. It was very dark, heavy rain and the smoke which our Artillery put over on the North of us blew in our direction and you could not see a man at a greater distance than 30 yards. There was very great difficulty in maintaining direction. I saw many Units in difficulty in this respect. My two attacking Companies and support Company were able to keep their direction and reached the Westerly edge of RONSSOY WOOD where they followed an East and West drive going through the WOOD. These three Companies were in the following position 10 minutes before the East and West barrage opened. My right was about F.15.d.6.5. my left flank on F.14.d.4.8. The East & West barrage was very straight though not thick was quite a good one. My right flank was very badly enfiladed by Machine Gun fire from F.15.d.6.9. A large number of Machine Gun emplacements were troubling us with direct fire from trenches running North West, South East on the Southern slopes of the North West portion of RONSSOY VILLAGE. Machine Gun fire from QUID POST and QUID COPSE also troubled considerably. The Battalion advanced until held up by Machine Gun fire when they held a North West, South East line on the North of RONSSOY WOOD. Under this Machine Gun fire one Company advanced by sections to a trench in F.15.a.6.2. The Battalion was then in great difficulties every sectional rush made by the other Companies being stopped by the enemy Machine Gun fire. A Tank then came into view at F.15.d.4.6 moving West. This Tank observed that we were in difficulties and wheeled round and moved down the MAIN STREET in RONSSOY. This gave us an opportunity. The whole Battalion then moved up by sectional and Platoon rushes and gained the whole of the N.W. portion of the VILLAGE. At the same time another Company attacked QUID POST and captured it and the advance was continued capturing QUID COPSE with its 2 FIELD GUNS, 14 Machine Gun posts taken the guns captured and in six cases the Gunners were killed. At the North West corner of the VILLAGE another Field Gun was captured and two Trench Mortars at F.15.a.8.6. and F.15.b.2.7. We captured a large number of Prisoners during our advance through the wood. Most of the

Prisoners were caught in the wood were between us and the Opening barrage. We also captured a number of prisoners in the Village, estimated between 130 and 140. After the capture of QUID POST on the north east of RONSSOY VILLAGE we were again held up by heavy shelling and Machine Gun fire from the direction of ZEBRA POST and FLEECEALL POST. We then worked our way up the trench from QUID POST and got into touch with the 12 Division at KNOLL POST also in touch with Royal Fusiliers on our right. The line was pushed to RIDGE RESERVE POST. On the night 18/19 we made several unsuccessful endeavours to get MAY COPSE. At dawn on the 19th we approached MAY POST from two directions and occupied it without resistance and we then advanced our whole line MAY COPSE. SOUTH WEST corner ENFER WOOD to Ridge Reserve trench at F.15.b.6.8; still maintaining in touch with Royal Fusiliers on our right and the 9th Royal Fusiliers on our left. At 11 am 53 Brigade went through us their Opening barrage was supposed to be on East edge of ENFER WOOD. It fell on WEST edge and we had 3 Casualties. The captured Machine Guns have been sent in by our Quarter Master to D.A.D.O.S. The sight off the Field Gun was sent in to Brigade. With regard to the other two, it was found that the dial sight had been removed and the angle sight could not be detached from the Gun.

1st Batt. Cambridgeshire Regt.

**Army Form C. 2118.**

# WAR DIARY
## or
## INTELLIGENCE SUMMARY.
(Erase heading not required.)

October 1918   Vol 4

Instructions regarding War Diaries and Intelligence Summaries are contained in F. S. Regs., Part II. and the Staff Manual respectively. Title pages will be prepared in manuscript.

| Place | Date | Hour | Summary of Events and Information | Remarks and references to Appendices |
|---|---|---|---|---|
| Sw. of WENDHUILE | 1st | 4 AM | The Bn. was finally relieved by the E. Surrey Regt. after a very strenuous period. The Bn then moved to RONSSOY and now bivouac'd in the Trench on the W. of RONSSOY WOOD and spent the remainder of the day resting and refitting. | C of H |
| RONSSOY | 2nd | 6 A.M. | The Bn marched to GUYENCOURT. | C of H |
|  |  | 11 A.M. | The Bn entrained | |
|  |  | 5 PM | The Bn detrained at MOISLIENS-au-BOIS where they were | C of H |
| MOISLIENS AU-BOIS |  |  | billeted | |
|  | 3rd |  | The day was spent in Bath & cleaning. | C of H |
|  | 4th |  | The Bn. rested and about the beginning areton | C of H |
|  | 5th |  | Reorganisation and introduction of Lays by County Officers | C of H |
|  | 6th |  | Church Parade not held as no Chaplain was available. | C of H |
|  | 7th to 9th |  | Institution of Congratulatory address by the County Officers. Training as the troops were attached. | C of H |

Army Form C. 2118.

# WAR DIARY
## or
## INTELLIGENCE SUMMARY.
(Erase heading not required.)

Instructions regarding War Diaries and Intelligence Summaries are contained in F.S. Regs, Part II. and the Staff Manual respectively. Title pages will be prepared in manuscript.

| Place | Date | Hour | Summary of Events and Information | Remarks and references to Appendices |
|---|---|---|---|---|
| MOLLIENS AU BOIS | 10 | | Training as per attached programme. Brigade Football Competition. 11 Royal Fusiliers 2, 6 Northants 2. | |
| | 11 | | Training as per programme. Brigade Football Competition. 2 Bedfordshire Regt 4, 6 Northants 0. | |
| | 12 | | Bde Sports - Fay day. | |
| | 13 | | Church Parade. Bde Football Competition 11 Royal Fusiliers 1, 6 Northants 5. | |
| | 14 | | Bn Inspected at work by G.O.C. Bde. Bde Football Competition 17th 2 Bedfordshire Regt 0, 6 Bn Northants Regt 1. | |
| | 15 | | Bn Parade for Instruction. Training in Bombing on the Marne - Outpost Duty etc. A, B Coys Bathed. | |
| | 16 | | Bn Parade for Instruction in Outpost Scheme. Transport moved off at 1700 to NURLU. | |
| | 17 | | Bn marched to POULAINVILLE and entrained at 1800. It Bn detrained at ROSELLE, arr. at 0200, + marched to billets at NURLU. The Bn rested during the morning and entrained at 1300 en route for YFRAIN. Bn found very comfortable billets here. Transport left NURLU at 1600 and arrived at YFRAIN at 2200 | |
| NURLU | 18 | | | |

# WAR DIARY
## or
## INTELLIGENCE SUMMARY.

Army Form C. 2118.

| Place | Date | Hour | Summary of Events and Information | Remarks and references to Appendices |
|---|---|---|---|---|
| SERAIN | 19th | | Bn. spent the day resting and cleaning up. | C.H.H. |
| | 20th | 1500 | In the morning baths prepared to work. Bn moved by march route to REUMONT arriving at about 1800. When they were billeted. Transport Limbers were at MADRAS and the Batt. H.Q. Limbers moved to ELAINCOURT. | R.A.9 |
| REUMONT | 21st | | Bn. spent the day resting | |
| " | 22nd | | Orders for Operation were received. Bn. spent the day resting | C.H.H. |
| " | 23rd | | The Bn moved off at 0410 and halted at Cross Road W. of LE CATEAU at 20:00 hrs. Bn. approached to assembly position W. of LE CATEAU at 0445 where they had breakfast. | |
| " | " | 0837 | The Bn. moved off and entered LE CATEAU at 0614 but were held up near the Church by the Queens Regt. for 15 mins. The Bridge over which the Bn. had to pass was not prepared so we had to head to head plans across the stream to enable the Bn. to cross. | |
| | | 1052 | Bn. H.Q. arrived at EPINETTE FARM with the Coys about 200x away and remained there until night. | |
| | 24th | 0030 | The Bn relieved 7th Bridge on E PINETTE FARM. | |
| | | 0315 | The Bn was on the morning of 24th by 0315. S.O.S. Coys were on the front line and had orders to advance 500x then consolidate. Immediately on halting they were to open rapid fire south every known German position to allow Co. D.15 drop forward. These two Coys had orders given them for rapid fire and the Berlitas and Lionism Cost gun were to pour them |

# WAR DIARY
## or
## INTELLIGENCE SUMMARY.

(Erase heading not required.)

Army Form C. 2118.

| Place | Date | Hour | Summary of Events and Information | Remarks and references to Appendices |
|---|---|---|---|---|
| | | | This Coy. object now to establish posts facing E to enable B. Coy. who following them to attack due South (See attached sketch) B. Coy. however now made to advance in a Southerly direction and C. Coy. had become hotly engaged with the enemy who were at A15.c.5.4. The enemy counter attacked about 0900 hrs but were repulsed. The tanks which were going to north of our area had previously further West and the advance of "B" Coy. was now held up by heavy M.G. fire from A15.C.5.4 and from the X roads at A15.C.0.5 just the Bedfords were unable to get South West of the main road running N. and S. and then gradually inch up Eastwards. B. Coy. seizing a favourable opportunity further along Southwards sending a platoon to work its way down the road from the North with consequently some trouble to establish a liaison post at A15.2.4.9. with the 2nd Middlesex who had also attacked this North meeting no at that point. A message was now sent objectives that been taken. About 1300 saying that our sent objectives about 1300 hrs. an objective their taken. the 2nd Bedfords and 11th Royal Sussex attacking S. on our right were also successful in gaining all their objectives and meeting the 50th Division who were attacking Northwards. | |

# WAR DIARY
## INTELLIGENCE SUMMARY
*(Erase heading not required.)*

Army Form C. 2118.

| Place | Date | Hour | Summary of Events and Information | Remarks and references to Appendices |
|---|---|---|---|---|
| | 24th | | C. & D. Coys who were following in close support were conferred owing to the nature of the ground to form up very close to the front Coys. The Right front and Support Coys had very little difficulty in forming up but the Left front & Support Coys owing to our barrage fire cutting their line had to withdraw 300x W. of it, in country which was very thick with hedges and this difficulty was considerable | |
| | | 4 am | The Barrage opened | |
| | | 4.45 | C. & D. Coys passed through A. & B. and nearest phase objective as per their orders, which are attached. C. Coy found their objective strongly held by German machine guns and wired, and when forced to fall back a few yds to the edge of Bonotes Wood the Enemy Counter attacked C. Coy but were repulsed much. | |
| | | 0800 | very heavy losses. At about 1300 At. F.W. HEDGES Comdg C. Coy by skilful manouevring was able to creep up a hedge towards a German M.G. Post paint Capture 4 guns and 4 prisoners. This enabled the Bn. to move forward and reach its objective as per orders attached. | |
| | | | During the night 24/25th the Bn. were relieved by the 8th Batt. Royal Berks Regt. and marched back to Bihucourt and adjacent Bousies. | |
| | 25th & 31st | | Refitting &c complete | |

**Army Form C. 2118.**

# WAR DIARY
## or
## INTELLIGENCE SUMMARY.
*(Erase heading not required.)*

Instructions regarding War Diaries and Intelligence Summaries are contained in F. S. Regs., Part II. and the Staff Manual respectively. Title pages will be prepared in manuscript.

| Place | Date | Hour | Summary of Events and Information | Remarks and references to Appendices |
|---|---|---|---|---|
| BOUSIES | 25th | | A list of the officers who were with the Bn. during these operations and shown as attached. (Casualties K & W.10667 & 63 S.M.6) | |
| | | 18:15 | The Bn. left BOUSIES and moved to camp in orchard near EPINETTE FARM. where they remained for the night. | |
| | 26th | 05:25 | The Bn. received orders to move at once and take up position near RENOUART FARM to support 53rd Bde under whose orders the Bn. was to be. | |
| | | | Col Turner re-assumed command of the Bn from Capt. GADSDEN after acting as Brigade Commander since the 24th. The Bn. arrived in position. | |
| | | 08:00 | | |
| | | 13:15 | The Bn. moved back to camp near EPINETTE FARM | |
| | 27th | 05:30 | The Bn. moved off from EPINETTE FARM and took over front line from 7th Batt. N.E. of ROBERSART. Bn. H.Q. in ROBERSART. Relief was completed by 07:30. D.M.B. Coys. were in the front line next C Coy. in support. During the day our line was advanced by about 200 ft. Enemy M.Gs. were very active throughout the day, and especially so during the night. Our patrols did not encounter any advance during the night 27/7/8/1. | |
| | | | Bn. still in the same position. Enemy shelling was chiefly confined to Back areas. ROBERSART was shelled at intervals throughout the day toward quietto. | |
| | 28th | | | |

# WAR DIARY
or
## INTELLIGENCE SUMMARY
(Erase heading not required.)

Army Form C. 2118.

| Place | Date | Hour | Summary of Events and Information | Remarks and references to Appendices |
|---|---|---|---|---|
| | 29th | | The morning was quiet. | |
| | | 1500 | The Bn. should that the Bde. on our left had moved forward 600x still occupied by enemy in turn, however, B Coy in front still occupied by enemy in turn, however, B Coy on the left pushed forward to Sniper Road in A.9.b. (Bns. attached) and A Coy on the right also pushed posts on to 100 yds. | C.H.Q. |
| | | | After these positions had been made good an intra Coy relief was carried out. "D" taking from "B" Coy, and "C" from "A" Coy | |
| | 30th | 0200 | Relief was complete. The Support Coys took up positions further forward. The enemy was fairly quiet during the day C.H.Q. | |
| | | 1930 | The Bn. was relieved by 2nd Bedfordshire Regt. and marched back to camp in the same position near EPINETTE FARM Nettlecomplete by 1930 hrs. | C.H.Q. |
| | 31st | | The Bn. rested and looked in Lorries at Le CATEAU. | |

R. Turner Lt. Col.
Comdg 6. Northamptons R.

ADDENDA to DIARY for 24th

During the operations of the 24th a Tank gave very valuable assistance around BOWSIES WOOD FARM. It continued circling round and making straight for German M.G. Emplacements. Although the Tank had been riddled with Armour Piercing bullets and all the crew except the Officer and Driver were wounded it went back and continued to give assistance to the Infantry.

# WAR DIARY or INTELLIGENCE SUMMARY

Army Form C. 2118/8

6 Northants R.

for November 1918

| Place | Date | Hour | Summary of Events and Information | Remarks and references to Appendices |
|---|---|---|---|---|
| EPINETTE FARM. | 1st | | The Bn. is still in the same position and also of the coys. reorganising and cleaning. | |
| | 2nd | | Bn. still in same position. | |
| | 3rd | 1600 | Bn. in same position. D Coy left Camp to relieve 3rd Bn. Royal Berkshires Reg't in the line. Rained (weather very showery and (?) rain then falling) Relieved the Royal Berks Reg't. | Out Out Out |
| | 4th | 0200 | A & B & C. Coys. left EPINETTE FARM at 0200 and arrived at the tunning off English rd in A.13.b (Sh 57A N.W.) 1:20,000. Zero hour before ZERO Z 0615 hrs The 4th and Devonshire opened 2 hours before ZERO. "D" Coy attacked due East with Royal West Kents on left and no one on right. 19" Coy advanced & a N. and S. line running through A14.b.8.8 at 0730 and consolidated. "A" Coy following 100 in rear, leapfrogged 19" Coy and carried on due E and consolidated on a line A15.b.2.8 to A15.b.3.9. The line was taken at 0815. The whole attack from Sunken Road covering a distance of scarcely 1 mile in 2 lines of platoons in Worm formation. "C" Coy following A. Coy in 2 lines of platoons in Worm formation. Some 70 m rear also leapfrogged B Coy and carried on to the front of the road at A15.a.4.0. They then reorganised the road SE on edge of road to A15.C.9.5. | |

# WAR DIARY
## or
## INTELLIGENCE SUMMARY.
*(Erase heading not required.)*

Army Form C. 2118.

| Place | Date | Hour | Summary of Events and Information | Remarks and references to Appendices |
|---|---|---|---|---|
| | | | French Inhabitants a very large percentage of the enemy captured were wounded. The 53rd Infantry Brigade carrying on (Sunnah) captured the Areas and Blue 2 and 3 and Claus details on the Red Line. The 55th Infantry Brigade having through them did not encounter the enemy for 2000 yds or so. At 15.00 the Bn. organised and arranged their forward positions having East in case of a counter attack from the enemy. The orders were brought up and the men made themselves as comfortable as they could for the night. Battalion HQrs were established at A.76.a.7.9. Cas— ualties during the day's operations were 3 Offrs wounded, + OR's 15 K. 96 W. 1 M. | |
| | 5.11 | 07.30 | "A" Coy. who had been in the forest during the night moved to Alkellor joined the Battalion at about 09.00 hrs. The weather all tender. | |
| | | 11.00 | The Battalion moved off in Column of Troops with Coys at 50 yds interval and marched via the Museum by Rue de PREUX to A.10.b. 3.3. arrived there at about 12.00. Raining hard all day. | |
| | | 14.15 | The Battalion moved off again + marched further on + NE. ford of MORMAL to about B.11.d. Coy. HQ was billeted at all MA. | |

# WAR DIARY
## or
## INTELLIGENCE SUMMARY.
*(Erase heading not required.)*

Army Form C. 2118.

| Place | Date | Hour | Summary of Events and Information | Remarks and references to Appendices |
|---|---|---|---|---|
| | 5th | 18.30 | Bivouac Sheets & Tents were sent up but they 7t darkness & rain that was great difficulty in pitching them. | |
| | 6th | 06.30 | The Battalion moved off & marched back to PREUX, where they halted for 2 hours to cook the breakfast & be served. | |
| | | 10.30 | The Battalion moved off again and marched via BOUSIES to billets in LECATEAU, arriving at 10.30. Still raining hard, every body being thoroughly drenched. | |
| | 7th | | Baths & Surplus stores Battalion sent off forward. The Battalion bathed in the morning. The rest of the day was spent in cleaning and resting. | |
| | 8th | | The day was spent in Organisation & Cleaning. | |
| | 9th | | Training under Company Commanders. | |
| | 10th | | Brigade Church Parade was held in the Theatre. The Battalion paraded 200 strong. A Guard of Honor of 25 men was detailed in honor of the proposed visit of the French President. This was cancelled later. | |

# WAR DIARY or INTELLIGENCE SUMMARY

Army Form C. 2118.

| Place | Date | Hour | Summary of Events and Information | Remarks and references to Appendices |
|---|---|---|---|---|
| LE CATEAU | 11th | 0805 | We received a verbal message from Brigade stating that HOSTILITIES would cease at 1100 hours. In parte was immediately issued that all parades for the day were cancelled. | |
| | | 1100 | HOSTILITIES CEASED (Germans ad opted  terms for an armistice) | |
| -"- | 12th | | Training as per programme attacked from carried out during the morning | |
| | | 1100 | Orders were received for the Bn. to move to SERAIN tomorrow | |
| | 13 | 0750 | The Bn. moved off and joined the Brigade starting point at 0805. A' Echelon thereof. accompanied the Bn. 'B' Echelon marched under Brigade arrangements. The Bn. arrived in SERAIN at about 1230 hrs and were billeted in the same billets they had used before. | |
| SERAIN | 14th | | Battalion training made by arrangement. | |
| | 15 | | Battalion training in "Platoon on the march" | |
| | 16 | | Battalion bathed at MARETZ | |

Army Form C. 2118.

# WAR DIARY
## or
## INTELLIGENCE SUMMARY.
(Erase heading not required.)

Instructions regarding War Diaries and Intelligence Summaries are contained in F. S. Regs., Part II. and the Staff Manual respectively. Title pages will be prepared in manuscript.

| Place | Date | Hour | Summary of Events and Information | Remarks and references to Appendices |
|---|---|---|---|---|
| SERAIN | 17 | | Battalion attended Brigade Church Parade under the command of B. Gen. BARRETT. DSO. | |
| " | 18th | | Battalion clearing the village of all Salvage and all ranks of Bourain celebrating. Who were down by A & B Coys. | |
| | 19th | | The Battalion carried on with Salvage and clearing of the village. Good progress was made. | |
| | 20th | | The Bn. still carried on with Salvage. | |
| | 21st | | The Bn. carried on with salvage. | |
| | 22nd | | Efforts were made to complete salvage work. | |
| | 23rd | | Bn. now clearing up trenches & shell holes in and around village. | |
| | 24th | | B'de Church Service. | |
| | 25th | | Bn. carried out training with the other 2 Bns. under the Brigadier. Div. Officers Cadet were told at PREMONT during the week | |

Army Form C. 2118.

# WAR DIARY
## or
## INTELLIGENCE SUMMARY.

(Erase heading not required.)

Instructions regarding War Diaries and Intelligence Summaries are contained in F. S. Regs., Part II. and the Staff Manual respectively. Title pages will be prepared in manuscript.

| Place | Date | Hour | Summary of Events and Information | Remarks and references to Appendices |
|---|---|---|---|---|
| SERAIN | Oct | | | |
| | 27th | | Bn. carried out training for the hours during the morning and parade for the remainder of the morning. | |
| | 28th | | do do do | |
| | | | Bn. practised for the Div. Review which is to take place on the 30th inst. | |
| | 29th | | The Bn. carried out training for 1½ hours during the morning. The remainder of the morning was spent in cleaning and improvement of Billets. | |
| | 30th | | Do. Do. Do. | |

R. Turner
Lt Colonel

Army Form C. 2118.

# WAR DIARY

6(S)Bn Northumberland Fus Regt

## INTELLIGENCE SUMMARY.

(Erase heading not required.)

December 1918

| Place | Date | Hour | Summary of Events and Information | Remarks and references to Appendices |
|---|---|---|---|---|
| SERAIN | 1 | 11.00 | Brigade Parade Service & under Brig. Gen. L.W. & V Sadleir Jackson CMG DSO | |
| " | 2 | | The Bn was reviewed by Major Gen. R.P. Lee Comdg 15 Div | |
| " | 3 | | A & B Coys employed in Platoon & Coy Training. C, D Coy employed on Salvage Work. | |
| " | 4 | | H.M. the King visits the Divisional Area. The Bn were stopped on the SERAIN - ELINCOURT ROAD. | |
| " | 5 | | A. B Coys employed in Platoon, Company training. C. D Coys employed on Salvage Work. | |
| " | 6 | | Baths at ELINCOURT & FREMONT allotted to Bn. | |
| " | 7 | | The Battalion carried out Bn Drill during the morning. | |
| " | 8 | | Brigade Church Parade under Brig Gen L.W. de V Sadleir Jackson CMG DSO | |
| SERAIN | 9 | 10.30 | Bn training - Platoon, Company & Bn Drill | |

Army Form C. 2118.

# WAR DIARY
or
## INTELLIGENCE SUMMARY.
(Erase heading not required.)

| Place | Date | Hour | Summary of Events and Information | Remarks and references to Appendices |
|---|---|---|---|---|
| SERAIN | 10 | | Bn. attended lectures by Dr Irving, on Reconstruction, etc. | |
| " | 11 | 10.30 | The Bn. moved to Billets at WALINCOURT. | |
| WALINCOURT | 12 | | Every effort made to clear rubbish from Billets and streets. | |
| | 13 | | Work on improvement of Billets continued. | |
| | 14 | " | | |
| SELVIGNY | 15 | 09.30 | Brigade CHURCH PARADE under Lt Col R TURNER DSO | |
| | | 12.00 | Divisional Race Meeting at SERAIN. | |
| WALINCOURT | 16 | | Salvage work on Bn. area WALINCOURT. | |
| | 17 | | Salvage work on Bn. area WALINCOURT. | |
| " | 18 | | Salvage work on Bn. AREA commenced but cancelled later on account of wet weather | |
| | 19 | | The Bn. spent the day improving billets, preparing Recreation Rooms etc- | |

**Army Form C. 2118.**

# WAR DIARY
## or
## INTELLIGENCE SUMMARY.
(Erase heading not required.)

| Place | Date | Hour | Summary of Events and Information | Remarks and references to Appendices |
|---|---|---|---|---|
| MALINCOURT | 20 | | The Bn. was employed on salvage work on the Bn AREA. | |
| " | 21 | | The Battalion Bathed at MALINCOURT | |
| SELVIGNY | 22 | 1100 | The Battalion attended Brigade Service Service | |
| MALINCOURT | 23 | | Christmas Holiday commenced. | |
| | 24 | | " | |
| | 25 | 1300 | B. C. Companies sat down to Christmas Dinner. | |
| | | | The W.Os & Sgts dined at 1900 hours | |
| | | | The Officers " 2000 hours | |
| | 26 | 1300 | A & D Companies sat down to Christmas Dinner | |
| | 27 | | The Battalion resumed salvage work on the Bn area, but owing to the heavy rain returned to billets before NOON. | |
| | 28 | | Platoon & Company musing | |

# WAR DIARY
## or
## INTELLIGENCE SUMMARY.

Army Form C. 2118.

| Place | Date | Hour | Summary of Events and Information | Remarks and references to Appendices |
|---|---|---|---|---|
| WALINCOURT | 29 | | Church Parade cancelled on account of the rain. | |
| " | 30 | | Battalion resumed dating Work in Pct. Area. | |
| " | 31 | | Battalion moved Platoon Company Drill | |

J. Kennett
Lt. Col.
6 (Sptb) Northamptonshire R.

PHOTOGRAPH OF "B" COMPANY AT DIVISIONAL REVIEW HELD ON 2ND DECEMBER 1918.

# WAR DIARY or INTELLIGENCE SUMMARY

Army Form C. 2118.

6 Northants Regt.

(Erase heading not required.)

| Place | Date | Hour | Summary of Events and Information | Remarks and references to Appendices |
|---|---|---|---|---|
| MALINCOURT | 1 | | Request Received | |
| | 2 | | 1st Bn arrived at Platoon - Company training | |
| | 3 | | 1st Bn received Draft of pte. at Ste Olle | cat |
| | 4 | | C.O. Lt Col Nunneley D.S.O. relinquished command of Battn - Major Duncan took | cat |
| | 5 | | Church Parade cancelled on account of rain | cat |
| | 6 | | Battn work continued | cat |
| | 7 | | Platoon + Company training | cat |
| | 8 | | Battn work continued. 15th Bn Battled at MALINCOURT | o.s.w |
| | 9 | | Battn work continued | cat |
| | 10 | | Conference of Infantry Company Commanders for Parade Draft | cat |
| | 11 | | 34 OR arrived | |
| | 12 | | Church Parade. Brigade Parade service | cat |
| | 13 | | Battn work resumed | cat |
| | 14 | | Platoon + Coy training football in the afternoon | cat |
| | 15 | | Battn work Platoon | cat |

Army Form C. 2118.

# WAR DIARY
## or
## INTELLIGENCE SUMMARY
(Erase heading not required.)

Instructions regarding War Diaries and Intelligence Summaries are contained in F. S. Regs., Part II. and the Staff Manual respectively. Title Pages will be prepared in manuscript.

| Place | Date | Hour | Summary of Events and Information | Remarks and references to Appendices |
|---|---|---|---|---|
| MALINCOURT | 16 | | The Bn. Bathed at MALINCOURT. Lectures by Company Officers on Demobilization. Authority received for the granting of the 1915 Star. | CSM |
| " | 17 | | Coy at disposal of Company Commanders from 0900 to 1100 hours. Capt Hoort M.C. Lectured to the Bn at 1200 hours on Demobilization. | CSM |
| " | 18 | | A Coy were employed on Salvage work. Remainder of Bn at Coy Commanders disposal | OR |
| " | 19 | | Brigade Church Parade & Service. H. Perkins Lft M. Bn. M. Demobilization | CSM OCM |
| " | 20 | | The Bn. carried on Salvage work until midday. Lecture on "Canada" in the afternoon Capt Ottewell of the Khaki University of Canada. | COH |
| " | 21 | | Coys at the disposal of Coy Commanders for general clean up. | OCH OCH |

**Army Form C. 2118.**

# WAR DIARY
## or
## INTELLIGENCE SUMMARY.
*(Erase heading not required.)*

Instructions regarding War Diaries and Intelligence Summaries are contained in F. S. Regs., Part II and the Staff Manual respectively. Title pages will be prepared in manuscript.

| Place | Date | Hour | Summary of Events and Information | Remarks and references to Appendices |
|---|---|---|---|---|
| MALINCOURT | 22 | | Bn arrived on Bn Salvage Area. | |
| | 23 | | Bn Bathed at MALINCOURT. | |
| | 24 | | Bn resumed Salvage Work in Bn Salvage Area | |
| | 25 | 0900 | The Bn was inspected by G.O.C. on Bn Bde in Square | |
| | 26 | | WALINCOURT. Brigade Church Parade cancelled. | |
| | 27 | | Bn resumed Salvage Work. Coys at disposal of Coy Commanders | |
| | 28 | | Coys at disposal of Company Commanders for cleaning billets & equipment | |
| | 29 | | Brigade Ceremonial Parade. Rehearsal for the Presentation of Kings Union Flag. | |
| | 30 | | The Bn Bathed at MALINCOURT. Lecture by M.O. Coys at disposal of Coy Commanders. | |
| | 31 | | Brigade Ceremonial Parade & rehearse the Presentation of the Kings Union Colour Cer | |

J. W. Pipon Maj or Commanding 1st Bn North Lancs

# WAR DIARY
## or
## INTELLIGENCE SUMMARY.
(Erase heading not required.)

Army Form C. 2118.

6 Northants B.

F&44

| Place | Date | Hour | Summary of Events and Information | Remarks and references to Appendices |
|---|---|---|---|---|
| WALINCOURT | 31 | 0100 | Brigade Ceremonial Parade for retrieval of Bivouackery Slopes | |
| WALINCOURT | Feb 1 | 1100 | Brigade Ceremonial Parade or Church Parade Lines east. For the Presentation of the King's Union Colour. The Colour was presented by H.R.H. Sir L. F. Morland Commanded XIII Corps. Lecture on AFRICA. | |
| | 2 | | | est |
| | 3 | | Inspection by Commanding Officers. | |
| | 4 | | Companys at the disposal of Coy Commanders for training. east. | |
| | 5 | | Bn. Parade for Ceremonial Parade under the Commander Officer | est |
| | 6 | | W.O.R. bathed at MALINCOURT. | est |
| | 7 | | Coys at the disposal of Coy Comers onders for training. est | |

Army Form C. 2118.

# WAR DIARY
## or
## INTELLIGENCE SUMMARY.
(Erase heading not required.)

| Place | Date | Hour | Summary of Events and Information | Remarks and references to Appendices |
|---|---|---|---|---|
| WALINCOURT | 8 | | Route March | cct |
| | 9 | | Church Parade. 195 OR attended service in PROTESTANT CHURCH | cct |
| | 10. | | BELVIGNY Lecture on "The New Erotics a Shaping the New World" by Mr Andrew Simms | cct |
| | 11 | | Inspection. Full marching order in Square by Commanding Officer | cct |
| | 12 | | Bttn. Route March | cct |
| | 13. | | Bttn. Bathed at MALINCOURT | cct |
| | 14 | | Companies at the Disposal of Company Commanders | cct |
| | 15 | | Company Training | cct |
| | 16. | | 150 men attended Divine Service in French Protestant Church | cct |
| | 19. | 1000 | The 54th Brigade were inspected by G.O.C. 54 Brigade Dress Full Marching Order | cct |

Army Form C. 2118.

# WAR DIARY
## or
## INTELLIGENCE SUMMARY.
(Erase heading not required.)

Instructions regarding War Diaries and Intelligence Summaries are contained in F. S. Regs., Part II. and the Staff Manual respectively. Title pages will be prepared in manuscript.

| Place | Date | Hour | Summary of Events and Information | Remarks and references to Appendices |
|---|---|---|---|---|
| WALINCOURT | 18. | | Brigade Dance at BRUSSELS. | |
| | 19 | | 1 Officer, 30 men of A Coy. Completed Salvage in Rot. AREA. Remainder of Coy. were at the disposal of Company Commanders. | aat |
| | 20 | | 1 Officer 30 men M.B Coy employed on Salvage. Remainder of Coys at the disposal of Coy Commanders for training. Mons Lens Achevelle Church Party marches the Btn. and were greatly appreciated. | aat aat |
| | 21 | | The Btn. Bathed at MALIN COURT. | aat |
| | 22 | | The Btn. was inspected by the Comm. ordery officer dress marching order. | aat |
| | 23 | | Route March. Church Parade in French Protestant Church. C Coy won second prize in Bde Cookery Competition. | aat aat |

Army Form C. 2118.

# WAR DIARY
## or
## INTELLIGENCE SUMMARY.
(Erase heading not required.)

| Place | Date | Hour | Summary of Events and Information | Remarks and references to Appendices |
|---|---|---|---|---|
| MALINCOURT | 24 | | The Btn organized into 2 Companies A + B under Command of Capt B. GILLOTT. M.C. + C+D Cy under Command of Capt. R.B. FAWKES DSO. M.C. Companies at the disposal of Company Comm-anders | |
| | 25 | | " " | |
| | 26 | | Route March. | |
| | 27 | | Btn Bathed at MALINCOURT. | |
| | 28 | | Inspection by the Commanding Officer | |

J.A. Piper. Major.
Commanding 6 Btn Northn Rgt

Army Form C. 2118.

# WAR DIARY
## or
## INTELLIGENCE SUMMARY.
(Erase heading not required.)

6 Northants Vol 45

| Place | Date March | Hour | Summary of Events and Information | Remarks and references to Appendices |
|---|---|---|---|---|
| WALINCOURT | 1 | | Conference at the disposal of Company Commanders. | |
| | 2 | 2300. | All watches clocks put forward one hour. | |
| | 3 | | 150 Other Ranks attended Divine Service in the French Protestant Church. | |
| | 4 | | Conference at the disposal of Company Commanders for Training. | |
| | 5 | | Inspection by the Commanding Officer | |
| | 6 | | 1 Officer & 50 other ranks employed at LANGSAART DUMP. Remainder of Coys at disposal of Coy Commanders | |
| | 7 | | 1 O[fficer] " " " " " " " " " Bn Baths at MALINCOURT. | |
| | 8 | | 1 Officer & 60 other ranks employed at LANGSAART DUMP. Coys at the disposal of Cy Commanders for cleaning. | |
| | 10 | | 150 men attended Divine Service in French Protestant Church. Selection [?] Coys but Disposal of Cy Commanders for training. | |

Army Form C. 2118.

# WAR DIARY
## or
## INTELLIGENCE SUMMARY.
(Erase heading not required.)

| Place | Date | Hour | Summary of Events and Information | Remarks and references to Appendices |
|---|---|---|---|---|
| WALINCOURT | 12 | | The Companies at disposal of Company Commanders for Training | |
| | 13 | 1000 | The Bn. was inspected by Commanding Officer. | |
| | | 1100 | Bn. Ceremonial Drill | |
| | 14 | | The Companies at disposal of Company Commanders for training | |
| | 15 | | The Bn. bathed at ELINCOURT. | |
| | 16 | | Coys. at disposal of Coy. Commanders. Farewell visit of Commander in Chief to XIII Corps. | |
| | 17 | | Church Parade in Church at WALINCOURT. | |
| | 18 | | Coys. at disposal of Company Commanders for training. | |
| | 19 | | Route March. | |
| | 20 | | Inspection by Commanding Officer. | |
| | 21 | | Bn. Bathed at ELINCOURT. | |

# WAR DIARY
## INTELLIGENCE SUMMARY.
*(Erase heading not required.)*

Army Form C. 2118.

| Place | Date | Hour | Summary of Events and Information | Remarks and references to Appendices |
|---|---|---|---|---|
| WALINCOURT | 22 | | 19 Other Ranks left Bn. to reinforce the Second Army. | |
| | 23 | | Church Parade in French Protestant Church WALINCOURT | |
| | 24 | | Route March. | |
| | 25 | | Companies at the disposal of Company Commanders for training - Inj | |
| | 26 | | do | |
| | 27 | | Bathing at Slincourt | |
| | 28 | | General Training. | |
| | 29 | | do | |
| | 30 | | Church Parade WALINCOURT | |
| | 31 | | General Training - | |

J. H. Pom Major.
Commanding 6th (S) Battalion
6th Northamptonshire Regt.

# WAR DIARY
## INTELLIGENCE SUMMARY

6 Northants

| Place | Date | Hour | Summary of Events and Information | Remarks and references to Appendices |
|---|---|---|---|---|
| Mullicourt | 1st April | | General Training and PT. | |
| " | 2nd | | " | |
| " | 3rd | | Cleaning up of kits and billets area. | |
| " | 4th | | Route March | |
| " | 5th | | General Training | |
| " | 6th | | Church Parade (150 OR) | |
| " | 7th | | Cleaning and Kit inspection | |
| " | 8th | | Battalion baths at Sipny | |
| " | 9th | | PT & Close order Drill | |
| " | 10th | | Route March | |
| " | 11th | | Battalion worked on Salvage dump at Maucourt | |
| " | 12th | | General Training. Inspection of billets by Commanding Officer. | |
| " | 13th | | Drafts of 59 and 114 Privates of War Corps proceeded to Rouen. Paraded on square at 0400 hrs & embused in lorries to Chauny | |

# WAR DIARY
or
## INTELLIGENCE SUMMARY.
(Erase heading not required.)

Army Form C. 2118.

| Place | Date | Hour | Summary of Events and Information | Remarks and references to Appendices |
|---|---|---|---|---|
| Wallincourt | April 14 | | Draft for 326th POW Coy paraded at same hour. Squad and proceeded to Rouen. 2 men for Strathatro also proceeded today. This left nothing of 6 Batt. under So Strength of POW Corps drafts were running 3 offr & 80 OR but now to season and command were they proceeded short of their number | |
| " | 15 | | Our Cadre Strick is considerably below strength awaiting to 80 hours. Draft of Camels for POW Coy was sent off on 24/4/19 | |

J. M. Phipps Major
Comdg 6th Nott R.

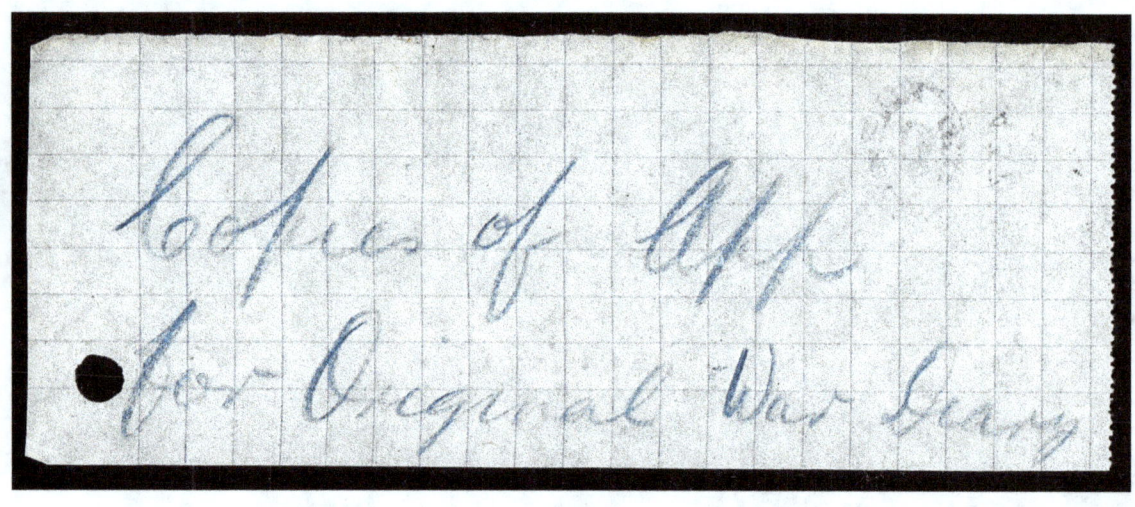

Copies of App
for Original War Diary